T0057953

ALSO BY NICHOLAS LEMANN

The Big Test:
The Secret History of the American Meritocracy

The Promised Land:
The Great Black Migration and How It Changed America

Out of the Forties

The Fast Track: Texans and Other Strivers

REDEMPTION

REDEMPTION

The Last Battle of the Civil War

NICHOLAS LEMANN

Farrar, Straus and Giroux

New York

Farrar, Straus and Giroux
18 West 18th Street, New York 10011

Copyright © 2006 by Nicholas Lemann
All rights reserved

Printed in the United States of America
Published in 2006 by Farrar, Straus and Giroux

The Library of Congress has cataloged the hardcover edition as follows:
Lemann, Nicholas.
    Redemption : the last battle of the Civil War / Nicholas Lemann.—1st ed.
    p. cm.
    ISBN-13: 978-0-374-24855-0 (hardcover : alk. paper)
    ISBN-10: 0-374-24855-9 (hardcover : alk. paper)
    1. African-Americans—Segregation—Southern States—History.   2. African
Americans—Civil rights—Southern States—History.   3. Violence—Southern
States—History—19th century.   4. Southern States—Race relations—History—
19th century.   5. Southern States—History—1865–1951.   6. Southern
States—Politics and government—1865–1950.   7. Ames, Adelbert, 1835–1933.
I. Title.

E185.61.L517 2006
975'.00496073—dc22

                                                              2006000091

Paperback ISBN-13: 978-0-374-53069-3
Paperback ISBN-10: 0-374-53069-6

Designed by Jonathan D. Lippincott

www.fsgbooks.com

P1

For Elisabeth Sifton

CONTENTS

A NOTE TO THE READER

When W.E.B. Du Bois wrote perhaps the best-remembered single phrase about American race relations—"The problem of the twentieth century is the problem of the color line"—it was by way of opening an essay about Reconstruction that appeared, in 1903, as a chapter in *The Souls of Black Folk*. Du Bois rightly perceived that the Civil War had been fought over slavery, but not so directly that it could produce a clear answer to what would seem to be the most obvious problem the Union victory posed: What would happen afterward to the four million black slaves who lived in the Confederate states?

When the war began, the national government had had no real policy about slavery in the South. The Union Army had had to make one up on the fly as slaves began to escape from the plantations and appear at its military bases. As Du Bois put it, "They came at night, when the flickering camp-fires shone like vast unsteady stars along the black horizon: old men and thin, with gray and tufted hair; women, with frightened eyes, dragging whimpering hungry children; men and girls, stalwart and gaunt,—a horde of starving vagabonds, homeless, helpless, and pitiable in their dark distress."

When the Union Army declined to return slaves to their masters, it forced the issue of slavery itself: two years into the war, Abraham Lincoln issued the Emancipation Proclamation and, in areas of the South that the Union controlled, black people became free.

Then, just a few months after the war ended, the nation ratified the Thirteenth Amendment to the Constitution, which abolished slavery. But that hardly settled matters. Freed slaves in the South generally had no money, no land, no jobs, no schools, no businesses, and no system of justice to protect them. How would they live? This question was intimately connected to the question of how the former Confederate states would be governed. The dream of "forty acres and a mule" for every black family—of a race of independent yeoman Southern farmers—depended on the availability of land, but in the end the United States government declined to take away land from its prewar white owners. When the Southern states quickly reconvened their legislatures, they passed new state constitutions and new laws meant to keep the former slaves in legal serfdom.

The U.S. Congress established a federal Bureau of Refugees, Freedmen, and Abandoned Lands, an ambitious though underfinanced effort to build a free black society in the South. And when it invalidated the South's new state constitutions and established military rule instead, the Freedmen's Bureau, a branch of the Department of War, essentially governed the former Confederacy: it taxed and spent; it created schools and courts; it controlled large tracts of land. Local organizations called Loyal Leagues, mainly black and affiliated with the Republican Party, served as the political arm of the Freedmen's Bureau. Southern whites despised the Freedmen's Bureau and the Loyal Leagues and, in the postwar years, increasingly took up arms against them. As Du Bois put it, "Guerrilla raiding, the ever-present flickering after-flame of war, was spending its forces against the Negroes, and all the Southern land was awakening as from some wild dream to poverty and social revolution."

As time passed, the United States untidily found its way to a different idea of Reconstruction, one that put electoral politics at the center. Southern states that were willing to commit themselves to full civil and voting rights for the freed slaves were readmitted to the Union; the essence of the bargain was that Southern whites could vote if they would permit Southern blacks to vote, too. The Fourteenth and Fifteenth amendments, adopted in 1868 and 1870, enshrined these rights in the Constitution. Direct military rule ended. As Du Bois put it, "So the Freedmen's Bureau died, and its child was the Fifteenth Amendment."

Du Bois limited his essay on Reconstruction to the period ending in 1872, and, after noting its shift to the political realm, ended by ominously repeating his first line: "The problem of the Twentieth Century is the problem of the color line." That is the point where this book picks up the story. The answer to the all-important question of what kinds of lives black people might live in the South now depended on the freed slaves' organizing abilities and on the reliability of their voting rights. From these, governmental power—and then schools and jobs and justice—would flow.

In the Southern states with the largest black populations, the tradition of white vigilantism, which had persevered among Confederate veterans despite, or perhaps because of, their defeat at Appomattox, began to evolve into an organized, if unofficial, military effort to take away by terrorist violence the black political rights that were now part of the Constitution. All across the South, raiders staged armed clashes with local forces of black political empowerment and federal authority, and everyone knew that through this scripted series of confrontations the final meaning of the Civil War would be determined.

This book focuses on a series of violent incidents—some of the most severe, outside of formal warfare, in American history—that took place within a limited time and space: Louisiana and Mississippi, in the two and a half years from the spring of 1873 to the fall of 1875. Together these incidents amounted to a long, bloody, climactic battle that settled the course of the political phase of Reconstruction and, therefore, of a major part of the next century of American history.

In telling the story of this crucial moment, and in aiming to make it vivid and resonant, I have used, as much as possible, contemporary rather than modern terminology (for example, the word "Negro"), and I have tried to present events from the inside, as they appeared to the participants—who of course didn't know how things would turn out or what their struggles would look like later. I hope that it has the feeling of history unfolding, not of history considered in retrospect.

REDEMPTION

PROLOGUE

The Negroes had been in control of the village for three weeks now, and it was plain that something terrible was going to happen. Their leaders had left for New Orleans on Wednesday to try to get help—meaning, they hoped, a detachment of police or, even better, federal troops, who would come to protect the people in the village. The white militia was encamped out in the countryside a few miles away, and every day it was being reinforced with volunteers, mostly Confederate veterans who had heard the whites' call for help, who had taken their shotguns and six-shooters and muskets and Springfield rifles from the Civil War down from the wall and saddled up their horses, and who had come to Colfax to fight for white supremacy. The Negroes, some of them at least, had guns, too, Enfield rifles shipped up from New Orleans in boxes and an assortment of lesser firearms, but by now there were many more people than guns to go around—hundreds of people, including women and children, who had come to Colfax because they feared the whites' bursting in on their homes and killing them. The Negro headquarters was the county courthouse, a two-story converted stable from a sugarcane plantation. At a short distance from it they had dug rudimentary breastworks, manned by sentries, to stave off the inevitable attack. All around, the Negroes from the countryside were camped out.

Deeply lodged in the consciousness of the South was the ever-present possibility of a race war in which, in each side's version, it would be mercilessly slaughtered by the other. If the anticipated deaths themselves were not horrible enough, unspeakable atrocities would make them more so. Now the inevitable was about to happen, and the cause was something that registered, in that time and place, as being literally a matter of life and death: politics. The Civil War was not yet ten years in the past. The Deep South was still in a raw condition not far removed from war. The two political parties and the two races were still violently opposed to each other. The great national questions the war had raised had by no means been settled. They were going to be settled now, with profound and lasting consequences for the whole United States, in places like rural Louisiana, by hard men with intensely local concerns, through the means of an armed struggle that, for all the potency of the load of racial fantasy it carried, was really about who could vote and hold government office.

Colfax, Louisiana, was not really a town—it was more a settlement, containing just five or six structures, and new even to that status. It was not insignificant, though. It sat in the exact center of the state on the banks of the Red River, a sugarcane or cotton planter's dream waterway because it was navigable in the countryside of central Louisiana, where roads were poor and railroads nonexistent, and because its floods had deposited a thick, rich layer of alluvial soil along its banks. The land around Colfax was lushly green and flat, and there was money in it. Local legend had it that Simon Legree, the plantation overseer in *Uncle Tom's Cabin* who, in the public mind, symbolized the cruelty of American slavery, was based on a man named Robert McAlpin, who ran a plantation near Colfax called Hidden Hill, which Harriet Beecher Stowe had visited while preparing her book. The area around Colfax was lightly settled, with nearly impenetrable swamps and uncleared woods and labyrinthine bayous; within easy memory, it had been wild country where desperate, lawless people could live free from social control, and even now it was common to hear about sightings of wild animals and to see families of settlers in covered wagons passing by on their way to Texas.

Politically, Colfax was part of an experiment, a new Louisiana that would resemble the abolitionists' prewar dream of how the South should be after its defeat in the Civil War. In 1868 a racially integrated (black-and-tan) Republican state legislature had created a new parish along the north bank of the Red River, drawing its boundaries so as to ensure that its local government would be Republican thanks to a Negro population majority. The parish was named Grant after the Republican president of the United States, Ulysses S. Grant, and its seat was named Colfax after the Republican vice president, Schuyler Colfax. To most local whites, these were unpleasantly resonant names: only a decade earlier, federal troops under General Grant's ultimate command—he was not far away, in Mississippi—had, as one white man from Colfax later remembered it, "ravaged" the Red River country using techniques taught them by the same "experts in extermination" that Grant's leading subordinate, General William Tecumseh Sherman, later used in his notoriously destructive march through Georgia. "If it were in my power, I would, as soon as possible, change the name of Grant Parish to Lee and the site of her dispensatory of justice to Davis," another white resident asserted, referring to the Confederacy's commanding general and its president.

On Easter Sunday 1873, Louisiana was in a state of low-grade warfare. In 1872, while President Grant was being reelected in a landslide, Louisiana had had a close and corrupt election. Both sides claimed victory, and now the state had two governors and two state legislatures, one Democratic and one Republican. A month after Election Day, federal troops dispatched by President Grant arrived in New Orleans, took control of the statehouse, expelled the Democratic government, and installed the Republicans. Grant Parish, appropriately enough given the condition of the state, had two political leaders, one from each party, each claiming control over the local police function—the Republican a black Union veteran, born a slave, named William Ward, the Democrat a white Confederate veteran named Christopher Columbus Nash. "In his face he bears the indications of all the worst qualities of his race and none of the better," a white organization later wrote about Ward; and, to judge by the one surviving photograph of Nash, he was a pretty rough character, too, with a full untrimmed black beard and close-set piercing eyes. Both men had had long, harsh experiences during the Civil War—extensive combat, injury, and imprisonment. They had come, separately of course, to the raw Red River country after the war because they saw opportunity there—specifically political opportunity.

One evening in 1871 Columbus Nash, then deputy sheriff of Grant Parish, led a mob of fifty armed white men to a house outside Colfax where two black Republican officeholders were living. The white men set the house on fire and shot the Negroes when they emerged; one of them survived by playing dead until the whites had left and then escaping. Legally, this incident fell under the category of law enforcement rather than crime, and Nash continued to serve as sheriff. William Ward was said to have killed a white man, or maybe two, that same year, though unlike the incident involving Nash, it was more a popular legend than a proven fact. In the version of the story most often told by the white people in Colfax, Ward had taken his victim out on the river in a skiff, hacked him to pieces with a hatchet, and dumped his remains overboard.

When the Republicans got the upper hand in New Orleans at the outset of 1873, thanks to the help of the U.S. Army, both Nash and Ward made it known that they wanted to be put in political authority in Grant Parish. The Republican governor, William Pitt Kellogg, vacillated, which was the worst thing he could do for the cause of stability in Grant Parish, and then appointed Ward's Republican forces. A meeting was held at the governor's office in New Orleans in March, with Ward, one of his lieutenants, and two Democrats allied with Columbus Nash. In the presence of the governor, the two sides started arguing, and one of the Democrats warned that if Nash was not made sheriff, there would be bloodshed. Ward returned to Colfax, called together his Republican political allies, and, unable to effect a peaceful transition of power because the Democrats wouldn't permit it, broke into the courthouse at night and took over the machinery of parish government, such as it was.

To the whites that was intolerable. They could not accept Negro rule in Colfax, with the freed-slave, plantation-hand majority having legal authority over their former masters. In fact, from the whites' perspective, the situation hadn't been tolerable for quite some time—probably since antislavery sentiment had become an important force in national politics, years before the Civil War began. Just after the war, white Louisianans had been able to establish firm political control over the state; then, from 1868 to 1872, Louisiana had been ruled by a biracial, moderate, and corrupt Republican regime, and so had Grant Parish. Whether that kind of government could have lasted is impossible to say, because it didn't last, but even before a blacker, more radical version of the Republican Party took power, whites in Grant Parish felt they were living in an upside-down nightmare world. In a deep-rural, almost frontier culture, where most communication was by word of mouth, where they were greatly outnumbered, and where racial issues carried the heaviest possible economic, political, and psychological load, rumor and myth were rife, and they mattered just about as much as reality—mattered enough, anyway, to determine what people thought and did.

A woman named Kate K. Grant, whose family owned a plantation just across the Red River from Colfax, wrote a never-published novel called "From Blue to Gray; or, The Battle of Colfax." The subtitle is "A Woman's Tribute of Admiration to the Heroes of Grant and Her Sister Parishes Who Fought So Valiantly Side by Side with Sheriff C. C. Nash." Nash himself, along with a few dozen of his comrades in arms, signed an accompanying endorsement of the work, evidently meant to be sent to publishers, that said, "In our opinion she has written a book which in point of literary finish and breadth of research would do justice to the most accomplished and famed litterateur of the land." That attests not to the merit of the novel, which is at best a routine Victorian potboiler, but to its standing as a true representation of the whites' preferred version of events in Grant Parish.

Negroes, in the view of "From Blue to Gray," are a simple people who thrive under conditions of forced labor, and who under other conditions deteriorate into idleness or, worse, violent rage at whites. Political activity—never the Negroes' own idea or preference, but instead something planted in their malleable minds by scheming, self-interested whites—is the prime force pushing them away from work and into mischief. In the first years after emancipation in 1863 and the ratification in 1870 of the Fifteenth Amendment, which gave Negroes the right to vote, this was not a terrible problem in Grant Parish, according to Kate Grant: "When the political fever has spent its force, when the simple Negro has been saturated with the pomp and excitement of mass meetings, barbecues, and the rest of the ridiculous hullaballoo, he will go back to his calm and he will work better if possible than before because of having learned the true nature of the men who pick him up and drop him at will. Old habits of industry will reassert themselves." But then Republicanism took a more ominous turn: "[S]trange white men appeared in the Quarters upon whose countenances the brand of Villainy was stamped. These tools of Radicalism sought the companionship of the black: ate with them; drank with them; lived with them on terms of perfect equality, embraced them also in the fulness of their new born affection. In a word they completely wormed themselves into the confidence of their unsuspecting dupes—the rascals gloried in their deception." After the 1872 election, when these Radicals took over the local Republican Party, "the negroes quit work; formed right societies to protest against the violence done their color on the other side, and with sullen looks and mutterings, showed the poison had done its work."

Just as political activity led inevitably to lassitude, so lassitude led inevitably to crime. In white accounts, the Negroes, beginning with the election, rampaged through Grant Parish, stealing, threatening whites at gunpoint, and despoiling plantations. After they took over the courthouse in late March, such incidents became epidemic, it was said. All of them took place—or not—far outside the realm of a formal law-enforcement system, so it is impossible to determine their veracity; they were supremely important as stories that white people told each other, more than as data.

The most widely repeated story was one of nightmare quite literally: A leading white citizen, whose custom it was to nap on a cot after his heavy plantation lunch, one postprandial afternoon during the political ascendancy of the Radical Republicans dreamed that a Negro mob came to his place, burned it to the ground, and killed his family. He woke up, told his wife about the dream—and just at that moment a "good Negro" arrived at the front door and reported that the mob was on its way. The man and his family escaped, just in time, to safety across the river, but in the pillage that followed (in the other side's version, it was merely a break-in by robbers when the family was out), the Negroes came upon a coffin containing the embalmed body of a long-dead daughter of the family. As the incident was breathlessly reported by the "good Negro" in "From Blue to Gray," "Dey picked dat pore little body outer hits coffin and flung hit out der winder, en sendin' der box after hit." Another horrified white report said, "They laid their destructive hands on the casket and threw it out of the house and left it there to the gaze of a howling mob, and at the mercy of the beasts or dogs that might come that way."

This kind of profound symbolic violation of decency, rumors of which have accompanied violent ethnic conflict forever, was a short step from the most fundamental violation, the sexual kind. The whites of Grant Parish, like whites just about everywhere in the South where there was a large and now politically empowered black population, believed that the Negroes were poised to take that short step. The most breathlessly dramatic moment in "From Blue to Gray"—and that is saying a lot—is this: "Subsequently, a plot was discovered by Adolphe Layssard [a local planter]. He overheard a conversation that took place one night on his plantation and was able fortunately to give warning of the premeditated diabolism. The white men were to be trapped and the women and children thus left without protection were to be captured by the dastardly wretches who proposed (to use their own words) raising a new race of people. That this attempt would have been made, there is not a shadow of doubt. But for Mr. Layssard's warning, God knows if I would have had the courage to write the horrible fate of my sisters in Grant. I shudder even at the thought that such was designed for them. The shock of such fiendish plots unnerved Mr. Layssard—the fear of their fulfillment haunted him. <u>To day he is the inmate of an Insane Asylum, driven there by the foul wretches whose atrocities led to the Battle of Colfax. His mental death, together with the blood of the slain, lies at their door</u>."

It is facile, perhaps, but irresistible to note that this unimaginable horror, the "new race of people," already existed copiously in Louisiana, which had a large, well-established mulatto population. Just across the river from Colfax, where Kate Grant lived, was a community of rich mulatto plantation owners. But these mixed-race Louisiana people had been born of black women and white fathers; the nightmare was the reverse, of a new race born of white mothers and black fathers. Perceiving how maximally high the stakes had become, far higher than most people would think a dispute over control of the offices of parish government entailed, the whites resolved to do what was required of them.

A distance up the Red River from Colfax, in northwestern Louisiana, lived a remarkable former slave and Army veteran named Henry Adams who managed to pull off the almost unimaginably difficult feat of organizing a committee of five hundred Negroes to travel through the former Confederacy and, as he put it a few years later, "look into affairs and see the true condition of our race." During the years immediately following the Civil War, the committee's investigators went to every state in the South and compiled a record, which is deadpan in tone to the point of being stenographic and all the more powerful for that, of violence done to Negroes—a "statement of specific cases of outrage," every one of which went unpunished. For the ten years after the end of the Civil War, just in the upper Red River parishes of Louisiana, Adams's list contains the names of 683 victims. A typical section goes this way:

220th. Sam Maybury, whipped near to death by Lord Hill and Henry Smith, white men. He afterward died from the effects of the beating. This was in Mansfield, in December, 1865. Several other white men helped to beat him.

221st. A young colored man was killed on John McMillen's place by a colored man, in 1873.

222nd. Henry West, badly whipped by Butler Williams, in or
near Mansfield, November 2nd, 1874, and since near beat
him to death.

223rd. An old man (colored) was killed by Hersel ——, a
white man, about cotton, while on their way to Shreveport, in the road, 1866.

224th. George, a colored man, killed on John McMillen's
place by white man, 1873.

225th. Nancy Brooks, badly whipped by Davis, a white man,
on Hammond Scott's place, in 1873.

In 1875 General Philip Sheridan, the great Union cavalryman of
the Civil War, was sent to Louisiana by President Grant to try to restore order; he made a careful investigation and reported that since
the end of the war 2,141 Negroes had been killed by whites in
Louisiana and 2,115 wounded—all these crimes, again, going unpunished. Henry Adams and his committee, concluding that the
freed slaves could not safely live among their former masters, formed
a "colonization council" and wrote to President Grant asking to
be given land where they could settle and live in peace by themselves. The anti-Negro violence was an expression of racial hatred
intertwined with, and intensified by, political conflict. Adams later
testified before a U.S. Senate committee:

"Now, in a great many parts of that country there our people
most as well be slaves as to be free; because, in the first place, I will
state this: that in some times, in times of politics, if they have any
idea that the Republicans will carry a parish or ward, or something
of that kind, why, they would do anything on God's earth. There
aint nothing too mean for them to do to prevent it; nothing I can
make mention of is too mean for them to do. If I am working on
his place, and he has been laughing and talking with me, and I do
everything he tells me to, yet in time of election he will crush me
down, and even kill me, or do anything to me to carry his point. If
he can't carry his point without killing me, he will kill me; but if he
can carry his point without killing me, he will do that."

———

On the morning of April 1, 1873, a white man named James Hadnot, who was known in Grant Parish as an especially active opponent of allowing the freed slaves to exercise their new rights, rode into Colfax. He wore a rather grand and military red sash and matching boutonniere and was leading a party of more than a dozen men armed with pistols (Hadnot himself also wore a saber) who intended (in the white version) to prepare for a peaceful mass meeting to discuss the crisis, or (in the black version) to carry his point by taking Colfax back from the Negroes by force. Ever since the Negroes had taken possession of the courthouse the week before, each race in Grant Parish had been operating on the assumption, fueled by reliable-sounding intelligence reports, that the other was planning a massacre. Negroes spotted two smaller parties of armed whites on horseback in the vicinity of Colfax that same day, and others on the following days. And the whites believed that the Negroes in Colfax were put through daily military drills by William Ward, in anticipation of the assault they were preparing to launch.

When Hadnot and his party saw what they were up against—a substantial encampment of Negroes, dozens of them armed—they retreated. On April 4, another, larger party of white men on horses with guns came to Colfax, bearing warrants for the arrests of the leading Negroes; they retreated, too. A white Republican planter named William Calhoun, on whose land Colfax had been established, had a visit from Hadnot and a couple of his fellow Democrats, armed, who induced him to go into the village and ask the Negroes to disperse. He did; they didn't; he left town.

On April 5, four Negroes from Colfax, led by William Ward, rode a short distance out of town—they were on mules because they had no horses—and met with four whites to try to negotiate a peace. While the men were talking, a Negro named Louis Meekin rushed up to report that one of the white posses roaming through Grant Parish had come upon a black man named Jesse McKinney—he'd been outside his house repairing a fence—and, in the presence of his wife and children, with no provocation, had shot him through the head. McKinney had "cried like a pig," one white witness to the incident said later, and then died, and the men who shot him hung around the scene of the crime "cavorting" for a couple of hours. (A white man who remembered the killing this way added the note of self-defense that was standard in white versions of incidents of violence against Negroes: "One of our boys rideing in advance, sudenly stoped and hallowed halt & then raising his shot gun to his shoulder fired, he hit this negro who was on pickett duty with one buck shot in the head killing him instantly.") Louis Meekin had a pistol, and he threatened to use it against one of the white men in the negotiating party. That ended the peace negotiations.

Later that day, and again the following day, brief, inconclusive skirmishes between white posses and black patrols occurred outside Colfax, the result of which was the whites being chased away from the town. Nobody died in these exchanges (the only injury reported was that a white man had had his thumb shot off), but the effect on the whites of encountering successful black armed self-defense, a thing constantly feared during the centuries of slavery but hardly ever realized, would be hard to overstate. One white participant later wrote, "You will most probably say why dident you fight it out but I assure you you would have been in the front rank making the mud fly just like I was, for in the front of us & on the side behind trees & logs were 50 negroes & behind us in the open field there seemed to be 4000 more coming our way." "From Blue to Gray" describes the most substantial skirmish, which took place next to a slow brown stream called Boggy Bayou, this way:

"The sight of those panic stricken youth fleeing from them aroused all the savage instincts which are innate in the [here the words 'inferior race' are crossed out on the handwritten manuscript] African and they clamored loudly for blood! blood! They thirsted for their victims as the veriest Cannibal does for human sacrifice. In anticipation, they wreaked vengeance upon them. How pain distorted those pale faces would grow as the writhing bodies vainly strove to evade the knife! What sweet music the shrieks of agony from defenseless womanhood when Death had claimed father, son, brother, lover, husband and they the victorious blacks had made good their threats against the weaker sex. The prize was well worth an effort."

The white patrols terrified the former slaves who were living in lonely, unprotected rural cabins in Grant Parish. Jesse McKinney's widow was afraid to have his body embalmed, so she and a friend loaded it onto a wagon and took it to a relative's place, where it remained long enough for turkey buzzards to detect the smell and start circling, and the women went into hiding. More and more Negroes made their way to Colfax to have the protection of William Ward's militia. A week into April there were four or five hundred of them. For one day, the courthouse actually opened and conducted government business, but that was not much more than a brave gesture; there was no mistaking what was coming. In the evenings the women would go out looking for provisions and weapons and bring them back to Colfax. Ward, using the impeccable penmanship and shaky English that was typical of ordinary people of both races in that time and place, wrote a letter to a friend living on a nearby plantation, pleading for help: "Hour Pepel are in troubel and I ask you in the name of hour Liberty and hour Children . . . I have Bin in gage 3 days and this day I had a Battle. Did not Amount to But Little one man I think wounded . . . Betwean now and Monday we will have heavy times and we are . . . in need of all the helpe We can get. If it was Grant Parish men we could Manage this but I seen Men to day from Winn Parish and the Rebels kill Jerry McKinney to day and they takeing Charley Harris and carry him off in the woods to day and I am Satisfide they have kill him."

As vivid as the whites' ideas about a coming Negro general assault were, Negroes actually made no unprovoked, proven attacks on whites during this period. All they had definitely done by force was take over the courthouse to which they had a right by gubernatorial proclamation, and the force involved had been merely that required to jimmy a window at night when nobody was there. It was the whites who openly treated one political party's assumption of the powers of local government as provocation sufficient to go to war. "From Blue to Gray" has Columbus Nash heroically taking charge of the white forces, at the rough headquarters he had set up in the woods, surrounded by like-minded men. " 'Arm yourselves!' " the book quotes him as saying, "his voice rising with excitement, his

eyes aflame. 'Drive the mob from their stronghold! If needs be, ex-
terminate them, that the lesson may be heeded by others as audacious as they are!'" Nash issued a call for reinforcements, which
couriers carried through the neighboring parishes; over the course
of a week, the white force grew to perhaps three hundred men.
Some of the Negroes said later that they had encountered members
of the Texas Rangers in Nash's little army.

On April 9, a steamboat called the *B. L. Hodge* came down the
river, bound for New Orleans. William Ward and his high command boarded it, hoping (in their version) to enlist military help, or
(in the white version) abandoning their people to what they knew
would be a losing battle. On April 12, a few of Columbus Nash's
men rode down along the river a few miles to the nearest sizable
town, Alexandria, where the captain of a steamboat gave them a
small wheeled cannon he had mounted on his deck for protection.
They brought it back to Grant Parish to use against the Negroes.
White people across the river sank the small ferry that traversed the
Red at Colfax, to prevent Negroes from escaping or coming after
them. In Colfax, the Negroes dug into their earthworks. Alexander
Tillman, one of the men leading them in Ward's absence, gave a little exhortation on Easter eve, saying that he was sure the Negroes
could hold off the white attack until help came.

On the morning of Easter Sunday—the one day when one could be
absolutely certain that armed reinforcements for the Negroes, if they
were on the way, would not turn up—Columbus Nash addressed his
troops. As one of them remembered it, "They were informed that
the action about to be taken could result in prosecution for treason
and those who were afraid to fight for white supremacy could step
out and return home. Some twenty five men took advantage of this
offer." The rest of them, two or three hundred men, rode toward
Colfax. Across the Red River, members of the local white gentry,
who had left their plantations during the Negro occupation of Colfax, gathered to watch the battle from the veranda of a stately home
overlooking the river and the town.

Another "good Negro," named Steve Kimbrell, according to the same memoirist, "went into Colfax and made a speech to the negroes, begging them to disband and go home, telling them of the necessity of white supremacy and that he would vouch for the white people giving them immunity from prosecution. All this was made light of, so he told his relations and close friends good-bye, that he never expected to see them again."

At noon, Nash rode into Colfax at the head of his force. He and a second, bearing a white flag, rode out to the earthworks, where the man who had replaced Ward as chief commander of the Negroes, Levin Allen, and his second met them. Nash demanded that the Negroes surrender, and promised them mercy if they did; Allen refused. As T. Morris Chester—the Civil War's best-known Negro correspondent—recounted this conversation at a later "meeting of colored men" in New Orleans, Nash "was reminded that it did not look much like [mercy] when they had killed several unoffending colored men at different times during their invasion, and further informed that the defenders did not feel safe in putting down their arms." Levin Allen returned to his men and told them about his refusal to surrender. "His course received the approbation of the whole posse," Chester said, "the men all believing that the proposal of their assailants was a ruse to trap them into disarming, that they might be incapable of retaliating in case of a massacre."

Nash announced he would wait half an hour to give the women and children inside the breastworks a chance to leave, and then he would attack. Early in the afternoon, with some of the escaping women and children still in view, the entire white force marched on Colfax. A horse-drawn wagon pulled the cannon into town, and it was wheeled into place. Soon nuts, bolts, and other bits of red-hot metal, in lieu of real cannonballs, were raining down into the earthworks. The Negroes had built two or three makeshift cannons of their own out of old steam pipes, which had stoked the white-hot alarm of the whites when they had been spotted, but in battle they failed to fire.

The town of Colfax sat right up next to the levee that ran along the north bank of the river. Nash split his force into three parts: one approaching from upriver, one from inland, and the third coming over the levee upstream from Colfax; that third force picked its way downstream along sandbars and bottomland, out of sight of the town until they were just opposite it, then climbed the levee and began firing down on the Negroes. Quickly, their comrades moved the cannon around to their position, more advantageous than the original one, and resumed firing on the Negroes. The battle raged for some time—"Old soldiers who were with Lee told me it was the hottest fighting they were ever in," one white man recalled—but the steady cannon fire from above finally led the Negroes inside the earthworks to conclude that their position was untenable. Some of them ran away by following the levee downstream, where there were no white troops, and tried to escape across the fields to the relative safety of a patch of deep woods. But whites on horseback pursued them; a few got away, but most were either killed or taken prisoner—as a white participant remembered it later, "pending a wholesale execution at such a time as the white citizens were able to carry out their plans." Another, larger part of the Negro force abandoned the earthworks and took cover inside the courthouse, where they began to fire at their assailants from the windows.

By now it was getting late in the afternoon, and although the battle was going against the Negroes, they were well defended inside the courthouse. Then one of the white men had an idea. He went into the building where the Negro prisoners were being held and said, as one memoirist put it, "You all know you're going to be shot. I want 6 men to volunteer to set fire to that building, and I will do all I can to save your lives. I think that I can do it. Will you take the chance?" Other white men, scavenging in Colfax's only store, found a can of coal oil and some rags. They soaked the rags in the oil, tied them to the end of a fishing pole, lit them, and sent a Negro prisoner named Pinckney Chambers on a mission that none of their own courageous number was willing to take on: walking unarmed and under fire to the courthouse. Pinckney Chambers reached up with his burning pole and set fire to the courthouse roof; the whites, from a safe distance, kept the place under such a heavy barrage that the Negroes inside the courthouse could not put the fire out. Soon the whole building was engulfed, and the Negro men inside were being burned alive. One man in the courthouse tore off his shirtsleeve and waved it out the window as a flag of surrender; another found a sheet of white paper and waved it. Through the tactic of inducing a Negro prisoner to set the building on fire, the whites had won.

What happened next is in dispute. In the white version, a few white men led by James Hadnot laid down their arms and approached the courthouse to receive the Negro surrender but were shot when they got to the front door. This, in the whites' story, was the last straw; they were, in the words of one account, "exasperated beyond endurance at the cowardly and treacherous murder of their comrades, thus lured to their death by the false flag of truce held out by the negroes." But "to believe this claim," as a report written later by Republicans in Washington mordantly put it, "would require us to find that the negroes, who so far in the fight had been unable to harm a single one of their adversaries, pent up in the building to which they had fled for refuge, with the roof blazing over their heads, compelled to choose between death by fire and the tender mercies of their *foemen*, fired on the men who were bringing them offers of quarter." Although James Hadnot did die, even the white accounts of the event acknowledge he was merely wounded at the courthouse door; he was taken by his comrades to a nearby house where he got medical attention, and later that night was put aboard a passing steamboat so that he could get better treatment downstream; he expired some time after that. These facts are not consistent with the idea of his being greeted at the door by a murderous Negro barrage. In the Negro version, the men in the courthouse were stacking their guns when the white men approached, and Hadnot was shot from behind by an overexcited member of his own force.

There is no disagreement, however, about what followed the surrender of the Negroes in the courthouse. The whites slaughtered them. Burning Negroes jumped from the second-story windows or ran out the front door "only to meet a savage and hellish butchery," as Morris Chester put it. Inside the building they pried up floorboards and tried, unsuccessfully, to hide beneath them. They were all killed, unarmed, at close range, while begging for mercy. Chester went on: "The escaping men were overtaken, mustered in crowds, made to stand around, and, while in every attitude of humiliation and supplication, were shot down and their bodies mangled and hacked to hasten their death or to satiate the hellish malice of their heartless murderers, even after they were dead." White posses on horseback rode away from the town, looking for Negroes who had fled, so they could kill them.

Up to the point where the courthouse was set on fire, Colfax was arguably a battleground, and from the start the battle went the whites' way. But what was happening now was not a hard military fight but a killing frenzy after the battle was over, after the outcome had been clearly settled, and with the defeated force unarmed. (Even the white accounts which say Hadnot was shot from inside the courthouse do not claim that any of the Negroes were able to inflict harm after that.) No attempt was made to care for the Negro wounded or bury the Negro dead.

When the steamboat that was to take the injured James Hadnot away first pulled up at Colfax, some of the white men asked the crew if they wanted to "see dead niggers." An alternate wording remembered by a few witnesses was "dead beeves." Some crewmen disembarked and crossed the levee, where they found the courthouse still smoldering, the ground littered with corpses, and the air suffused with the sickening smell of burning flesh. The whites gave them a tour of the battlefield, kicking the occasional Negro body to make sure the man was dead.

Even in the triumphant white accounts of the battle, a defensive, or embarrassed, note creeps in when this part of the story comes around, but the excuse is made that the white men had been pushed far past the ordinary bounds of wartime behavior. One memoirist said, "It was a sorry blunder the negroes made in fireing on our men after surrender, for only their leaders would have been dealt with, but after their treachery the order went forth let none escape." A report by a group of Louisiana Democrats said, "That excesses were committed by the outraged and exasperated whites, there can be no doubt. But let it be remembered . . . that, in the heat of the fight, they saw two prominent citizens, their comrades, go upon an errand of peace, summoned by flags of truce displayed by the negroes, unarmed, with words of peace upon their lips, shot down, killed by the very persons they wished to save, by the very hands that held the white flags of peace! . . . Then, is there not palliation for the excesses of the whites in the Colfax affair, who, in heat of blood, visited upon the treacherous murderers of their comrades swift and terrible vengeance?"

When night fell, the white soldiers who were old enough to have families to return to began to leave Colfax; some young bachelors, who had been drinking heavily to celebrate their victory, were left in charge of the Negro prisoners who had been captured. During the night they told the prisoners they were going to take them downriver to Alexandria. Then, as they marched the prisoners out of the house two by two, they shot them point-blank from behind, killing all but one of them. The prisoner who managed to survive, by playing dead, remembered a white man responding to a plea for mercy by saying that "he did not come 400 miles to kill niggers for nothing." A few white versions of the story make a feeble attempt to portray the murder of the prisoners as a foiled escape attempt; but as a more candid participant remembered it, one captor said, "'I can take five,' and five men stepped out. Luke lined them up and his old gun went off, and he killed all five of them with two shots. Then it was like popcorn in a skillet."

The next morning the whites sent word around the countryside that any Negro families who wanted to come to Colfax to claim their dead could do so. Understandably, since there was no evidence that the whites were not still in the full grip of bloodlust, nobody came. When the help the Negroes had been waiting for finally arrived a day later, on Tuesday, April 14—a boatload of "Metropolitan Police" dispatched by the Republicans in New Orleans—the town was littered with unburied bodies. Wild dogs and buzzards were picking at the flesh of the corpses. James Longstreet, the Confederate general best known for having unsuccessfully advised General Lee not to attempt a frontal attack on the Union Army at

Gettysburg, was now, to the bitter consternation of his unapologetic former comrades, a Republican supporter of President Grant, and commander of the Metropolitan Police in New Orleans. He dispatched a colonel named T. W. DeKlyne to lead the force to Colfax. This was DeKlyne's first impression of Colfax after the battle:

"About one-third of a mile below the courthouse we came upon a party of colored men and women carrying away a wounded colored man upon a sled. At a little distance in the field were the dead bodies of two colored men. About two hundred yards nearer the courthouse were three dead bodies of colored men, and from that point to the courthouse and its vicinity the ground was thickly strewn with dead. We were unable to find the body of a single white man or to ascertain the loss of the whites . . . Many were shot in the back at the head and neck; one man still lay with his hands clasped in supplication; the face of another was completely flattened by blows from a gun, the broken stock of a double barreled shotgun being on the ground near him; another had been cut across the stomach with a knife after being shot; and almost all had from three to a dozen wounds. Many of them had their brains literally blown out . . . We caused to be buried in the ditch near the ruins of the courthouse, the remains of fifty-four colored men, three of whom were so badly burned as to be unrecognizable." One of DeKlyne's men, William Wright, later described the scene this way: "The corpses laid around indiscriminately; bodies had begun to decompose; . . . there were unusual marks of violence on the bodies; the wounds numbered as high as six, mostly in the head and neck; found six bodies under a warehouse; three charred bodies were beyond recognition; . . . found one body with skull crushed in; the stock of a shotgun laid alongside; found no armed colored people; it was difficult to obtain assistance to bury the dead; . . . have been in battle fields after a fight; the wounds in this case were different from those given in regular fights."

DeKlyne's men turned the Negro earthworks into a mass grave and buried most of the dead there. On his second day in Colfax, DeKlyne got a message from Columbus Nash, who was hiding out in the countryside. If DeKlyne would promise not to arrest him,

Nash would meet him at a spot outside of town and give his version of the battle. So DeKlyne heard the white version of what had happened, which he found implausible, and then Nash slipped out of view again.

On April 21, Captain Jacob H. Smith of the U.S. Army, with a hundred men under his command, arrived in Colfax. The next day, he wrote his commanding officer: "The place I found to be almost entirely deserted, a few negro families only remaining. The troubles here have quickly quieted down with only the attendant excitement which necessarily follows any such fatal riot, as appears to have taken place." Soon Captain Smith had a visit from Columbus Nash, who, he wrote, "informed me that he was Sheriff of this Parish and would return in a day or two and give me his version of the affair." Even after hearing Nash's account of the battle, Smith reported that "there is no doubt but that quite a majority of the killed were shot down after the surrender."

Smith had arrived in Colfax thinking he might find Grant Parish in a state of general armed insurrection against the authority of the government, accompanied by indiscriminate violence against Negroes. But by mid-May, he concluded that the place had calmed down enough for him and his men to leave. In his final report, Smith put the number who had died on April 13 at Colfax at seventy-three—seventy-one blacks and two whites. He was probably too low by one on the white death toll, and in later years white people in Grant Parish claimed to have killed many more Negroes than seventy-one: a hundred and fifty, or two hundred, or three hundred. (It is a sign of the special racial charge that the political conflict carried that no white Republicans were harmed.) Because the power of local law enforcement now rested in the hands of Columbus Nash, there was no question that any white would be charged with murder. Instead, they were heroes, and they were running the parish. The Negroes who remained in Colfax had no choice but to live meekly under the rule of the men who had killed their husbands and sons and brothers.

In June a federal grand jury in New Orleans began issuing indictments in connection with the Colfax massacre. Since conventional criminal charges, which are a local responsibility, were not an option, the indictments were for violation of what was supposed to be a revolutionary new form of federal authority, the Enforcement Act of 1870. This was one of a series of what were known colloquially as "Ku Klux laws," which a Republican Congress had passed specifically to combat the proliferating activities of the Ku Klux Klan all over the South and generally to empower the federal government to do what local Democratic governments in the former Confederacy would not: guarantee the former slaves their civil rights. In July, a state Republican judge tried to convene a court in Colfax to look into the massacre, and an armed mob of white men appeared to prevent that from happening. It was clear that if justice was going to be done, it would only be done by the federal government.

In October, Louisiana's "state steamboat," the *Ozark*, arrived in Colfax, filled with troops who had come to find and arrest as many of the indicted white leaders of the massacre as they could. In Colfax as in most of the rest of the South, especially areas with heavy black populations, any federal presence was presumed to have an insurrectionary effect on the Negro mind, so by the time the *Ozark* arrived, the whites were in a state of high alarm. One white memoirist later wrote, "Negroes knew long before we did that this military force was coming and they were jubilant. They would sing at the work, or as they strolled in a lordly manner over the neighboring roads, a taunting song, composed by themselves, in which dire revenge was broadly hinted 'when the Ozark comes' . . . The air was a throbbing lilting melody, that was enthralling, beautiful and hideous, full of malice and hatred, this awful time is embedded in my soul, and after all these years, this throbbing, jouncing rippling music is living in my inner consciousness. I can still hear the wild exultant shouts of the malicious singers." One officer on board the *Ozark* wrote to his superior, "Soon after the expedition reached Colfax, scattering reports began to come down the river, indicating the commission of many crimes, and among others the ravishing of three respectable white women . . . these reports were afterwards ascertained to be false and exaggerated"—and he tartly noted that the whites' indignation about lawlessness might be easier to take seriously if it were also applied to the events of April 13 in Colfax.

The soldiers went hunting for the leaders of the Colfax massacre and arrested eight men, but not Columbus Nash, who hid out in a pasture until an informer gave up his location—whereupon, according to white legend, "he swam Red River on his horse amid a patter of bullets. Reaching the opposite shore he waved his slouch hat in defiance to them and was off." He was soon back in Colfax. The arrested men were taken to New Orleans on the *Ozark* and put in jail. In February 1874, a federal court began to hear the Colfax case, but it ended in a mistrial. The unacceptability of the idea of convicting whites for killing blacks can be adduced from the white prosecutor's apologetic summation to the jury: "This is the first time, and God grant it may be the last, that all testimony has been from colored men. Aside from their lack of intelligence, I was apprehensive that by their aggressive sense of wrong and their disposition to exaggerate, a vindictive feeling might be manifested. But of all the witnesses placed on that stand and confronted with their murderers, not one of them manifested in any instance the degree of malice that a white man would. I confess I don't understand it."

Some combination of outrage that the federal government had dared to try to punish the perpetrators of the Colfax massacre and of a sense of invulnerability because the effort had failed thus far emboldened white Louisiana. By now it was an election year again, and that presented the alluring possibility of inflicting a crushing, undisputed defeat on the Republicans. On March 28, 1874, only a few miles from Colfax, in Alexandria, three former Confederate officers started a newspaper called the *Caucasian*, which was dedicated to the proposition that it was time for white supremacy to be reestablished by force in Louisiana. As an early editorial put it, "[W]e, having grown weary of tame submission to this most desolating war of the negro upon us, propose to take a bold stand to assert the dignity of our manhood, to say in tones of thunder and with the voice of angry elements STOP! THUS FAR SHALT THOU GO, AND NO FURTHER!" The advent of the *Caucasian* led quickly to the appearance of similar sentiments in newspapers all over the state. Within a month a group of whites had convened in another Red River town, Opelousas, and established a new organization called the White League.

Nearly overnight the White League became a substantial statewide operation. Many Confederate veterans in Louisiana, as elsewhere in the South, had never fully accepted the outcome of the Civil War, if that was defined as full citizenship for the former slaves, and they had continued the conflict locally, informally, and sporadically, through the Ku Klux Klan and similar mystically titled terrorist organizations (the leading one in Louisiana was called the Knights of the White Camellia). The White League was something more: it was less secret, better organized, and more explicitly political in its aims. Its purpose was to use extralegal violence to remove the Republican Party from power, and then to disenfranchise black people. Although it drew emotional sustenance from the old idea that it was protecting white womanhood from black despoliation and trying to restore the proper order of the races, its main activities were in the public realm. It tried to drive Republican officeholders out of power, to disrupt Republican campaign activities, and to prevent Negroes from voting—all aims that were to be accomplished by any means necessary. The risk of being Republican in Louisiana was escalating so quickly that even William Ward soon renounced his membership in the party. As one historian aptly put it, the White League was "the military arm of the Democratic Party."

In May 1874 a second trial of the Colfax prisoners in New Orleans resulted in a victory for them that only increased white Louisiana's sense of possibility. An associate justice of the U.S. Supreme Court, Joseph Bradley, came to New Orleans to attend the trial, and after the verdict came in (five acquitted, three convicted), he ruled that the Enforcement Act of 1870, under which the convictions had been obtained, was unconstitutional. He had all the prisoners released—not just the five acquitted, but the three convicts as well. In Colfax, the whites celebrated at a mass meeting, after which white men went out into the countryside to terrorize Negroes. They slit the throats of two black men, without provocation, and left them lying dead on the ground. Once again the U.S. Army had to come in to apprehend the murderers, in lieu of a functioning local criminal justice system, but the suspects were released because no Negroes would testify against them. Louisiana's Republican governor later said that the acquittal of the Colfax prisoners "was regarded as establishing the principle that hereafter no white man could be punished for killing a negro." The federal government appealed the case to the Supreme Court.

On the forty-eighth anniversary of the Colfax massacre, April 13, 1921, the white townspeople of Colfax erected a monument—a white marble obelisk placed at the most prominent location in the town cemetery—to commemorate the most dramatic day in their local history. Engraved on the shaft were these words:

In Loving
Remembrance

Erected
To the Memory of
The Heroes

Stephen Decatur Parish,
James West Hadnot,
Sidney Harris

Who Fell in the Colfax
Riot Fighting for
White Supremacy

April 13, 1873

A lengthy dedication ceremony included five speeches, a musical program by the high-school band, a rendition of "Dixie" by the high-school choir, and an unveiling of the obelisk itself by the elderly widows of Harris and Hadnot. Then everyone marched to the "riot tree," a short distance from the cemetery, from whose branches several Negroes who had attempted to escape on the day of the battle had supposedly been hanged, and officially consecrated it.

Colfax by then was a pretty little town, with towering pecan trees, streets laid out in a few neat rectangles, a commercial block next to the levee with solid two-story brick structures, and a handful of gracefully columned white houses where the most substantial citizens lived. A few surviving veterans of the battle paraded through the streets in automobiles, and then attended a luncheon in their honor at the LeSage Hotel. As always at important battlefields, the blood and bones had disappeared, the stench of death had faded away, and it required some imagination to picture this moist, slow-moving, remote Louisiana hamlet on fire, and attracting the attention of the whole country.

At the time, though, the Colfax massacre laid a gauntlet directly before President Grant. The territory he had personally conquered just ten years earlier—a legendary military feat that propelled him to the position of general of the Army and then to the presidency—was unconquering itself. Grant's own view of what had happened was obvious from a statement he later issued about the state of affairs in Louisiana: "A butchery of citizens was committed at Colfax, which in blood-thirstiness and barbarity is hardly surpassed by any acts of savage warfare." For the dour and minimally moralistic Grant, to say this was to say a lot. He went on: "To hold the people of Louisiana generally responsible for these atrocities would not be just; but it is a lamentable fact that insuperable obstructions were thrown in the way of punishing these murderers, and the so-called conservative papers of the State not only justified the massacre, but denounced as federal tyranny and despotism the attempt of the United States officers to bring them to justice. Fierce denunciations ring through the country about office-holding and election matters in Louisiana, while every one of the Colfax miscreants goes unwhipped of justice, and no way can be found in this boasted land of civilization and Christianity to punish the perpetrators of this bloody and monstrous crime."

The debate about what the main purpose of the Civil War was—union or the abolition of slavery—is too large ever to be entirely settled. But at just this moment a more specific, and equally impor-

tant, point about the meaning of the war was going to be settled
definitively through a series of military and political moves in a contained corner of the United States. The abolition of legal chattel
slavery, through the Emancipation Proclamation of 1863 and then
the Thirteenth Amendment to the Constitution in 1865, had evidently taken hold. But the next two constitutional amendments,
the Fourteenth and Fifteenth, which guaranteed the former slaves
civil and voting rights, were still in contest, especially in the most
deep-Southern and heavily black parts of the former Confederacy.
Whites there had in mind instead a social compact under which Negroes would not formally be slaves anymore, but under which they
would be unable to vote, hold office, or have legal rights—in which
they would be completely powerless, subject to the will of whites
without any protection or recourse, even when that will was expressed in individual violence and sexual violation. It had become
impossible to enforce the Fourteenth and Fifteenth amendments
through conventional political means, so the question became a
military, or paramilitary, one: the U.S. Army, which still maintained
minimally staffed posts in the former Confederacy to enforce federal
law, versus the surging new White League. That the Civil War had, in
effect, broken out again in one region of the South raised the question of union again, along with the question of race: Would the
country unite around full Negro citizenship even if it meant a re-
sumption of war? Or would it fall apart once more? Or would it find
another principle around which to become a functional single nation again?

For many former Confederates, this was a glorious time. After
years of defeat and loss of power and control, it looked as if they
might be winning again, and winning not in the mundane realm of
civil life but militarily, heroically. They were taking their homeland
back from what they saw as a formidable misalliance of the federal
government and the Negro. The drama of it was so powerful that
killing defenseless people registered in their minds as acts of brav-
ery, and refusal to obey laws that protected other people's rights
registered as acts of high principle. That was why white Southerners cheered about what happened at Colfax: finally someone had

had the courage to take up arms against Negro depredation and win. They could see the lopsidedness of the death toll as a sign of valor rather than cruelty. The date of the massacre, with its connotation of divine sanction and of rising from the dead, only added to its resonance.

Negroes, with their dark puissance, their ineradicable "nature," were on the other side of a gulf too wide to be bridged by empathy, so it was impossible for the whites to see how Colfax looked from across the racial divide, with the whites as the powerful, incorrigibly violent ones and the Negroes living in a condition of terrified unprotection. But in that case, of course, the religious symbolism played quite differently. As T. Morris Chester put it in his speech in New Orleans after the massacre, "On Easter Sunday, when the Christian world was chanting anthems in commemoration of the resurrection of the world's Redeemer, when from every sanctuary the gospel of love and peace was proclaimed, it was then that angels veiled their faces, and devils howled at the bloody and revolting scenes that were enacted on the banks of the Red River."

1

ADELBERT AND BLANCHE

One function that politics serves is to embody, through parties, the sometimes startlingly different ways in which people can perceive the same situation. To a Republican during the Reconstruction era, Adelbert Ames would have seemed to be a very promising young American. He was the son of a sea captain, born in the port town of Rockland, Maine, in 1835; his family had been in America since the seventeenth century and, by the time Adelbert was a young man, had acquired enough influence to get him an appointment to the United States Military Academy at West Point, where, when he arrived, the superintendent was Robert E. Lee. Ames had the good luck to graduate in 1861, just one month after Confederate forces fired on Fort Sumter, and thus he was able to command troops in battle immediately. At the first Battle of Bull Run, a few weeks after his graduation from West Point, a Confederate bullet went through his thigh. He could no longer sit on a horse, but he insisted on remaining in the field, being wheeled about on a caisson by his men. At Gettysburg he led a brigade of Union troops at the front line for all three days of the great battle. He fought at Chancellorsville, Fredericksburg, Petersburg, and Antietam—in sixteen battles in all. And in early 1865 he led the force that finally captured Fort Fisher, a crucial Confederate redoubt at the mouth of the Cape Fear River near Wilmington, North Carolina, which for four long years had protected the Confederacy's importation of munitions from Europe. Thirty years later his aide-de-camp at the battle for Fort Fisher described Ames this way for a Maine newspaper:

"He was the beau-ideal of a division commander, and as such there was no more gallant and efficient officer in the armies of the Union. Every one who rode with him soon discovered that Ames never hesitated to take desperate chances under fire. He seemed to have a life that was under some mystic protection. Although he never permitted anything to stand in his way, and never asked men to go where he would not go himself, still his manner was always cool, calm, and gentlemanly. Under the heaviest fire, when men and officers were being stricken down around him, he would sit on his horse, apparently unmoved by singing rifle-ball, shrieking shot, or bursting shell, and quietly give his orders, which were invariably communicated in the most polite way, and generally in the form of a request."

At the end of the war Ames, still not yet thirty, had won the Medal of Honor, the highest decoration for military valor, held the rank of brevet brigadier general, and had attracted the admiring notice of General Grant himself. A photograph taken at the time shows him looking like a dark-haired version of another of the "boy generals" of the Civil War, George Armstrong Custer: he is in a dramatic profile, with long hair brushed behind his ears and touching his collar, a big, bulbous, pale forehead, a prominent brow, a pointed nose, sharp clear eyes, and a luxuriant walrus mustache and goatee.

During the years after the end of the Civil War and before the onset of the Indian wars in the West, most leading officers in the U.S. Army spent time in the former Confederacy; they were there to enforce the peace and reestablish order. This was partly a military task, since the former rebels had by no means all accepted the outcome of the war, and partly a civilian one, involving tasks like trying to help freed slaves get on their feet. Adelbert Ames was posted to South Carolina, where, he wrote his parents, his duties "consist of little more than aiding the agents of the Treasury Department and the Freedmen's Bureau"—the economic and welfare agencies for the former slaves—"and in trying white men for killing negroes, of which work we have more than we can well do." He went on:

"They think about as much of taking the life of a Freedman as I would that of a dog . . . I am in hopes that in course of time the pious people of this State will be convinced that according to our law it is, if not a sin, at least a crime to kill what they term a—'nigger.'"

In the summer of 1866 Ames obtained a year's leave from the Army and went on a tour of Europe, traveling both as questing young man and as visiting dignitary. In England he heard Charles Dickens lecture and had audiences with the Prince of Wales and with the American ambassador, Charles Francis Adams. In France he was presented to Napoleon III at court. He kept a diary, in which he occasionally mused on what he had seen in postwar South Carolina. Once he wrote: "In affairs of state, I approve of the policy of taking a half if the whole is unattainable. Yet, I know many say unless we have all we will take nothing. This is illustrated by those who in the present crisis cry for negro suffrage. Foolishly, they would let such a plank in a platform be a source of great insecurity—fatally so. But I do not believe in negro suffrage." Another entry said, of the Radical Republicans who were the leading advocates of Negro suffrage, "The extremists seem to me to be almost crazy on many points."

The closest the usually matter-of-fact Ames had to an epiphany during his *Wanderjahr* came during a visit to the Luxembourg Palace in Paris, where, while looking at the works of art, he ran into an old friend from Maine who had moved to Europe, married, and become an aspiring painter. Ames noted that his friend, though he "has not mounted so high the ladder of fame as to attract universal attention yet," seemed completely happy, whereas he—General Ames!—had "accomplished much—but to what end? Instead of having that which gives peace and contentment, I am adrift, seeking for what God only knows. I do not. Thus far life has been with me one severe struggle and now that a time of rest is upon me, I am lost to find my position. I seek to know the particular object of living. I suppose I have to exist yet longer to be fully convinced that to suffer is the beginning and end of life. It is a sad lesson but one I am now being convinced for the first time which must be learned to the very letter."

Ames had the self-awareness to realize that a life of free creative questing like his friend's was not for him. He needed a mission. He had a particularly Yankee blend of ambition (he devoted a good deal of space in his journal to worrying over his next military promotion) and idealism, almost to the point of aspiring to sainthood. What best united the two traits was an official assignment to a difficult mission. When he returned to the United States in the summer of 1867, he accepted the military rank of brevet major general and an assignment to the Fourth Military District—formerly the states of Mississippi and Arkansas.

Like other Confederate states, Mississippi had, just after the war, with the tacit encouragement of President Andrew Johnson, convened a legislature made up mainly of unrepentant Confederates, and it had passed "black codes" that legislated the freed slaves into a condition as close to their former one as it was possible to get without actually reinstituting slavery. The Mississippi codes essentially prohibited Negroes from renting land or quitting their jobs—the object was to force them to remain as plantation hands instead of becoming independent farmers—and also restricted their rights of assembly and voting. In retaliation for its failure to ratify the Fourteenth Amendment, the Republican U.S. Congress, which had impeached President Johnson over his open sympathy for the white South, had refused to readmit Mississippi to the Union as a state: that was why it was still under federal military control.

In January 1868, under the supervision of the occupying federal troops, a Mississippi version of another Southern institution of the time, a black-and-tan convention (in this case, with sixty-eight white and seventeen Negro delegates), convened in Jackson to write a new state constitution in which freedmen's rights would be protected fully enough to persuade Congress that Mississippi could become a state again. The convention produced a constitution in May 1868, but a month later, because of white intimidation of black voters, it failed to win the approval of more than half the theoretically black-majority Mississippi electorate. After that election, General Grant—then secretary of war, preparing to run for president—appointed Adelbert Ames provisional governor of Mississippi. In March 1869, on the day after Ames was inaugurated as governor in

Jackson and Grant was inaugurated as president in Washington, the latter gave the former the additional title of commander of the Fourth Military District. Ames's main assignment was to supervise—with the backing of a new president, who seemed prepared to be much tougher on the former Confederates than his predecessor had been—a fall election in which Mississippi would approve the new state constitution, accept the new federal Fourteenth and Fifteenth constitutional amendments, which guaranteed Negroes civil and voting rights, and elect state officials, after which it would, at last, be readmitted to the United States.

In late October, a few days before the election, Ames reported to his superiors in Washington that the troops under his command were mainly engaged in putting down violence that was aimed at the two goals, which were actually one goal, of suppressing Negro rights and preventing the Republican victory that a truly open election would almost certainly entail. He wrote:

"By the numerous reports at this headquarters it appears that the disturbances and lawlessness have their origin in political animosities, and the incapacity or unwillingness of many to recognize the change, resulting from the late war, in the condition of the freed people.

"A prevailing sentiment in many sections of the State has been that the whites who entertain political sentiments different from the community should be driven therefrom, and that the blacks should be, if not deprived of rights undeniably theirs by law, at least seriously curtailed in the exercise of them."

Of course Ames was himself one of those whites "who entertain political sentiments different from the community." In the parlance of the former Confederacy, he was a carpetbagger, and as such he belonged to a class whose members, Southern whites supposed, were motivated by anything but idealism. However valorous his record in the war might have been and however upright his bearing and high-minded his expressed sentiments, most white Mississippians at first presumed him to be, like all carpetbaggers, a cynical opportunist, out to attain personal wealth and power by exploiting both the powerlessness of the defeated South and the malleability and pathetic delusions of the freed slaves. Physical threats against carpet-baggers who occupied less elevated positions than Adelbert Ames were driving them out of Mississippi and other Southern states constantly. Whether that would work with a general who was in Jackson on direct orders from the president of the United States remained to be seen.

The country then was lustily political. Newspapers were, unapologetically, party organs. Other than a few major railroad companies, which were new, there was still not much big business or organized labor to counterweight government. There was no federal civil service. Rich "special interest groups" were only beginning to manifest themselves in politics, to the shock of the nation, and the lack of them meant that the parties were all-powerful. Although the federal government was small—the Army was the only "federal agency" in the modern sense, which was why it was running the Freedmen's Bureau in the South—it controlled much of the country's land-mass, as well as such vital matters, in a society of farmers, shopkeepers, and craftsmen, as tariffs and the amount of public currency in circulation. Economically well-off people who were in such businesses as railroads, bonds, foreign trade, and mining depended completely on government favor. A government job or contract was a precious thing, and obtainable solely through political influence.

So much was at stake in politics that just about everybody who could vote did. Campaigning was a mass popular activity; office-holders were celebrities who had the oratorical skill to hold a crowd's attention for hours. Getting the right to vote was quite literally, as Ames reported, a matter of life and death, at least in Mississippi. Many forms of political maneuvering and intrigue short of violence were available to the forces opposing Reconstruction in the South—though that certainly didn't mean violence wasn't a constant possibility or that the former Confederates considered it wrong.

Ames's own view of himself had no room for any consciousness of personal, let alone selfish, interest, but in his journal and his letters home during the years just after the war ended, it is possible to detect, in the growing number of references to Republican Party as well as Army matters, the dawning of his political ambition. In Mississippi he became deeply engaged in his duties as provisional governor, more so than as district commander. Perhaps the core thought process of politicians is to align their sincere convictions as closely as possible with their political interests—an accomplishment requiring not much less creative imagination than an artist would use in getting the world onto a piece of paper. In Mississippi one could envision a political future in which, with Negroes voting freely, the Republican Party would be as solidly in control of the instruments of government as it was in states like Massachusetts and Ohio, because the 445,000 Negroes in Mississippi made up a majority of the population. Nationally, the Confederate states with the biggest Negro populations might become an additional base, after the Northeast and the upper Midwest, for the Republican Party.

The horrors that Ames witnessed in the South—the racial killings with impunity, the physical intimidation at election time, and the unwillingness on the part of the Civil War's losers to obey law or authority—would only have reinforced the political logic that caused him to reconsider his earlier opposition to Negro enfranchisement. He also had cause to reconsider his earlier opinion that Radical Republicans were crazy, since, in Mississippi, the non-Radical Republicans were led by a very wealthy plantation owner, James Lusk Alcorn, whose recent switch to the Republican Party from the Democratic looked to Ames more like a tactical move meant to keep the state's elite in power than evidence of a genuine change of heart. Ames the practical-minded military occupation officer was quickly becoming Ames the idealistic Mississippi politician, passionate about bringing rights and education to the Negroes and fully in tune with the Radical ascendancy of his party in Washington.

In November 1869, with General Ames overseeing the election, the new Mississippi constitution and the guarantees of rights for Negroes did pass, and a heavily Republican legislature was elected. It was so obvious that the next election would produce a Republican victory that the Democrats did not even put up a major candidate for governor; instead, the race was between Alcorn, the Democrat-turned-Republican, and Louis Dent, the pathetically weak and exploitable brother of President Grant's wife, Julia Dent Grant, whom unrepentant Democrats had put on the ballot as a ruse, believing that naive Negroes would vote for him because of his association with the president, but that as governor he could easily be subverted and Democratic control in fact restored. The embarrassed President Grant publicly disowned his brother-in-law's candidacy, and Alcorn won.

Those were the days before direct popular election of U.S. senators; since the founding of the nation, senators had been chosen by state legislatures. In January 1870, Mississippi's new Republican legislature convened and selected two new senators, who of course were both Republicans: a prominent Negro minister named Hiram Revels, who took the seat that had been vacated by Jefferson Davis when he became president of the Confederate States of America, and Brevet Major General Adelbert Ames, who was thirty-four years old at the time.

On a visit back to Washington in the spring of 1868 to consult with his superiors, Ames had dropped by the visitors' gallery of the Senate to see something of the drama that had the capital transfixed: the impeachment trial of President Johnson, essentially for being too forgiving of the former Confederates and too willing to let the South return to something like its old racial order. Although the impeachment failed by one vote to produce a conviction, it was a sign of the power of the Radical Republicans in national politics. Republicans who hadn't previously been Radical—like Ulysses Grant and Adelbert Ames, who had earlier written his parents that he was unsympathetic to the impeachment—were moving in the Radicals' direction.

Everybody who mattered in Washington went to see the impeachment trial, including the city's most prominent women, who, though they may not have had the right to vote, certainly had the right to be as interested in politics as everybody else in town. One regular attendee was Blanche Butler, the twenty-one-year-old daughter of Representative Benjamin Franklin Butler, Republican of Massachusetts and one of the impeachment managers. Blanche was already a figure in Washington in her own right by virtue of her beauty, her forthright intelligence, and her social prominence. A sketch appeared in a Washington newspaper that spring showing Miss Butler sitting on a bench in the gallery, beautifully costumed in a hat, veil, and gloves, holding a fan in one hand, and, on the bench behind her, General Ames, in frock coat, top hat, and sleek mustache, leaning over the back of Miss Butler's bench in conversation.

Blanche's father, Ben Butler, would have ranked at the very top of the South's pantheon of resentment—or perhaps just behind Representative Thaddeus Stevens of Pennsylvania, who was believed in the former Confederacy to be a deranged clubfoot who tortured rebels to please his Negro mistress. The rampaging General Sherman was by then well on his way to becoming a Southern sympathizer and opponent of Reconstruction; General Grant, at that point, appeared to be magnanimous in victory; the South had persuaded itself that President Lincoln, had he lived, would have been forgiving (meaning, not inclined to insist on Negro rights) as well. But Ben Butler was a different story. A rich lawyer-politician from the textile mill district of northeastern Massachusetts, he had served as a general in the Union Army during the war. As commander of Fort Monroe, in southeastern Virginia, in 1861, he established the principle that not-yet-freed slaves who managed to make their way into the custody of the Union Army would not be returned to their owners. Of Butler's many wartime assignments, the one the white South remembered best was his service as commander in charge of the unusually harsh—at least in Southern legend—Union occupation of New Orleans. "The little children of New Orleans, when they are very good, are treated by their grandmothers not to the thrilling adventures of Blue Beard and Jack the Giant Killer, but to tales of the Federal general in command of the city during the war," a local author wrote thirty years later, and the tale-telling went on well into the twentieth century. Butler—who was rheumy-eyed and weak-chinned, rather than being a dashing career officer like Ames—had ordered the society women of New Orleans to register as enemies of the United States, and to surrender their family silver so that it could be melted down into bars that would be sold to finance the Union war effort. This got him the nickname of Spoons Butler, or, putting it more directly, Beast Butler.

All through Reconstruction, opponents of the Radical Republicans accused them of "waving the bloody shirt," meaning, trying to drum up support for their Southern policy by reminding Northern voters that it wasn't so long ago that their fathers, brothers, and sons had been killed on the battlefield by the people who were now trying to wriggle free from the war's results. (This worked much better than a direct appeal on behalf of Negro rights would have.) The phrase originated when Ben Butler actually did wave the bloody shirt of a murdered federal tax collector on the floor of the House, as a prop for a speech he was making. To his daughter Blanche, watching from the gallery as her father lengthily accused Andrew Johnson of conduct unbefitting the presidency, Butler may have been a bit distant and forbidding personally—his substantial household operated on the principle of maneuvering around him—but he was one of the great statesmen of the age, a superb political strategist and steadfast opponent of the egregious secessionists.

Soon Adelbert Ames had adopted the same view of Butler. "His great genius—his resources, his tact, his courage strike me as something remarkable and worthy of the highest admiration," he wrote to Blanche, whom not coincidentally he had also begun to admire highly. Ames came from a plainer, more provincial realm than the one the Butlers occupied. General Butler's air of mastery, his confidential friendships with all the chief Washington figures, beginning with President Grant, his large home near the White House where there were nightly sessions of billiards, cigars, and high-level political talk—all this made a great impression on Ames, and so did Blanche.

Ames arrived in Washington as senator-elect from Mississippi in early 1870; on February 3, Blanche and her mother made an appearance in the Senate gallery, and after that day's adjournment Ames was invited to the Butler home for dinner. The Butler women were a far cry from the sort of person Ames had met in his career as a military officer. Blanche's mother was an accomplished amateur

actress who had performed Shakespeare all over the Northeast, and
an expert in the realm of elegant household management and dress.
Blanche herself was a painter, a witty conversationalist, and a clothes-
horse. During that season several portraits of her were on display in
Mathew Brady's photographic gallery in Washington, and a full-
length oil painting, showing her dressed in an expensive and beautiful taffeta gown trimmed with lace and embroidered with violets,
hung in the National Academy of Design in New York. A press clipping Blanche saved into old age declared that she possessed "a
beauty that is the event of a century, and deserves celebrity with
that of the immortal women whose portraits the great painters have
hung on the walls of European galleries—so radiant and rosy it is,
so dazzling with the sunshine of dimpled smiles, so dark and splen-
did are the eyes, so bright and golden is the profuse hair." She was
confident and unconventional enough to be willing to flirt with
old-maidhood (she was twenty-three) rather than settle for a less
than thrilling husband.

The Democrats in the Senate tried to prevent Ames from being
seated, on the grounds that rather than being a bona fide resident
of the state he claimed to represent, he was a "military dictator"
who had arranged the legislative elections so as to ensure, at gunpoint, that he would be elected to the Senate. (And it was true that
Ames did not own a residence in Mississippi, though he planned to
correct that shortcoming soon.) The Republicans prevailed and
Ames was sworn in, but the fight took up most of February and
March; during that time, Ames consciously avoided public activities
in Washington that might come across as presumptuous and hurt
his cause. What he was really up to then, besides fighting for his
seat, was courting Blanche Butler.

In early April, when he was finally seated, his mother wrote to
congratulate him, but also sounded this somewhat wounded note:
"The papers say you are engaged to be married to Miss Butler. We
suppose it is all a hoax, as had it been so you would have informed
your parents before you had the public." Whether or not they were
secretly engaged at the time, within a couple of weeks they were
officially so, and Ames had duly informed his parents, who by

then had moved from Maine to Northfield, Minnesota—in wheat-farming country—to open a flour mill. With the arrangement completed, Blanche and her mother returned to the Butler family home in Lowell, Massachusetts.

Adelbert Ames spent his first months in the Senate sitting at his desk and, as the debates droned on, writing love letters to his fiancée. He almost never missed a day; on many days he wrote two or three times. Blanche wrote back at a rate that would have seemed remarkable, too, if only the point of comparison had not been Adelbert's production. (He was, perhaps, ever so slightly more earnestly in love with her than she with him.) "Do you blacken your finger when you write?" Blanche wrote one day in May; letters then were handwritten, in a flowing script, with ink dipped from a well. "I am very unfortunate that way. A ring on one hand, and a big ink-spot on the other are the tokens of my engagement." The two lovers teased, gossiped, offered up bits of political and business news, exchanged declarations and little gifts and endearments (Adelbert called himself the "Old Jew" because he held Blanche's love with such a fierce possessiveness), feigned wounds at each other's hands, and made giddy, limitless plans for their wedding day and beyond. Blanche, who was not inclined toward self-effacement, wrote Adelbert that she planned to drop from the wedding ceremony the wife's traditional promise to obey the husband. "I thought I had better write and ask if you have any objection—at the same time to inform you that I have not the least intention of making that promise."

To the extent that the couple had an issue to settle, it was when the wedding would take place. The Congress adjourned sometime in July, but one couldn't be sure in advance of the date. Blanche did not want the wedding to be held in August, because everybody in her circle of acquaintance went away to the mountains or the beach then. If they waited until September, then there might not be time for the couple to take the long trip Adelbert planned—first to Northfield to meet his family, then to Iowa to look into the possibility of starting a second Ames flour mill there, then to Mississippi to spend time with his constituency—and still be back in Washington by the beginning of December, when Congress reconvened.

General Butler believed there was a strong possibility that the president and first lady might travel all the way to Lowell to attend the wedding, if a date convenient to them could be found.

Although the post-wedding journey, particularly the part in Mississippi, was far less important to Blanche than to Adelbert, she generously set July 21 as the date, never mind the president's convenience, and even suggested (displaying a degree of political canniness that was, generally, higher than that of her husband-to-be) that if the congressional adjournment were postponed, he might pair with an absent Democrat and thus not miss any recorded votes.

President and Mrs. Grant did not come, but the wedding was nonetheless glorious (and the Ameses, on their way west, called on the Grants soon afterward). There were six hundred guests, and, according to press reports, ten thousand people gathered outside the church to cheer the bride and groom when they emerged. The Ameses were a gleaming, famous young couple, which they didn't mind at all—they'd send each other press clippings about themselves. (Adelbert's plain country mother had written to chastise him when she saw his name on a newspaper's list of the best-dressed men in the Senate.) In Washington, Adelbert was intensely proud of his reputation as a rising man; once, after reporting to Blanche that he had called upon the president privately, he wrote, exultantly, "Am I not getting rapidly into the political circle when at this early day I go to the Executive to point out his errors and to indicate the proper path for him to pursue?" During their wedding trip, small crowds sometimes gathered to stare at them.

They could see, because it was obvious, that they were living on the verge of a great change in American life. The Civil War was hardly over and the careers of General Butler and General Ames were, as the titles they preferred to use connoted, retrospectively connected to it, but the world of carriages and lockets and duels and quills in which Blanche and Adelbert had been raised was giving way to a faster one of telegrams and railway cars and big cities filled with factories, and even more dramatic changes were plainly coming. The transcontinental railroad had been completed the year before they were married. On the wedding trip Blanche, who was forced by proximity to Adelbert to redirect her inexhaustible writing energies from letters to a journal, recorded this musing at a train station: "The engines with their great Cyclops eyes and fiery mouths rushed by us snorting and throbbing. Three on the right, two on the left would glower at us out of the darkness, then pass and repass each other hissing and screaming like devils. The engineers looked so puny and impotent on their iron steeds. Yet man's ingenuity framed these wonderful machines, and a child's hand can control their motions. What is there that human mind is not capable of fashioning? Ere long the Heavens may be used as the common highway and Jove's own thunderbolts—no longer simply for destruction—may be utilized for the benefit of mankind, in the form of light and heat." If you were young and in love and prominent, it sometimes looked as if all these miracles had been made just to provide you with maximal possibilities. "Our lives have been marked, yours as no other young lady of the country—and mine as no other young man," Adelbert wrote to Blanche, just before their wedding. "Both qualities of head and heart have made us so. Why may we not expect, hope certainly, to be unlike the masses in our future?"

Blanche's relief was palpable in her letters home from her postnuptial visit to the Ames family in Northfield. They live in a large and solid home and use table linens and good silver just as we do, she reported; she'd been worried, obviously, that her in-laws were going to be uncomfortably rough-hewn. But her reassured feeling dissipated when the couple arrived in Mississippi.

First the trip was delayed because there were reports of a yellow fever outbreak in New Orleans. Because it might spread north to Mississippi, it was felt prudent that the Ameses should remain in Northfield until the arrival of the first frost down South, which would reduce the danger to their health. Safety was another concern: Blanche's mother, mindful of the former Confederates' unrepentance and their violent proclivities, advised her, "I should be a little careful in Mississippi. Some of those people are very brutal." Blanche had never been much entranced with the project of reforming Mississippi anyway. She loved Adelbert very much and liked being the wife of a U.S. senator, but she was far more cosmopolitan and sophisticated than her husband and far less animated by the idea of self-sacrificial gallantry or missionary work. Adelbert had been educated at a military academy, and loved it; Blanche had been educated in a convent, and hated it. Her correspondence was funny, eloquent, astute, and heartfelt, but never moralistic.

During the engagement Adelbert wrote to Blanche, "Are you glad that the time passes, bringing the days when we shall be working together for the interests of Mississippi?" Blanche replied, "I don't know that I look forward with great delight to 'working for the interests of Mississippi.'" What she was looking forward to was "an eager, passionate existence—not listless, monotonous, selfish." She had trouble seeing a life of battling Ku Kluxers in a pestilential backwater, on behalf of Negro rights, as meeting her adjectival requirements.

In Holly Springs, Mississippi, Blanche wrote, "the fleas . . . took breakfast, dinner, and supper from my poor flesh," and in the local cuisine "lard was the basis of everything." In Vicksburg, "There are perhaps some twenty houses in the town superior to cottages of our ordinary mechanics, but not one of them can compare in elegance and richness with Father's place in Lowell." Even Natchez, a prosperous river port that was the Mississippi town Blanche found least objectionable, offered no real escape from "the baleful climate, the lack of good will and refinement in the people. No amusements, no librarys, no social intercourse." She remarked wistfully that it would be far preferable to winter in Havana than anywhere in Mississippi. Everything about Mississippi annoyed her: the people's petty, importuning complaints about the war, when they had started it; the open disloyalty to the Union that local ministers encouraged in their Sunday sermons; the endless round of dull public engagements and meetings that a senator's visit home entailed.

Blanche realized that her feelings about Mississippi presented a problem, given Adelbert's position; at one point in her journal she hopefully reported that Adelbert was considering the possibility of moving to Iowa and running for office there. For the moment, Mississippi was the one real point of disagreement in what was thus far a very happy marriage. Blanche kept up the front as a politician's wife must, and reserved her true opinion of Mississippi for her journal: "The malarious atmosphere, with its baleful influence upon mind and body, the red, clayey, turfless soil, filled with watercourses and gullies, the slothful indolence of all its people, would be insurmountable reasons why I could never regard it with favor, as a permanent place of residence."

Once during their disastrous tour of Mississippi the Ameses called upon a family of transplanted Northern liberals—the kind of people the locals, but never the Ameses, called carpetbaggers. These Northern émigrés were a part of Adelbert's electoral base, and they lived in constant physical danger. This family was called Gill; the husband was a former Union soldier turned local postmaster, thanks to Republican patronage. They simply were not Blanche's type of people. She reported in her journal: "This Mrs. Gill chooses to consider it her mission to superintend and aid in the education of a large number of Negroes, and has established a school, in which she has four assistants. Not content with that, however, she invited the colored people to her house, has them eat at her table. In fact seems to consider them as fit associates for her in every respect. I do not feel sure whether she is actuated by a feeling of spite or philanthropy."

The Ameses' contact with Negroes was limited to Adelbert's somewhat awkward public speaking appearances before Negro audiences, in which he would proudly note how much progress the colored race had made under Republican government thus far, and would promise more of the same in the future. Adelbert, eleven years older than Blanche, had imbibed more of the prewar abolitionist culture—*Uncle Tom's Cabin* and the like—than Blanche had, and now he represented a Negro-majority state and his career depended entirely on the Negro vote. Blanche tended to see the Ku Klux Klan activity in Mississippi as an example of the general uncivilizedness of the white South; Adelbert was very slowly freeing himself from the deep-seated conviction of Negro inferiority with which most white Americans, no matter where they lived or how they had felt about slavery, were imbued, and he was developing a crusading feeling about the cause of Negro rights. He told Blanche that he wanted President Grant to "buckle on his armor and begin to fight." He expended a good deal of effort to obtain a commission at West Point for a colored boy from Mississippi.

Adelbert was more high-principled than Blanche to begin with, more shocked by the senatorial vote-selling he encountered in Washington, less nuanced, astute, and canny in his political judgments, and more attracted to noble causes that might turn out to be lost ones, though it remained to be seen just how far he would be willing to pursue a political crusade into the realm of personal sacrifice. There was something abstract about the Negro to him—a feeling of collectivity, as if the moral weight of the race and its struggle inhered in the question of its overall status more than in the pursuit of interest by individual Negroes, though in fact by that time Mississippi had a substantial, complex, rivalrous black political culture. Once, in his customary spirit of manful candor about his shortcomings, he reported to Blanche after they had been together in Washington for a time and then she had gone back to Lowell to visit her family:

"The colored girl who was here as chamber maid the last few months of our stay here came to me yesterday requesting me to recommend her for some office. I did not recognize her and in declining said I do not know you. She replied, you ought, I was in the house long enough. I did not, and it was only afterwards in thinking it over that I recalled her.

"She was dressed in a walking costume with a flat hat on, and did not seem half as large as she used when going about the house. Of course I felt very cheap and would willingly give the letter of recommendation to regain what was lost—to avoid even the appearance of being neglectful or unduly forgetful toward one so lowly."

Word began to reach Adelbert Ames that back in Mississippi, Governor Alcorn was behaving in a manner unbefitting someone who had been elected to high office under the banner of the Republican Party. Alcorn would have called himself a "fusionist"— someone who was trying to build a Republican political coalition that was not limited to Negroes and carpetbaggers. But to Ames, Alcorn was a Republican in name only, and out of convenience, and he was sullying the party's name and principles by inviting into it unrepentant rebels whose aim was to subvert the party's program of supporting Negro rights.

The rich, round, venerably Mississippian Alcorn was nothing if not canny. In those days of not very highly developed election laws, he had arranged to have himself elected both governor, the position he was now occupying, and U.S. senator, which he would become in 1871 when the brief tenure of Hiram Revels ended. (Revels, the first Negro U.S. senator and Mississippi's leading black politician, had been elected to fill out Jefferson Davis's term.) This gave Alcorn the choice of remaining in Jackson, where he could best control patronage, legislative, and state party matters, or going to Washington to take part in national affairs. Because of his power within the state, he seems to have established a complete domination over Revels, who, like other Mississippi Negroes, was poor and badly needed a new job once his Senate term expired. Ames felt as if it was really Alcorn, rather than Revels, who was his fellow Mississippi senator, because Revels simply did Alcorn's bidding. By then plenty of other black Mississippi politicians were available to hold high office who were much more loyal to the program of the national Republican Party. And Alcorn was also beginning to remove from appointive public offices in Mississippi the loyal Republicans Ames had installed, and to replace them with men who Ames believed were not committed to upholding the nation's new laws guaranteeing full Negro citizenship.

As freshman senators are supposed to do, Ames waited a suitably long time—until March 21, 1871—before making his maiden speech. It was a brief in support of one of a series of what were popularly known as "Ku Klux laws" or "Force Acts," providing for federal (meaning, U.S. Army) enforcement of Negro civil and voting rights in the South in cases where the local authorities would not enforce them, and federal prosecution of violators of the Fourteenth and Fifteenth amendments. Ames knew that Mississippi Ku Kluxers were trying, by means up to and including murder, to keep Negroes from organizing and voting, and to drive carpetbaggers out of the state. He warned his colleagues that they should not assume that the Civil War had entirely ended in the South: "Hatred to the Union, treason, cannot be whipped out of men. Defeats, disasters, and humiliations are not likely to generate love for our Government . . . The country makes a sad and grievous mistake when it supposes that all the evils of slavery and rebellion vanished on that day of surrender at Appomattox Court-House." He complained in particular about Governor Alcorn, whose claims that he was vigorously pursuing the Mississippi Ku Kluxers were belied by a total lack of results. In a second speech, delivered the following month, Ames reported that during Alcorn's governorship thirty Negro schoolhouses and churches in Mississippi had been burned down, with no one punished for it, and that in the first three months of 1871 alone, the Ku Klux Klan had murdered sixty-three Mississippi Negroes, again with complete impunity.

"Gen'l Ames will not go down to Mississippi this summer, I think," Blanche wrote to her mother. "His speech is very radical, and the whole society is so unsettled by the outrages which have been and are being committed that he concludes it wise not to go at present,—especially as his being there will be no use to the people." The *New-York Tribune*, whose editor-owner, Horace Greeley, was maneuvering himself into position to run for the presidency at the head of a breakaway branch of the Republican Party that was much more sympathetic to the South than the Radicals, published a brief summary of Ames's speeches, and soon afterward Governor Alcorn sent the *Tribune*, and it published, a lengthy defense of his conduct. Mississippi's two most powerful politicians were openly at war with each other.

In the fall of 1871 Ames returned to Mississippi, and what he saw caused the confluence of his moral passion, his political interests, and his natural competitiveness to become more powerful. In his letters to Blanche, he treated the idea that Alcorn represented a threat to him as ridiculous. "Alcorn is intensely disliked by all Republicans," he reported; and, the next day, "What was I going to say of Alcorn—I have forgotten—whatever it was matters little. He is dishonest and everybody knows it. Therefore his influence is on the wane." And a few days later: "I find the political situation perfectly satisfactory. In fact, I was never so strong as now."

Beneath these protestations, though, was an unmistakable note of worry. While he was in Mississippi, Ames heard that Alcorn had decided to come to Washington in December to assume his Senate seat. The governor's office would be occupied by Ridgley C. Powers, another former Democrat, the sincerity of whose political conversion to Republicanism Ames doubted and who, anyway, appeared to be merely a cat's-paw for Alcorn. Hiram Revels would be leaving his Senate seat to become president of a new educational institution for Negroes called Alcorn College. It appeared to Ames that Alcorn had seduced Revels and his followers, through the use of patronage, into abandoning the politician who represented the true interests of their race. Ames knew that many of Mississippi's rising Negro politicians shared his scorn for Alcorn and Revels, and would prefer a governor who was stronger for Reconstruction.

Because they were legislatively rather than popularly elected, senators who had a broad following back home but weakening support among local politicians were in real peril. Ames had to consider the awful possibility that a state legislature mainly made up of Democrats and ersatz Republicans controlled by Alcorn would not return him to his seat in Washington. Politicians always tell themselves that it isn't for their own sake that they fear defeat, but for the sake of their constituents and their cause; Ames told himself this—but, although he certainly liked being a U.S. senator, in his case more than almost any other one could imagine, the idea that his defeat would be harmful to people other than himself was no self-delusion. Hardly a week passed in Mississippi when a freed slave or a carpetbagger was not murdered, with no evident response from Alcorn. There was only one sure way for Ames to strengthen the long-term security of his Senate seat, and that was to return to Mississippi and run for governor. That would lay to rest the suspicion that he was not really a resident of Mississippi (he still did not own a home there); he would be able to shore up the real, mainly Negro, Republican Party; he could bring in a legislature that would support him; and, as Blanche pointed out, he could "show that the power of the bayonet had no part in your first election," the one to the Senate.

In August 1871, a year and a month after their wedding, Blanche gave birth to the Ameses' first child, a boy. They named him Butler, which was a sign of the almost worshipful esteem in which they both held Blanche's father. Although she was a wife and mother, Blanche was still living as a member of her parents' household. She spent most of the time at the family's house in Lowell, as part of a large, warm circle of family, friends, and servants, and during the relatively brief congressional sessions, in the winter and then again late in the spring, the whole household, including Blanche, would move to Washington, where General Butler would take his seat in the House, General Ames would take his in the Senate, and Adelbert and Blanche would reside in an apartment that her father had added to his house there. (The first time little Butler Ames was brought to Washington, two hundred and seventeen callers came to the Butler home to view him.) At other times Adelbert was usually far away, either helping his family look after its interests in the flour business in Minnesota and Iowa, or looking after his own political interests in Mississippi, or making the long journeys between those places by steamboat, railway, and coach. He was still a young man, and he had not entirely decided what kind of life he wanted to lead. He had supervised the construction of a new flour mill in Fort Atkinson, Iowa, and he had also become entranced with the idea of inventing and producing a shallow-draft steamboat that could travel in canals. His commitment to either Mississippi or politics was not total. Blanche was more definitely interested in politics than he, but less in Mississippi, which she regarded with a mixture of horror, scorn, and fear. They went back and forth in their letters about what to do with their lives. "Sometimes I feel like abandoning for once and all, all further thoughts about political matters in this state, and so preparing that we can transfer ourselves to a more civilized people and a more congenial latitude," Senator Ames confessed to his wife in one letter.

Senator Alcorn's maiden speech, in May 1872, was, like Senator Ames's the previous year, about a Ku Klux bill, except that Alcorn took the other side from his colleague, and he opposed federal enforcement of Negro rights. Senatorial courtesy had made some progress since the immediate prewar period—when, for example, Representative Preston Brooks, of South Carolina, had savagely beaten Senator Charles Sumner, of Massachusetts, with a cane on the floor just after the end of a day's session—but not enough to prevent Alcorn from lengthily and sarcastically excoriating his fellow Mississippi senator. "My colleague is not connected with my State by any of the ties which make up the genuineness, the reality of representation," he said. "He is not a citizen of Mississippi. He has never contributed a dollar to her taxes. He is not identified with her to the extent of even a technical residence." Ames gave an equally bitter and personal reply.

In the fall of 1872, when Ames was next in Mississippi, he found himself regularly listening, as politicians considering a race often do, to importunings to try for it. Mississippi's Negroes, though whites saw them as the political pawns and dupes of carpetbaggers, had in fact organized themselves with impressive speed. The first formal statewide meeting of Negro Republicans had been held back in 1868, in Vicksburg. Since then nearly every county in Mississippi had developed a strong local Negro Republican organization, which was often built on a foundation laid by one of the leading black religious denominations: the African Methodist Episcopal, the Baptist, or the Methodist Episcopal. The Freedmen's Bureau, the Loyal League, and an informal cadre of educated Negro ministers and educators who had moved to Mississippi from the North all helped in the project of political organization. Politically active Negroes found safety in numbers. They liked to stage parades and rallies, and to come to polling places en masse to make it less likely that white vigilantes would attack them.

Black politics and black economics went together. And what ground Negroes were gaining in organizing and voting, they were losing in the struggle to find alternatives to plantation employment. Instead, the sharecropper system—in which Negro field hands lived on plantations, often the same ones where they had been slaves; owned no land; and split the proceeds of the cotton they raised and picked with their former masters on highly unfavorable terms—was rapidly emerging as the dominant economic form of post-emancipation Mississippi. To escape the sharecropper system would require schools to be built, a real justice system to be established, and access to patronage jobs, and all those would be impossible unless Negroes first attained political power. That was why so many black Republicans were no longer willing to put up with the bargain Alcorn and Revels represented, and why they turned to Ames as an alternative. It was still such an early moment in black politics that nobody could imagine a Negro winning the governorship. Ames couldn't imagine it because even as he was beginning to see Negroes as admirable, he still saw them as simple; and most Negroes couldn't imagine it because they thought the prospect would be so horrifying to whites as to lead to a race war that they would lose. So, for now at least, Ames's political ambition and the political ambitions of Mississippi's bolder Negro politicians converged on the idea of his running for governor.

Ames also listened to horrifying reports of the misdeeds and malign intentions of his political enemies and to assurances that he, but only he, had the popularity to carry the forces of good to the governorship. As he traveled through the state to campaign for the reelection of President Grant (at an agonizingly slow pace, because transportation in Mississippi was so primitive, that offered ample time for reflection), Ames sensed that his connection with audiences was deepening, that he really meant something to Mississippi's former slaves. Not much earlier he had reported to Blanche that colored voters were simple and unsuited to listen to real oratory—which was fine with him, because he had limited confidence in his ability in that area. Now, however, he detected a growing stature in himself and in his constituency. His speeches became ever longer—an hour, two hours—and the response to them deeper and more enthusiastic. He saw now that he could run at the head of a ticket on which would also be some of the new Negro politicians who had begun to appear in Mississippi—not Revels and his type, but men who were true representatives of their people, and who had been among those urging him to run. He began looking for Mississippi property to buy.

"As I look about I am being convinced that it would be wisdom to run for Gov. next year, though I have been trying to decide that I would not," he wrote to Blanche in October, in a gingerly tone because he knew how unenthusiastic she would be. "Many of my friends insist that such a course would be the surest way to the Senate." That, rather than taking possession of the Governor's Mansion in Jackson, was the prospect he knew would appeal to Blanche. "I am still hesitating. I shall decide before I start north." A week later Blanche replied. On matters of both business and politics, she was far more knowledgeable and far less quixotic than her husband. As Adelbert was endlessly away working on three projects about which she was skeptical—Mississippi politics, the flat-bottomed steamer, and the new flour mill in Iowa—Blanche made her views known gently and carefully, never offering an overt opinion but never leaving it entirely mysterious what she really thought. In this case she wrote: "You speak of running for Gov., Del. Of course, I need not tell you that I am with you in anything you think best to undertake. I cannot advise, because I cannot judge the way things are with you. Looking at it as an outsider, I should say the chances would be against your being returned to the senate—if you have a colored man as Lieutenant Governor."

On the day before the 1872 election—which would be, actually, the first time in his life that Adelbert Ames ever voted—Ames crossed the Mississippi River with a friend to observe the voting in a small town in Louisiana, whose election was held a day earlier. He saw what was obviously a game that had been rigged to produce a Democratic victory, with very few black voters. In reporting his reaction to Blanche, he tried to demonstrate that he understood and sympathized with her preferences about his future, but also that higher concerns were pushing him in the other direction: "It causes two different and conflicting emotions to rise up within me—the one, to abandon a life of politics where such things alone may find place, and another, to buckle on my armor anew that I may better fight the battle of the poor and oppressed colored man, who is regarded by the old slave holder as an inferior, and not fit for the duties of citizenship."

On Election Day, President Grant carried Mississippi by a substantial margin, thanks to the Negro vote. A few days later, before he left the state to return to the North, Adelbert Ames purchased a large, handsome house in Natchez, the one town in Mississippi that Blanche, on her previous visit, had found at all tolerable.

In retrospect, Ames saw his decision to run for governor of Mississippi as a simple matter of answering a call to protect Negro rights. "When I took command of this military district," he explained, a couple of years later, "I found that the negroes who had been declared free by the United States were not free, in fact that they were living under a code that made them worse than slaves; and I found that it was necessary, as commanding officer, to protect them, and I did. They were never permitted to go into a jury-box until I put them there. They had no rights that were respected by white men. I found it was necessary to protect them, and I did protect them. I found that their freedom depended on the success of the republican cause, and circumstances grew out of the election which made me believe that I might be of service to the race, in giving them the rights that every American citizen is entitled to all over the country; and so my purpose in becoming a citizen of the State of Mississippi grew out of the necessity of the case. That is my conviction, that I might be of use and advantage to the colored people of the State in securing their actual freedom."

At the time, at least in his intimate life, Ames was not quite so entirely noble, but circumstances were leading him inexorably, if so slowly as to test the limits of the modern imagination, toward a recognition of the humanity of his constituency that was hardly common among white Republicans of the day. In March 1873, Blanche Ames gave birth to a second child, a daughter named Edith. By that time Adelbert had dropped any pretense that he was still trying to make up his mind about running for governor. In May, Blanche and the baby traveled to Mississippi to inspect their new home and to let the state see that the Ames family really was now residing there. But after just a few weeks, Blanche came to the conclusion that the Mississippi summer presented an unacceptable risk to Edith's health, and she returned to Massachusetts. She was not being irrational—the Ames correspondence is full of reports of babies dying, and cholera and yellow fever regularly swept through the Deep South—but it wasn't as if she had to be torn away from a place she was coming to love, either. Shortly before Blanche was to leave for Mississippi, news of the Colfax massacre in Louisiana had reached her in Massachusetts, and that did not increase her eagerness to relocate in the Deep South. Her letters home to her mother, once she had arrived in Mississippi, were brave, but with horror always discernible in the background. On one occasion, she reported, a woman approached Edith's nanny and said she'd like to hold the beautiful baby—whose was it? When she heard that it was General Ames's daughter, she changed her mind in a hurry and, besides declining to hold Edith, lined up her six grandchildren and had them sing "The Bonnie Blue Flag," the Confederate national anthem. This kind of thing happened regularly: "Everyone on the street asks, 'Oh, whose sweet baby is that?'" Blanche wrote. "When they learn it is Gen'l Ames' the noses fly up and they start back as from an adder."

So Adelbert spent the six months leading up to Election Day in Mississippi by himself. Within the Ames marriage, a subtle dynamic of mutual adjustment set in. Adelbert knew that Blanche despised Mississippi, and in his letters he had often offered up sarcastic bits about the "Southrons" for her delectation. But he had the bit in his teeth by now. Having entered the race, he very badly wanted to win it. He was being drawn out of the comfortable life of his class into the dangerous life of his times. His opponents were not just competitors, but evil and corrupt (and they really were). Something vital was at stake (and it really was). Like any public performer, he sensed the presence of wisdom in audiences that responded to him. His accounts of his encounters with Mississippi Negroes shifted in tone. He once had played them to Blanche for humor, using the minstrel-show dialect that most white Americans then found innocently amusing. After a few weeks of campaigning, he emphasized his constituents' simple moral nobility. Soon he was writing to

Blanche, after an evening political event in a Negro church, "I imagine early Christians met and worshiped in the same manner—there was a sentinel to guard our building. It was sad because it showed how much they had been oppressed, and how eager they were for light. The church we were in was not half built. It was covered in, but there were no windows, and stars shone through the cracks. They were so poor that they could not complete the building. Yet they sat and cheered and laughed in turn, probably enjoying the meeting more than meetings are enjoyed even when the audiences sit on velvet cushions."

Blanche, sensing the movement in her husband, began accustoming herself to the possibility of being Mississippi's necessarily resident first lady. As people in a successful marriage do, each struggled to find a way to be supportive without merely surrendering to the other's will. In Adelbert's case this meant reassuring Blanche that he was a skillful politician moving surely and adeptly toward high office, not just a crackpot idealist. To register this version of him, it helps to note that the political power of Blanche's adored father was ebbing while that of her husband was growing: Ben Butler failed to get the Republican nomination for governor of Massachusetts that year, even though he had invested $10,000 of his own money in the attempt, while Adelbert, in Mississippi, was investing just $250 in his promising effort. Adelbert rather hesitantly mentioned that it would be wonderful if Blanche and the children would return to Mississippi for the final stages of the campaign. Blanche did not respond directly, but she began at least to find words with which to express sincerely the hope that Adelbert would win. Shortly after returning to Massachusetts, she cautioned him, "I hope you have not felt obliged to make any statement or promises as to what you will or will not do in the future. I should desire to be unfettered if I were you in all personal plans and actions." But within a few weeks, having sensed how much Adelbert wanted the governorship, she was able to write: "It is better to take care of the present, and the future can take care of itself. I want you, if possible, to be elected Governor *this fall.*"

At the end of August, the state Republican convention nominated Ames for governor by a vote of 187 to 40, at the head of a slate mainly made up of Negroes. (Alcorn, humiliated, switched his party registration again and announced for governor as an independent.) Blanche offered her congratulations without mentioning her previous view that it would be a mistake for her husband to run on a mixed-race ticket, and Adelbert was positively exultant. "Could the victory be more decided?" he wrote Blanche. "Of course it was made unanimous. This is a death blow to Alcorn. Our banner prevails. We are the master of the field."

Adelbert and Blanche occupied two different places geographically that were also, in a sense, different places temporally. In Mississippi, Adelbert was consciously engaged in trying to resolve the most terrible event in the American past, the Civil War. Slavery, secession, the devastation of the war, and, more generally, the problems associated with life in a premodern agrarian society were a palpable daily presence in his life. Just a decade earlier, Grant had been in Mississippi fighting at the head of his army, and the state had presented a tableau of slaughter, starvation, physical and economic devastation, and the upsetting of the world's harshest system of chattel slavery.

Blanche, in Massachusetts, was in a setting where the nearness of the war was not so overwhelming and where, on the other hand, the oncoming rush of a sophisticated, urban, industrial society was impossible to miss, even from the vantage point of a pleasant house in Lowell. In September 1873, a financial panic that had begun in Europe caused the failure of Jay Cooke and Company, the leading American investment banking concern, and that, in turn, led to the closing of the New York Stock Exchange for ten long days. Ben Butler was an active investor, and the panic immediately engendered an air of crisis in his household in Lowell. (However, Butler was able to immunize himself so successfully that within a few weeks he had bought a half share in the famous and grand yacht *America*, which required a crew of twenty, for his family's recreation.) In Mississippi politics, these financial developments were so distant as to go unnoticed at least in the short run. Even Adelbert and Blanche's epistolary flirting gives a feeling of people occupying two different cultural eras, hers one in which the twentieth century seems to be spreading its light over the horizon, his one that calls to mind the early days of the Republic.

One day Blanche and her sister decided to be adventurous, and afterward she gave this account of the adventure to Adelbert: "About half past nine, if you had been lingering near the flagstaff, you would have seen two grey figures picking their way along towards the rocks through the darkness, and four or five colored girls following. Katie and I had determined to try the water boy-fashion, without bathing suits, and of course night had to be our covering. When we reached the shore, the waves looked black enough, but were filled with sparkling phosphorescence. We put our feet in to try the temperature—it was cold, but the determination not to be baffled was strong, and off came the grey flannel drawers and shirts and into the frightful-looking water we rolled. It was a lovely sight I know, for every movement lit up the waves about us as with heat lightning, and the sparkles fell from our arms and finger tips like showers of gold. The white flesh in this pale light had a soft indistinct gleam like pearls. The freedom from all restraint was delightful, but having bathed once before, we did not dare to remain but a moment. The colored girls acted as sentinels, to guard against all comers."

Adelbert, a few weeks later, attempted to answer in kind, with an account of a nighttime swim of his own in the Gulf of Mexico: "After viewing the dancing for a few minutes, we went a-bathing. The water was delightful. We of the north do not know the luxury of bathing. Here one is inclined to remain in the water any length of time. I can understand how it is the savage inhabitants of islands under the equator are half amphibians. The water last night was full of phosphorous and often a rapid motion of the hand under water would leave a small luminous ball behind. As we swam along, little sparks like electric sparks were thrown off, or would roll up the arm. Finally we came out, and I went to bed, thinking of you and in my sleep dreamed of you." But this was an explorer's account of an exotic encounter with the primitive, the sexuality saved for later—not an arousing dip into a coming world where people like the Ameses one day might plausibly dwell.

For the month leading up to the 1873 election, Ames was soaring, as a politician does when things are going his way. His letters to Blanche were full of ecstatic reports on the reaction that he—not so long ago a stiff, inept public speaker, especially uncomfortable around colored people—was getting from Mississippi crowds. In a time when there was no scientific way of gauging public reaction, Ames tended to measure his success by the length of his speeches. In Holly Springs, he wrote to Blanche, he held an audience of more than two thousand people for over two hours, and "I find I am producing a wonderful effect, and none more marked than on the white people. Even the most bitter are compelled to acknowledge that I am honest, which goes a great way. I am astonished every day at the results of my appeals."

In Grand Junction, "it seemed as if every colored man in the county had presented himself"; the word "Ames" was emblazoned everywhere from hatbands to horse-drawn wagons, and, Ames wrote, "they lost no regard for my name in listening to my speech." In Vicksburg, he spoke for three hours and forty minutes to a standing crowd—"a sea of upturned faces before me, which I could and did make assume the sad or gay at my bidding." In Greenville, he spoke for four and a half hours. When he traveled down the Mississippi River by steamboat, which was the only way to get from the northwestern part of the state to Jackson, because there were no reliable roads, a crowd appeared at every landing to cheer him. "My leadership of the party, the qualities which have made me such—my unexpected success as a speaker—one and all compel deference and respect," was the way he summed up the situation to Blanche.

Just before the election, Alcorn's forces, seeing that there was no doubt what the result would be, introduced a bill in the Mississippi legislature to postpone the selection of a governor by a year. Alcorn controlled the state House of Representatives, so Ames would have to stop the bill in the Senate. That was difficult, because that body's presiding officer was an Alcorn man who made all rulings on procedural matters so as to inflict the maximum harm on Ames. A wild week or two ensued in Jackson, full of parliamentary maneuvering, intrigue, and bribery. "Money and whiskey are used plentifully," Adelbert told Blanche at the height of the confusion, "and last night one of our senators was taken to New Orleans by an enemy to be plunged into a debauch if possible." And, two days later, "Money, threats, flattery, promises, everything is being used by the enemy." Two days after that, Adelbert reported that a Republican senator on whose vote he had been counting had disappeared—"He had previously refused to sell himself for one thousand dollars, and it is believed he did sell himself for five thousand"—and another had been expelled from the Senate. But the Ames forces countered by sending a search party to New Orleans, finding the missing, debauch-prone senator, bringing him back to Jackson, and putting him to sleep in a big bed, with a loyal Republican lying next to him on each side, in an Ames safe house that was under armed guard.

Ames prevailed in the state Senate through the uninspiring but effective means of putting up so many legislative roadblocks that the bill to postpone the election could not come up for a vote before the deadline for its passage: October 31, 1873 (which was Ames's thirty-eighth birthday). Then the election itself was a wonder. Mississippi's Negro voters turned out in a great mass and gave Ames his victory over Alcorn by a margin of thirty thousand votes. (After the returns were in, Governor Powers tried to have them invalidated, but the state Supreme Court upheld Ames's election.) The new legislature elected along with him had a heavy Republican majority and a substantial Negro membership—55 of 115 state representatives, and 9 of 37 senators, were black. Never mind the aspect of personal triumph for Ames—it seemed, at least for the few days after the election during which Ames remained in Mississippi (he was soon off to Minnesota to attend to his flour-milling business), as if a new political order had emerged, and one so solid that, at last, the rebels would have no choice but to stop resisting the outcome of the Civil War and the authority of the U.S. government.

In Lowell, three days after the election, General Butler called his family into the library, made everyone sit down, and read out loud a telegram containing the great news from Mississippi. In the Butler home, Mississippi may have been poorly regarded, but the attainment of official power and rank got immediate and full respect. There was some joking conversation about which of the three grand honorifics to which Adelbert Ames was now entitled was preferable, General Ames, Senator Ames, or Governor Ames. Presently, little Butler Ames was sent into the library to call the family to the dinner table, and in his hurry he slipped and hit his head on the floor and began to cry.

"Never mind, my boy," said General Butler, to console his grandson. "Your father is Governor of Mississippi."

2

VICKSBURG TROUBLES

As if it were the capital city of a small and self-important independent nation, Jackson, Mississippi, had state buildings of a proportion and grandeur far above anything surrounding them. At the eastern edge of town, set on top of a bluff with a commanding view, was the state capitol, an elegant, oblong stone structure with a metal dome. In the north side of the building was the chamber of the Mississippi House of Representatives, a two-story-high room with big columns flanking the speaker's podium, and a curved balcony with wrought-iron railings; on the south side was the Senate, a more intimate circular room, and the governor's office, an oversized, chandeliered rectangular chamber with tall windows and imported furniture, fit for a continental prime minister. A couple of blocks west on Capitol Street, taking up an entire block at the center of Jackson, was the Governor's Mansion, built of white-painted brick, with a tall semicircular colonnade, broad front steps, and surrounding grounds planted with graceful shade trees. The capitol and the mansion both were built in the early 1840s, when Jackson was just a small town, and even now the state had fewer than a million people. Beyond its being war-ravaged, it was still substantially wild and unsettled. Parts of it were nearly jungle; slavery and the taking of the land from Indians were so recent as not even to deserve to be called memories. Most Mississippians were illiterate; most Negroes worked as hands on the land where they had been slaves; violence and justice were as much in the control of individuals as governments.

It was the state buildings, with their presumptuous air of consequence standing in contrast to the rough conditions in the hinterland, that formed the orbit into which Adelbert and Blanche Ames moved in the first days of 1874. While governance in Mississippi was notionally quite grand, as the out-of-scale buildings indicated—the governor was routinely addressed as "Your Excellency"—Blanche nonetheless immediately noticed a lack of the sort of gentility to which she was accustomed. She sent her mother little sketches of the layout of the mansion, and together they made plans for importing Northern standards of social behavior to Jackson, to the extent that would be possible. Convicts under armed guard did the heavy cleaning work on the house and grounds. The cook was difficult to persuade, Blanche complained, "that lard is not the staff of life"; in general, "the colored people are not nearly as well trained as they are in Washington." Most of the proper ladies of Jackson were obviously hostile: "All are lynx-eyed, and one is always polite and kindly, but constantly on guard."

Blanche began holding croquet parties for carpetbaggers on the lawn of the mansion, and inviting the prominent Negroes who were her husband's most important political supporters to social events inside. Sarah Butler constantly urged Blanche to spend as much time as she could in the North—"A sallow, Southern woman cannot compare with the bright, glowing color of a Northern one," she admonished her daughter—and reminded her of the high political prizes that would make their Southern exile both temporary and worthwhile. It was not much time, really, until the next elections, when Adelbert could return to Washington as a U.S. senator and Ben Butler (here it was Blanche reminding Sarah) could run for the governorship in Massachusetts and then for president. It was a sign of both the family's prosperity and its political confidence that Butler had undertaken to build what would be the largest private residence in Washington, a five-story house just a short distance from the White House.

Adelbert, the family idealist, laid out for the people of Mississippi, as he took office, a dream of a government that would create a public education system good enough to defeat the illiteracy that pervaded the state; that would operate on a sound financial basis; that would find a way to turn the former slaves from peasants into landowning farmers. Railroad companies, in those days, were by far the most powerful interest group in American politics—no less so in Jackson, where the right to build the lines that would transport the state's agricultural riches was at stake, than in Washington. Ames planned to reverse Mississippi's practice of taking on public debt to finance railroad construction, which was essentially a way of subsidizing the railroads in return for the railroad men's own personal subsidies to the state legislators. His ideas on this score did not represent the consensus among white Mississippians, to say the least, including those who had enough money and influence to challenge Ames directly.

Mississippi's prosperous whites, nicknamed Bourbons by their opponents (and they didn't find the comparison to prerevolutionary French kings offensive), believed so deeply that racial hierarchy was the natural order of things that they considered themselves not as prejudiced against Negroes but merely as protectors of that natural order; and they had economic and political as well as racial motives for wanting postwar Mississippi to take a profoundly different form from the one Ames had in mind. Literacy and land tenancy would be disruptive to the plantation tenant system that they wanted to emerge as a workable successor to slavery. Clean, railroad-resistant government would dampen the kind of deal-making they wanted to be in on.

It might have seemed that Ames had the force of history on his side. The Union had crushed the Confederacy less than a decade earlier. Its chief general was now president. Grant had been easily reelected in 1872, even though his opponent, Horace Greeley, had run as the candidate not only of a breakaway group of Republicans but also of the Democratic Party. Ames himself had been elected governor by a wide margin, and Mississippi was a Negro-majority state. The social compact he was proposing—public education and the rights of citizenship for all—was not so different from what other parts of the country had, at least outside the South.

Politics produces an endless rush of events that take a definite form only retrospectively, so Ames could not see this, but now it looks as if the country's commitment to Reconstruction was already flagging at the time he was taking office as governor of Mississippi. The financial panic of 1873 had turned into a sharp economic ache that distracted attention from reformist projects, and also President Grant's heroic reputation had been damaged. The men who owned the railroads, bipartisan seekers of close relations with those in power, were as closely allied with the Republicans in Washington as they were with the Democrats in Mississippi, and in the time since Grant's reelection the Crédit Mobilier scandal had erupted, in which it was shown that high Republican and administration officials had been bribed by the Union Pacific Railroad. Simultaneously, another great national scandal had developed, perhaps less important but certainly no less interesting or well publicized: the exposure by the feminist reformer-troublemaker-publisher Victoria Woodhull of a "free love" relationship between the country's most famous liberal clergyman, Henry Ward Beecher of Brooklyn, New York, brother of the author of *Uncle Tom's Cabin*, and one of his married female parishioners. The destruction of Beecher's good name, through a series of sensational trials initiated by the cuckolded husband, was a setback to Northern white support for the cause of Negro rights that Beecher had championed, though of course it hardly caused Negroes to change their minds about the justice of the Fourteenth and Fifteenth amendments to the Constitution.

If, before the war, the abolition of slavery had been the leading cause of Northern intellectuals, academics, clergymen, journalists, and public-spirited patricians, "reform" was becoming their leading cause now. Reform meant sound money on the gold standard, free trade, a civil service free from patronage, limited government, low taxes, and a generalized suspicion of the uneducated masses and their political style (like the political machines and the spoils system that awarded government jobs to political cronies) and causes (like tariffs and inflation). If there was one leading reformer, it was probably Carl Schurz, the former German revolutionist, Union general, journalist, leader of the German immigrant community, and politician, and it was he who had organized the breakaway Liberal

Republican Party and helped to engineer its support of Horace Greeley, another ex-abolitionist, as Democratic presidential nominee in 1872. In December 1865, Schurz had published a celebrated "Report on the Condition of the South," which was the result of a trip he had made at the behest of President Andrew Johnson, and warned that the South would never grant the freed slaves their rights unless forced to; now Schurz had turned against Reconstruction, in the name of reform.

The embodiment of the tendencies in the Republican Party that the reformers found repulsive was Benjamin Butler; to them, "Butlerism" meant big government, corruption, and toadying to the immigrants who were then coming to the United States in increasing numbers. And the enforcement of the constitutional rights of America's new Negro citizens fell, in the reformers' minds, into the category of corruption rather than reform, because it entailed just what they found so disturbing in the Northern cities, the political empowerment of illiterate men and the expansion of government power. It was difficult, anyway, for even the most liberal-minded white Northerner to look on the spectacle of black people not just voting but holding political power—something generally known as "Negro domination"—without an instinctive revulsion. The reformers had gone in just a few years from abolitionism to anti-Reconstructionism. So, just as it was becoming clearer to Adelbert Ames that political morality resided mainly in supporting the cause of ensuring the former slaves' civil and voting rights, that was becoming less clear to the country as a whole, if it had ever been clear at all.

On the same day that Adelbert Ames was elected governor, the voters of the First District of Mississippi elected Lucius Quintus Cincinnatus Lamar, of Oxford, to the U.S. Congress. Lamar was the model of the Southern Bourbon politician. Scion of a prominent Georgia family (in 1838 his uncle Mirabeau Buonaparte Lamar had succeeded Sam Houston as president of the short-lived Republic of Texas), lawyer, politician, arch secessionist and defender of slavery before the Civil War, Confederate general, he had a big square marble block of a head set off by long, flowing brown hair and a Vandyke beard. He was, naturally, deeply opposed to Reconstruction. His son-in-law and biographer imagined his state of mind in the early 1870s, in the wake of the passage of one of the laws providing for federal-government suppression of the Ku Klux Klan, in this way:

"[H]ere was a great heart greatly suffering. In those darkening twilight hours when nature gathers the wandering thoughts of men into the narrow circle of their inner selves, what mighty passions wafted him upon their currents! What inaudible threnodies of sorrow for those deeply loved and uselessly lost! What mocking, pale-faced visions of blooming hopes and vaulting ambitions, now death-stricken forever! What thrills of hot hatred, holy in its intense fire if there be such a paradox in the spiritual world as a hatred at once profane and sacred, for the vile vampires who were drawing the lifeblood from his prostrate State! What surging waves of contempt for those friends of old whose venal knees had bent before the golden calf of power and pelf, and what pangs in tearing out their friendships from his heart! What swirling vortices of passionate and generous reproach for the tragic past, the dreary present, and the frowning future! What agonized searching of the inscrutable mysteries of the coming years! What sickening despair as the tortured mind groped for clews that might lead out from this Stygian darkness into light!"

Lamar had been a Mississippi congressman before the war, and it would have seemed fair to assume that he would use his return to the Congress, once the "deliverance of the state from Military thralldom" (as he put it in a letter to Edward Clark, his protégé and former law partner, who was now practicing in Vicksburg) was accomplished, to take up the postwar version of his prewar cause. A couple of weeks before the election, having read an account of Ames's speech in Jackson accepting the Republican nomination for governor (one of those speeches about which Ames had written so exultantly to his wife in Massachusetts, because it had gotten an enthusiastic audience response that made him feel he had successfully transformed himself from remote military officer to popular leader), Lamar set down his feeling about Ames and Mississippi politics at length in a letter to Clark.

"[Y]ou will find that his mission in Miss., as proclaimed by himself, is the exclusion (by means of the ballot in the hands of the freedmen) from any share in the government, of the only class in which reside the elements of dignity virtue & the welfare of society," Lamar wrote. As the letter went on, Lamar's temper rose: "The real effect of his scheme is that the white people of the state shall be for four years longer practically denied the privilege of self government, their voice silenced, and their interests and their honor confided to strangers who neither comprehend the one nor believe in the existence of the other. I say strangers, for Gen. Ames admitted in his speech here, that his party of Northern men and enfranchised negroes were new to the political interests & institutions of the State . . . Draw a line on one side of which you see property, intelligence, virtue, religion, self-respect, enlightened public opinion, and exclusion from all political control; and on the other the absolute unchecked political supremacy of brute numbers, and there you will behold not one attribute of free government, but the saddest & the blackest tyranny that ever cursed this earth."

Lamar, who was neither ignorant nor naive, did not misjudge his adversary as someone embodying the crude stereotype of the rapacious carpetbagger. "Let it be conceded, which I am always glad to do," he wrote Clark, "that Ames & the men he carries into power are not corrupt personally"; but "it is impossible, and certainly unprecedented, for a body of men to be invested with such vast powers and irresponsible control over the entire wealth of a State without becoming corrupt and criminal. Where is the constituency to which these men will be responsible? Negroes!" By the end of the letter, as he went into his peroration, Lamar's handwriting had gone from its customary beautiful precision to a kind of mad scrawl. "It does seem to me that if there ever was a time when the white people of this state, the men in whose veins flows the blood of the ruling races of the world, should rise & with one unanimous voice protest against the domination about to be piled upon them the present is that time. Can it be that the soul of our proud people which a few years ago rose with such keen sense of wrong and heroic effort has, by long oppression, been dulled into indifference & sullen despair?" L.Q.C. Lamar did not seem to think so. The proper course for men like himself in Mississippi politics, in his view, should be anything but passive.

When Lamar took up his seat in Congress, only a few weeks after writing that letter, he kept quiet for a while, in accordance with etiquette. When he gave his first substantial speech, on April 27, 1874, it was, to Washington's surprise (and possibly to Edward Clark's as well), a lengthy and deeply respectful eulogy for Senator Charles Sumner, one of the best-known Radical Reconstructionists and a man whose name had been associated with the violent proclivities of the white South because it was he who had been brutally clubbed into unconsciousness on the floor of the Senate by a South Carolina congressman in 1856. In the sort of long, ostentatiously eloquent address that represented the pinnacle of a politician's art in those days, Lamar praised Sumner's moralism and magnanimity, came awfully close to hinting that he harbored a certain warmth of feeling toward Reconstruction itself, and grandly suggested that the great man's passing be the occasion for sectional reconciliation. Lamar had never met Sumner, but the deep feeling of his eloquent eulogy transformed him, in the public mind, from Southern diehard to national statesman. And that made him a far more significant enemy to Ames than he would have been otherwise.

At the beginning of June 1874, the Ameses left Mississippi to spend the summer in the North. Adelbert had to attend to his Midwestern business interests and visit Washington, Blanche wanted to spend time with her family at its summer residence, in Bay View, Massachusetts, and even if they had been inclined to remain in Mississippi, they both believed that doing so would put their young children's health in danger because of the heat and pestilence. Ames probably should have been more on guard than he was. He had been receiving alarming letters from Negroes all over the state. "I think you act to do something to give the colored people protection," a man from Holmes County, who identified himself only as John, wrote, "I am a hard working colored man and lost my wife and before I died send a cry for help." A man named L. D. Penn, from the town of Aberdeen, wrote, "If we don't have better treatment than we had well we'll petition Congress to give us a territory off to our self. We cannot comport with our condition here." During the spring of 1874, the neighboring state of Arkansas had been through a short Louisiana-style internal war, with two governors— one Democratic, the other Republican—battling, in the literal military sense, each with his own militia, for control of the state; the Democrat won. Nonetheless, in June, Ames left his black lieutenant governor, A. K. Davis, in charge in Jackson. The state legislature was not in session, and he believed it would be a quiet summer.

He was wrong. At a July 4 celebration held by Negro Republicans in Vicksburg, whose population of eleven thousand made it Mississippi's largest city, a group of whites with guns turned up and started shooting. The celebrants scattered, and the whites went on an open-ended rampage. Peter Crosby, the county sheriff in Vicksburg—the most important position in local government, since it carried both tax-collecting and law-enforcement power— was a thirty-year-old black veteran of the Union Army who had been elected to his position by a large Republican majority on the same day Ames was elected governor. Crosby had warned Ames back in April about unstable conditions in Vicksburg: "There is great excitement among the colored people and seems to be a settled determination among reckless, desperate white men to repeat 'Meridian'"—a well-known incident of anti-Negro political violence in another Mississippi town, in 1870—"here in our midst. Unfortunately the whites are thoroughly armed with State guns which are to be seen in every home and office." Crosby had thought it would be a good idea if federal troops came to Vicksburg to maintain the fragile peace.

Now, on July 5, Crosby sent A. K. Davis an alarmed letter, its hasty scrawl communicating as much as its words, saying, "It becomes my painful duty to again state to you that news comes to me that several has been killed upon the streets of Vicksburg today and several wounded also . . . The killed and wounded all being colored. Who they are and how many is yet unknown." On July 20, Davis wrote President Grant about the situation in Vicksburg: "Armed bodies of men are parading the streets both night and day, the City Authorities, are utterly unable to protect the lives and property of the Citizens—regretting the necessity—I am constrained to ask that Two (2) Companies of United States Troops be at once ordered to Vicksburg to ensure the Citizens against domestic violence which is imminent. Please answer at once."

When word of the Vicksburg disturbances reached Adelbert Ames, he hurried back to Mississippi, but that took a while. He arrived in Jackson on July 29, finding the city full of prominent Republican refugees from Vicksburg, and he immediately sent Grant a long telegram that urgently repeated the request for federal troops. "Regret to inform you that I find upon returning here that a serious & alarming condition of affairs exists at Vicksburg. Infantry and cavalry organizations exist & it is reported that a number of pieces of artillery have been sent to the city & these bodies organized & armed without authority and in violation of law . . . Of the causes of this lamentable state of affairs it is now useless to speak. I only seek peace & protection for all. Can there be any serious objection why troops can not be sent there . . . Will it not be the best (least?) of evils to have troops there for any emergency."

We don't have access to President Grant's thoughts as he considered these requests—his response came, tersely, through his secretary of war, William W. Belknap—but the irony of the situation was surely inescapable: the Vicksburg disturbances had broken out on the eleventh anniversary of the greatest military victory of Grant's career and one of the greatest of all time, which was obtaining the surrender of the city of Vicksburg after a campaign that had lasted more than half a year. Vicksburg is dramatically situated on high bluffs overlooking the confluence of the Mississippi and Yazoo rivers. The Confederate Army had placed an imposing battery of cannons on top of the bluffs, which made it impossible for any Union boat traffic to move past Vicksburg. The bluffs also gave the

Confederates an enormous advantage in defending Vicksburg itself from attack. Grant had made a long, grim, messy, determined overland advance on Vicksburg from the north; had run a flotilla carrying his troops past the cannons on the bluff in the middle of the night; had landed some distance below Vicksburg; had led a march to the city from the inland side; had tried unsuccessfully, twice, with great loss of life, to dislodge the Confederate forces from their favorable location; and, finally, had laid siege to the city and forced a surrender on July 4, 1863. That victory had cut the Confederacy vertically in half and given the Union control of the Mississippi River.

And now Vicksburg was, evidently, seceding all over again.

Municipal elections were scheduled in Vicksburg for August 5. The Republicans had put up a ticket that looked like the statewide ticket that Ames had run on, indeed like Republican tickets over much of the South—with a white man at the head, running for mayor, and the rest of the candidates mostly black. Two recent incidents had inflamed white opinion in Vicksburg: the daughter of a prominent white planter in a nearby town had married a Negro state legislator, after which the Negro city clerk gave a speech endorsing the idea of interracial marriages and predicting that there would be many more of them; and a grand jury had refused to indict a black official on corruption charges. The prospect of a Republican local government being added to the list of indignities pushed Vicksburg's whites into a state very close to armed uprising. The usual rumors about the Negroes' perfidious designs spread through the city. "Talk of bloodshed and slaughter of the whites on election day was common and open," a white Mississippi historian, J. S. McNeily, later reported. "There was no urgent need after this for the white men to organize and take up the color line gauge of battle. The trouble was to restrain them within the limits of peace and order."

An account with obviously different (that is, Republican) sympathies, written just a few months after that tense summer in Vicksburg, does not contradict McNeily's anti-Reconstruction version: "For four weeks or more this self-constituted and unlawful organi-

zation held the streets of Vicksburgh under show of force. They pa-
trolled the streets by day and especially by night; they placed sentinels and released guards; they had their passwords and their
countersigns; they admitted whom they pleased and kept out
whom they pleased; they watched the steamboat-landings, the fer-
ries, and the roads; they attended in armed bodies at the registration of voters, in clear violation of law; and impressed upon the whole
city that fear which comes naturally from an organized and irresponsible mob, prepared for violence, and the more to be dreaded
by peaceable people, because of the mystery which surrounded their
numbers, their leaders, their purposes, and their threats." Democracy, in other words, was being nullified by the whites of Vicksburg.

Secretary of War Belknap had sent an officer from the Army post
in Holly Springs, Mississippi, to Vicksburg to inspect the situation,
and had his inconclusive report forwarded to President Grant. Less
than a week before the city election, a telegram arrived at the Governor's Mansion in Jackson with the news that the president would
not be sending troops to Vicksburg. "I have tried to get troops, but
the President refuses," Adelbert Ames wrote Blanche. "It is thought
he wants the support of the Southern Democrats for a third term.
Most true it is that they are generally for him in this state. And they
in Vicksburg who are rioting, who are ready for murder and frauds,
laud him to the skies." A few days later Ames bitterly remarked in
another letter, "This house"—the Governor's Mansion—"does not
seem a natural place for you and the children. It almost requires an
effort to locate you and them in the rooms. It seems more like a hotel where we stayed, but for a day. This is not a home and never can
be. Where our own vine and fig tree are to grow I know not, but it
is true that in imagination I plant them *not* here."

Election Day, August 5, brought a sweeping Democratic victory
in Vicksburg. "The election at Vicksburg passed off quietly only because the Democrats, or white man's party, has both intimidated
the blacks and perpetrated frauds of registration, which made their
success a certainty, so, of course, they had no cause to commit murder," Adelbert wrote Blanche. "Had there been a doubt as to the issue, a bloody riot would have resulted." Whites did not disagree as

to the significance of the election. J. S. McNeily put it this way: "The result, moral and political, extended far beyond Vicksburg. The significant and signal overthrow of a radical ticket, that followed the administration's refusal to back it with troops, revealed the fatal weakness of the whole reconstruction fabric of government. It pointed to the certainty of the recovery of white rule whenever the pressure of Federal force should be lifted."

Just after Governor Ames had returned to Mississippi that summer, Blanche shipped him a pistol in a box. She had just discovered that she was pregnant again, so, when the summer ended, she and the children remained in Massachusetts.

President Grant's decision not to send troops to Vicksburg appeared to have the immediate consequence of emboldening the armed white resistance to Reconstruction that was spreading everywhere in the South where Republicans still held political power: not only in Arkansas, but in Louisiana and Alabama and South Carolina in addition to Mississippi. Less than a week after the Vicksburg election, a Colfax-like incident occurred in Austin, Mississippi, a hamlet in the cotton plantation country just south of Memphis, Tennessee. A white doctor could not sleep, because two Negro men were singing loudly in their house nearby, so he took down his gun, marched over, and shot and killed them. Negro local officials put the doctor in jail; his white friends took up arms, marched on the jail, and freed him; the Negroes, feeling the need for a safe haven, took over the municipal building; the whites raised a militia and took it back. "I suppose they will now hunt the Negroes through the swamps as they did in slavery days," Adelbert wrote sourly to Blanche. "Unfortunately, I have no means in my power to suppress this kind of disturbance." Evidently Ames's prediction came true: McNeily reports that the whites in Austin killed "eight or ten" of the Negroes after taking back the town, and, as usual in these incidents of supposed martial valor by the whites, there were no reported white casualties.

The public flouting of government authority by the white citi-

zens of Austin, which together with the Vicksburg incident put
Ames's hold on state power into question, had an embittering effect on the governor. In his letter about it to Blanche, he declared:
"Mississippi, which has commanded my thoughts and time for the
last six years, has lost its power over me forever." Blanche continued
to think of the governorship as a wonderful opportunity for political advancement for her husband, and therefore urged him not to
think of the failure of his request to the president for troops as a
crushing blow, but Adelbert had a much bleaker view of the future
course of Mississippi politics, if the Army would not enforce Negro
voting rights. He was becoming less inclined to behave with the
prudence of someone whose future is at stake. The day before
Vicksburg voted, he sent out a confidential feeler to a friend in
Washington to see whether Frederick Douglass, America's most
prominent and accomplished Negro citizen and, not coincidentally,
probably the one most unpopular with white Southerners, might be
interested in coming to Mississippi as president of the state's fledg-
ling university for Negroes. (Douglass wasn't.)

That summer President Grant was receiving reports both official
and unofficial from all over the South about increasing white-on-
black violence, and it appeared to be much better organized and
more political in its aims than it had been during the Ku Klux Klan
heyday a few years earlier. Well-financed terrorists, armed, increasingly, with the latest in military technology—Prussian needle guns,
Winchester rifles, and Colt revolvers—were engaged in what
seemed to be a planned campaign to unseat the Republican Party,
and undo Negroes' civil rights and voting rights, by means of violence against its officeholders and voters. In July, the Red River
valley of Louisiana began to destabilize in just the same way as Vicksburg; Grant was entreated to send federal troops there, too. In late
August, in Coushatta, Louisiana, not far north of Colfax on the
Red River, a white mob operating under the flag of the White
League (and, as usual, under the fantasy of self-protection from marauding Negroes) killed five black men, one of whom was tortured
over a fire, and then six Republican officeholders, two of whom had
already surrendered. Nobody was punished.

Letters poured into the White House from ordinary Southerners describing horrific conditions, and in those days letters to the White House were likelier to get a presidential reading than they are now. A man from Silver Creek, Mississippi, reported to Grant, "Thae tak up the Corlded Peapel and Haung thim . . . We are Prass so We Cant Stand it. If the law Woant Pertect ous We don't What to do." A letter from a "Committee of 1000 men" in Caddo Parish, Louisiana, close to the site of the recent massacre, said, "We as Soon to be Sunk in the Bottom of the red Sea and to live here in the Southern States in the condition that we have been in for the past 9 years and we protend to be free, as Mr. President it seems to Us, and furthermore it seems to Us, that it gets worst, and worst . . . if we go to law for our rights we are either shot or hung or runned off the place, of out of Parish or county." On September 2, Grant appeared to modify the course he had set in response to the Vicksburg troubles in July, for he publicly instructed Secretary of War Belknap that he was empowered to send troops anywhere in the South where it looked as if the local authorities might not protect the legal rights of all citizens.

On September 15, as Grant was preparing for a trip to his summer residence in the oceanfront town of Long Branch, New Jersey, word reached the White House that in New Orleans, the White League had made its boldest move yet—mustering an open, full-dress militia with more than five thousand members and officially demanding the resignation of the Republican governor, William Pitt Kellogg. Kellogg refused, and the White League defeated thirty-five hundred Republican troops in a formal military battle that took place on Canal Street, the main commercial thoroughfare of the largest city in the former Confederacy. Grant, whose family's packed trunks were sitting in the White House hallway waiting to be shipped to Long Branch, canceled his trip, issued a proclamation commanding "turbulent and disorderly persons to disperse and retire peaceably to their respective abodes," and called an emergency Cabinet meeting for the next morning where he briefly considered calling the Congress into special session. Within three days, thanks to the arrival of federal troops, Governor Kellogg was back in office, and by the end of the month Grant had dispatched the Seventh U.S. Cavalry to restore order, finally, in the Red River valley.

Major Lewis Merrill, a remarkable officer (much hated by white Southerners) who had fought in "Bleeding Kansas" and the Indian country before the Civil War, in Kansas and Missouri during the war, and against the Ku Klux Klan in South Carolina during the past few years, arrived in the principal Red River town, Shreveport, in October, and reported to his superiors: "The leaders here are some half-dozen reckless, passionate men of broken fortune, who miss no chance to foment trouble, and whose whole time is occupied in setting afloat disturbing rumors and blowing into a flame every ember of sensation and excitement that they find . . . [T]he whole community seems to have become impressed with the notion that it is practically a state of war, in which all law is to be ignored, and is fast drifting into a state of anarchy, in which any crazy fool could precipitate a condition of things which is fearful to contemplate." Major Merrill believed that the White Leaguers actually wanted the cavalry to attack and defeat them, because that might set off a great regional conflagration—essentially a continuation of the armed conflict of the Civil War years. His superiors didn't disagree that this was a real possibility, so they kept Merrill on a tight leash.

About the Negroes in the Red River country Merrill wrote, a few weeks after his initial report, "The condition of these poor people is pitiable. They are systematically plundered of their crops and driven away from their homes at best, when they escape personal violence or death, in such numbers that it is not an exaggeration to say that the entire black population of this section is absolutely terror-struck, and, if remaining at their homes at all, doing so in almost hourly apprehension of the visits of White Leaguers. Large numbers of them dare not go to their homes at all, and in several instances that I have seen families are scattered to the four winds—the father here, and wife and children somewhere hidden in the woods. There is absolutely no hope for them from the enforcement of any local law; from this they can get no protection whatever. It moves me deeply to hear their sad stories of wrong, outrage, and lawless violence, and their pleading for protection against the devlish vengeance of these people, but I am as powerless to help them as they are to help themselves."

November 1874 brought a stunning result in the national congressional elections. The Democrats, who had been politically marginalized since the Civil War and who only two years earlier, despite their alliance with the Liberal Republicans, had lost the presidential election badly and wound up at a 110-seat disadvantage in the House of Representatives, swept to victory. One hundred and seventy seats in the House changed parties, which made 1874 the most realigning national election of the century. Such stalwart Republican states as Ohio, New Hampshire, and Grant's native Illinois elected Democratic governors. The Democrats took back Alabama, by virtue less of changing sentiments in the electorate than of intimidation of black voters; even a leading anti-Reconstruction historian later wrote that "there was abundant evidence that the whites had demonstrated their superiority . . . by methods that would have no place in the North." In Massachusetts, Benjamin Butler, who had run for both governor and Congress, lost both elections, which meant he was out of office for the first time since the end of the war. The economic depression and the Crédit Mobilier scandal were obviously factors in the election result, but most people in politics thought that President Grant's decision to send more troops to Louisiana just a few weeks before Election Day had badly hurt the Republicans as well.

The day before the election Adelbert Ames was visiting the Mississippi State Fair in Jackson when whom should he run into but Jefferson Davis ("traitor," he wrote Blanche), the former president of the Confederate States of America. "I did not wish to meet him, but could not well avoid it," Adelbert wrote. "His coming (and he is visiting the state) I have no doubt is for political reasons . . . I have no doubt that one and all will do him honor should the opportune moment occur." And the day after the election Adelbert was walking along the street in Jackson and overheard a young man saying to his companion, "They have beaten Ben Butler, that is glory enough for one year." The meaning of the election couldn't have been clearer to Adelbert: the great Union victory of 1865 was coming undone. "What sorry times have befallen us!" he wrote. "The old rebel spirit will not only revive, but it will make itself felt. It will roam over the land, thirsty for revenge, and revenge it will have . . . the war is not yet over."

The Butler family, being deep-in-the-bone politicians as Adelbert Ames was not, had a somewhat different reaction to the disastrous election results. To them it simply meant that Adelbert's future political success was now of consuming importance. Mississippi's next legislative elections would be in a year. Blanche and her parents had a definite plan in mind, which was for Adelbert to engineer a Republican sweep in 1875 and then have the state legislature send him to the U.S. Senate to replace his hated accommodationist Republican rival, James Lusk Alcorn—whereupon the Ameses would take up residence in the Washington mansion whose construction Ben Butler, somewhat overoptimistically it now seemed, had undertaken. Blanche reported to Adelbert that her mother had declared, "If Gen'l Ames can only be returned I shall feel that the great barn of a house is of some account."

In most of the substantial towns of Mississippi, the equivalent, and ally, of Louisiana's White Leagues were springing up. The purpose of these "White Line" organizations was to reestablish white (which was to say, Democratic Party) control of the apparatus of government, and their means was the violent disruption of Republican (which was to say, Negro) political organizing and voting. After the war, the mainly black supporters of Reconstruction had set up "loyal leagues" all over the South dedicated to maintaining Negro rights. Widespread white legend had it that the loyal leagues were actually organizations sworn by secret blood oath to the mass slaughter of white people, and the White Liners, who partook of the white Southern tradition of locating their own violent impulses in the other race, imagined themselves as a counterweight to the loyal leagues. But in fact the loyal leagues did not engage in the violence that was the White Liners' signature technique.

The White Line organizations were plainly in communication with each other, and Governor Ames, at least, believed they were also in communication with the Democratic Party. Certainly they had a well-formed political purpose. Although they drew deeply from the psychological well of white Southern justifications for killing Negroes—rumors of incipient organized bloody revolt, an urgency in protecting white women from sexual depredations, and so on—the murders were not random or local. The killing was terrorism in service of a coherent cause, the overthrow of Reconstruction, which was beginning to seem plausible.

A Negro farmer named Moses Kellaby who lived in the countryside outside Vicksburg offered this account, to the somewhat incredulous questioners from a congressional investigating committee, of how the White Liners looked to Negroes:

Q: What do you understand to be the object of these clubs?
A: I cannot say. I have been traveling right smart with the white people . . . East Tennessee is my home—and I have been looking over that thing—what the foundation was; with what little brains I have got, I could not see except that the white people want to kill all the darkies out.
Q: Do your people stand in fear of these clubs?
A: They do stand in fear.
Q: Why?
A: They think they are not safe.
Q: Why?
A: They think they will kill them . . .
Q: Do they interfere with your voting?
A: If a man does not vote as they want him to, he stands a poor hack. If a man does not vote the democratic ticket, he is gone up.
Q: Do you think he is not safe if he does not vote that ticket?
A: He is not safe . . .
Q: When there is no fighting and no trouble around, no danger to anybody, do the negroes ever go to the canebrakes to hide?

A: No, sir; but a black man is hardly ever safe.

Q: Is that the general feeling among the black men in this county?

A: Yes, sir.

Q: That they are not safe?

A: Yes, sir.

Q: Is that not what you mean when you say that your folks are afraid of things all around in the air?

A: No, sir. They are not afraid of things in the air; but since they got these clubs in the country that is what the black people are afraid of.

Q: Do you mean the white men's meetings?

A: Yes, sir, white men; you may have twenty or thirty in your club.

Q: Since these clubs have been formed the colored people are more afraid?

A: They are more afraid, sir . . .

Q: And when you say they don't hunt you because you are a smart darky, what do you mean by that?

A: I mean that I know how to keep out of the way.

Q: Is that all you mean by being a smart darky?

A: Yes, sir.

Q: Smart in protecting yourself by hiding?

A: By hiding.

Somewhere between the White Line organizations and the Democratic Party on the scale of respectability were "taxpayers' leagues," which were also springing up all over Mississippi. Theoretically, the taxpayers' leagues—like similar groups organized elsewhere in the South, even during President Johnson's administration—were merely concerned with what their members found to be excessive taxation levied by Republican authorities, but their membership was all white, and they seemed to operate in coordination with the White Liners. Also, although the taxpayers' leagues always insisted that their goal was simply to put a stop to stealing by Republican officeholders, they opposed the main purpose to which the increased government spending favored by Republicans was directed: public education for the Negro population, which was meant to give the children of freed slaves the means to escape plantation peonage. In Vicksburg, after the municipal elections in August, Democrats controlled the city government, but the county—including the all-important office of sheriff—was still under Republican control. One of Peter Crosby's duties as sheriff was to collect taxes, and taxes were next due on December 2. In anticipation, as J. S. McNeily, the white historian, put it, "a storm of cyclonic intensity was gathering in Warren County and Vicksburg. Goaded by the tax burthen, with the evidence of robbery by a gang of negro officials flaunting in their faces, emboldened by a recent successful city election, patience ceased to be looked on as a virtue."

On November 17, a local grand jury indicted three Negro officials on charges of corruption. The best known of those charged was Thomas W. Cardozo, a mixed-race scion of the same South Carolina family that later produced Benjamin Cardozo, the second Jewish justice on the U.S. Supreme Court. Cardozo by then was no longer a Warren County official but state commissioner of public education. He was charged with stealing two thousand dollars in public funds (which, by all accounts, he had done) and other misdeeds—but his importance was as much the point as what he had done wrong. To whites the indictments confirmed their view that Mississippi was under the intolerable control of thieving Negroes. As McNeily put it, "The grand jury report was the spark that fired the train."

The very day of the indictments the taxpayers' league in Vicksburg issued a call for a mass meeting on December 2—not, presumably, for the purpose of paying the taxes that were due that day. The meeting produced a resolution demanding the immediate resignations of Peter Crosby and the other Negro county officeholders. A messenger walked over to the county courthouse—an improbably grand, tall stone colonnaded and cupolaed structure, built by slave labor just before the war, set in a lush park on the highest spot in town—and presented the demand. The county officials, who after all had been duly elected in a county with a large black majority, politely refused to comply. The messenger left, and soon the entire attendance of the taxpayers' meeting, more than five hundred white men, marched on the courthouse to ask them to resign again, less politely.

Crosby later recalled his reaction to the taypayers' visit: "I set to work, and the conclusion my brain worked out was that it might be intended to lead to my assassination." He signed a letter of resignation, and the white mob took over the courthouse. Crosby got hold of a horse, rode to a friend's place out in the country, stayed there until three o'clock in the morning, when he figured he could travel in safety, and then rode on to a small country depot where he caught a train to Jackson, forty-five miles away. He appeared at the Governor's Mansion on the afternoon of December 3, having been up all night, and told Ames the whole story. Sometime that same day, a Negro from Vicksburg named Tom Broadwater came riding up to the Governor's Mansion and pulled out of his boot a message from a Republican judge in Vicksburg reporting that an armed mob had taken over the courthouse and a "general riot" was imminent unless Ames did something.

That night Ames convened a group of his advisers and political allies. He could accept the overthrow of Vicksburg's elected county government, but that would encourage White Liners all over the state to try the same thing, setting off a rolling coup d'état that would wind up at the Governor's Mansion. He could ask President Grant again to send federal troops, but the likely result of that would be another humiliating public rejection that would, again, embolden the White Liners. He could send the state militia to Vicksburg, but if they were white troops, would they agree to carry out his orders, and if they were black troops, would they do more harm than good in the aggregate if they wound up killing whites? The course Ames decided upon was to send Peter Crosby back to Vicksburg with instructions to assemble a *posse comitatus*—a temporary militia—that would help him regain the courthouse. The posse would surely be made up entirely of Negroes.

That evening meeting in the Governor's Mansion wound up being one of the most elaborately parsed hours in Mississippi history. Lengthy depositions were eventually taken from most of the participants about what had taken place. The reason for this special scrutiny was that most of white Mississippi believed fervently, and wanted to prove definitively, that Governor Ames had endeavored to set up a situation in which Vicksburg's whites would massacre ordinary black people—thus generating wider sympathy for the Republican Party and for Reconstruction.

During the meeting Ames sat in a large, crowded room that people wandered in and out of, so not everyone heard clearly every word he had said. No formal minutes were recorded. What everyone agreed upon afterward was that Ames, who had a heroic view of himself and of the times, who was grandly ambitious on behalf of a cause he believed in and perhaps for himself as well, and who was in no personal danger, was openly impatient with Sheriff Crosby, who, from what we know, merely wanted to do his law-enforcement job and was quite upset to discover that if you were a Negro, holding the sheriff's office meant you were in constant danger of being taken out and hanged by vigilantes. Crosby wasn't so sure he wanted to return to Vicksburg to gather a posse and face down a large, heavily armed, violent company of whites who, no matter how ragged the opposing force, would believe that anything they did was in self-defense. The governor reminded him that not so long ago Ames himself had been exposed to the possibility of death for the sake of Negro freedom, and that great struggles demanded personal courage.

What Ames said after that was in dispute. The rumor that went all over white Mississippi was that when someone pointed out that members of Crosby's posse were likely to be killed, Ames had replied, serenely, "The blood of the martyrs was the seed of the church." Or, in an only slightly tamer version of the story, that if twenty-five or thirty Negroes died in Vicksburg, it would be a good thing for the Republican Party. Governor Ames of course hotly denied that he had said anything of the sort—but the supposed remark took on the force of truth with his opponents, because it perfectly fit their view of white Reconstructionists as cynical power-seekers who were willing to use Negroes as cannon fodder, under the cover of a damp, pious concern with their rights.

On December 4, a Friday, Crosby returned to Vicksburg. On

December 5, Blanche Ames, who had arrived in Jackson a few days earlier, having given birth to another daughter, Sarah, on October 1, wrote her mother, "Gen'l Ames is quite troubled about affairs in the State. Perhaps you have seen by the papers that the white men in Vicksburg have intimidated and driven away some of the colored office holders in that county. Of course, this is perplexing and annoying, but it will soon be settled I hope." Blanche was being far too optimistic. In Jackson, Governor Ames issued a proclamation calling on the whites holding the Warren County courthouse to disperse. In Vicksburg, a printed circular appeared over Crosby's name (though it had been written, he later said, by a colored Cyrano he'd engaged), which in high-Victorian prose put the matter in starkly political terms and called for bold action. It ended this way:

"Citizens, shall we submit to violent and lawless infringements on our rights? No; let us with united strength oppose this common enemy, who, by all the base subterfuges known to political tricksters, and the audacious mendacity of heartless barbarians, are trying to ruin the prospects and tarnish the reputation of every republican, colored or white, who aspires to fill any office of prominence, and who are daily defying the constituted powers of the law, and insulting those charged with its administration.

"Fiat justitia ruat coelum!"

On Sunday, December 6, black ministers all over Warren County read the proclamation to their congregations and urged them to join Crosby's effort. By Sunday afternoon, the *posse comitatus* was taking form out in the countryside surrounding Vicksburg.

Warren County, Mississippi, at the southern end of the rich Mississippi Delta, had three or four times as many Negro inhabitants as white, because it was in cotton plantation country. The city of Vicksburg physically embodied the county's economic and social condition: the small, elegant, prosperous city center, with its lovely verandaed and columned houses and its substantial brick shops and offices, sat high up on the bluffs overlooking the Mississippi and Yazoo rivers; but then, after a few blocks in each direction, the land fell steeply away and the ramshackle Negro part of town began, and beyond it lay a mysterious maze of bayous and backcountry roads, home to thousands of Negroes. As the Confederate Army had during the Civil War, the whites of Warren County now held the almost impregnable high ground in Vicksburg, and they were literally, as they had been psychologically since the war ended, surrounded by Negroes whom they assumed to have nearly infinite numbers, horrifying intentions, and terrible powers—though, oddly, at the same time, they were also viewed as incapable of exercising free will, and therefore helpless to resist the malign influence of men like Adelbert Ames and Peter Crosby. As one white memoirist put it, "The dread of Negro insurrection, which has at one time or another darkened every hearthstone in the South, took possession of the people, and they saw visions of slaughter, rape, arson, and robbery." If General Grant himself had failed, twice, in leading Union troops against Vicksburg, the odds against a small, hastily assembled, untrained, haphazardly armed militia of country Negroes were almost unimaginably long, but the whites in the courthouse saw themselves, with absolute certainty, as the courageous ones in the coming clash.

Early on Monday morning, December 7, a sentinel posted in the high cupola of the courthouse reported that he had spotted a column of Negro militia approaching Vicksburg from the south. The mayor declared martial law, and placed Colonel Horace Miller, late of the Confederate Army, in charge of the city. Miller found Sheriff Crosby, arrested him, and put him in jail, and then he took command of an armed company of whites who had assembled outside the courthouse and marched to meet the Negroes at a bridge over a deep ravine at the southern edge of the city. In the white version of the story, the Negroes—four hundred strong, heavily armed, and commanded by Andrew Owen, a Union veteran, friend of Crosby's, and "a bold, desperate character" who had "threatened to wade knee-deep in the blood of white men"—had plans under which Vicksburg would be "given over to plunder and the flames, and the women become the prey of the infuriated passions of the invading negroes." Negro accounts had the size of Owen's force much smaller and its intentions of course entirely different. As a pro-Reconstruction Northerner remarked, in a tone meant to parody the white Southerners' endless, knowing disquisitions about the immutable traits of the Negro, "With that curious inconsistency which seems to be part of their nature, they [the whites] had left their wives, children, and property unprotected in a heavily black settlement, and gone to defend Vicksburgh, which was already armed to the teeth, against an imaginary invasion."

In that full, still moment when two armed forces are facing each other but theoretically could still choose not to fight, Colonel Miller rode up to Owen and asked him to disband his forces. Owen replied that he was acting on orders from Peter Crosby, the elected chief law-enforcement officer of Warren County. Miller said that Crosby no longer held the office and was now a prisoner in the county jail. Owen asked to see him.

While each side's troops waited uneasily at the bridge, a white man brought Andrew Owen to the county jail, where Crosby told him he had better disband his posse. Owen returned to the bridge, he later testified, stood before his troops, and said, "Men, go right back home." Some of them shouted out that they wanted to fight. "Boys, go back peaceable and quiet," Owen told them, and the Negroes turned and began to retreat. A white man fired at them. Some of Owen's men asked if they could form a line and fire back. "If you do it you will have to put a bullet in me," Owen said. "Everything is settled, let us go home."

But the whites kept firing. Several of the Negroes fell; Owen himself jumped into a muddy ditch and crouched there until the advancing whites took him prisoner. As the report of a Republican-instigated congressional investigating committee from Washington later put it, "It was no battle; it was a simple massacre, unutterably disgraceful to all engaged in it." Blanche Ames wrote in a letter to her mother: "They were shot down like dogs, and those that fell wounded were murdered."

As was invariably the case with what whites called "Negro uprisings," a story was soon in circulation that had the whites exhibiting incredible valor in repulsing an advancing Negro force. But, as the investigating committee's report sarcastically put it, "To lead eighty or one hundred men under heavy fire down an exposed hill, to cross a bridge and storm the opposing height in the presence of a foe superior in numbers, is an exploit worthy of the heroic days of the republic, but the truth of history compels your committee to say that there was no enemy in sight or reach during the wonderful evolution, and, further, no white man was killed or wounded, or in any danger except from the careless shooting of his own comrades."

There were two other armed encounters at entry points to Vicksburg that afternoon of December 7, one on the road leading east to Jackson, the other at the northern edge of town at a monument marking the site of the Confederate surrender to General Grant. Each was about as brief as the incident at the bridge. White Vicksburg had repulsed its Negro invaders, and the county government remained under the control of those who had extralegally ousted Peter Crosby. Afterward, remnant groups of men from the white force roamed through the countryside, seeking vengeance and searching for Negro arms caches. A Negro named William Wood later gave the investigators this account of the aftermath of the battle:

Q: You are afraid, are you?
A: I am afraid, I acknowledge it.
Q: What are you afraid of?
A: I don't intend to tell you. I don't care to be hunted from one part of the world to the other, nor to have them come along and shoot me down just like I was a rabbit. I have got a family to support.
Q: Have you been shot down like a rabbit?
A: You ought to have been here about the 7th of December, and you would have seen that on every pathway; you would have been scared, too, I know.
Q: Do you say men were shot down here on the 7th of December like rabbits?
A: I call it like rabbits . . .
Q: You mean, then, that men were pointed at with guns?
A: Yes, sir; a man pointed his gun at me just like I was a bear.

Out on the road from Vicksburg to Jackson, a Negro family named Banks was living in a cabin set far back in the fields. Five white men on horses rode up to the house and asked Robert Banks, the head of the household, to produce his eighteen-year-old son, also named Robert, whom the white men believed had marched in Andrew Owen's posse. Then they dismounted and asked the elder Banks to hold their horses. When the younger Banks came outside, the white men asked him if there was a gun in the house. He said there was, hidden in the rafters. One of the white men went inside, got the gun, and hit young Robert Banks with it. When Banks turned and tried to run away, another white man shot him dead, in the back.

Then the white men asked the elder Banks to tie up the horses to a tree and walk out to an open spot in the yard. His wife, Louisa, who had just watched the men kill her son and could see what was coming next, testified later that she implored the men not to kill her poor husband. One replied, "They have killed our husbands," and another shot Robert Banks, point-blank, through the neck. The men rode off.

Another Negro woman, Lucinda Mitchell, testified that she had been standing outside her place that same day when a group of white men rode up to the home of one of her neighbors, "an old crazy man" named Tom Bidderman. As she told the story: "They asked him for his gun. And the old man said, 'Yes, sir, there is a gun.' And they said they wanted it. Then he shut the door, and one of the men said, 'God damn you, I will push the door down'; and opened the door and shot right through the door and killed him. I was standing there, and my little girl was crying and screaming, and they said, 'By God, be quiet.'"

A woman named Matilda Furman testified that she heard her husband had been killed by whites and had gone out to look for his body. She encountered a white man she knew, who told her that if she didn't go back inside her house, he would shoot her on the spot. She told him that all she wanted was to claim her husband's remains; the white man said, "Go to Crosby and Ames for that political carcass!" The bodies of most of the Negro dead rotted in woods and fields because their families were afraid to venture out and bury them. William Wood testified, "Others were killed and eaten by buzzards, and the only way they found them was by the birds sitting in the trees. The birds had got all the meat off their bodies, and the only way you could recognize them was by their clothes; and there were some killed that never have been found; only missed them out of the settlement, and never knew where they were; never have been seen there." Many Negro men left their families and hid out for days in the canebrakes until the killing had ended. The best estimate of the final death toll during those early December days in Vicksburg was twenty-nine Negroes and two whites.

Governor Ames could hardly permit Vicksburg to remain in the hands of the white uprising, so he called the Mississippi legislature into special session. Given the condition of communications and transportation in a rural, quasi-frontier state, it took until December 17 for its members to assemble in Jackson. Ames greeted them with a long, impassioned proclamation about the events in Vicksburg, which he called an "insurrection in the fullest sense." He pointed out that there was nothing in the state's power that could bring to an end the "reign of terror" in Warren County, and that its authors had the clear intention of fomenting a revolution in Mississippi and instituting a new order "founded entirely upon the degradation and serfdom of a class." On December 19, Ames telegraphed to President Grant the text of a resolution passed by both houses of the legislature, urgently requesting the dispatch of federal troops to restore order in Vicksburg.

This time Grant complied right away. How could he not? To do otherwise would mean permitting a force of armed rebels to install itself in the seat of government in an American county. As he had in September after the battle in downtown New Orleans, he issued a presidential proclamation calling upon the "disorderly and turbulent persons" in control of the Warren County courthouse to "retire peaceably to their respective abodes" within five days—which, of course, they did not. (The order to disperse was required under the federal Insurrection Act, which dated from the early days of the

Republic.) On December 24, Grant ordered General Philip Sheridan to go to New Orleans, take command of the Army's Department of the Gulf, investigate the reports of disorders in Louisiana and Mississippi, and take whatever actions he deemed necessary. At the same time, the House of Representatives, lame-duck but still Republican, sent an investigative committee to Vicksburg to hold hearings. It arrived on December 30. Sarah Butler wrote to her daughter that Ben Butler had been at the White House for a long visit with the president, during which there had been considerable discussion of Governor Ames and his troubles. "The President says he believes in Gen'l Ames, in his honor and integrity and his ability, and is glad there is one Governor who means to carry out his work and govern his state," she wrote. "He believes every word that the officer telegraphed for, has stated that he, the President, will sustain Gen'l Ames."

So it seemed as if the president was now, at last, going to crack down on the White League and White Line organizations that were taking back the Deep South. On January 4, 1875, Sheridan telegraphed Ames from New Orleans: "I have to-night assumed control over the Department of the Gulf. A company of troops will be sent to Vicksburg to-morrow." The troops, under the command of Major George Head, a veteran of Major Merrill's recent operations against the White League in the Red River valley of Louisiana, arrived on January 19. They removed A. J. Flanagan, a Confederate veteran who had been elected sheriff in a hasty, white-only vote in late December, and reinstalled Peter Crosby in the office to which he had been elected.

In Louisiana, though, opponents of Reconstruction, perhaps emboldened by the apparent success of their confreres in Vicksburg, were on the move again. General William Tecumseh Sherman, now the Army's commander in chief, who had gone from despoiler of the South during the Civil War to opponent of Reconstruction afterward, sent Lieutenant Colonel Henry Morrow to the Red River valley to peer over the shoulder of Major Merrill. On December 24, 1874, the same day that President Grant ordered General Sheridan to Louisiana, Morrow produced a report severely chastising Merrill, whom he accused of behaving more like a Republican politician than an officer, and calling for the withdrawal of federal troops from the area. "The political condition of the State is the one subject of conversation everywhere, in public and private, and among all classes, except the negro, who feels no interest in it, because he does not comprehend it." In Morrow's rather restrictive frame of reference, there could be no legitimate Negro political activity because it was not within the capabilities of the race, while the White Leagues were liberationists and self-protectors, not terrorists. Therefore, the restoration of Democratic Party control would represent the reestablishment of democracy—even if most Louisianans would then not be able to vote. General Sherman passed Morrow's report on, with an enthusiastic endorsement, to President Grant.

"I shall not be astonished if two legislatures are organized in New Orleans on the 4th of January next," Morrow wrote in his report. He was wrong only on the specifics. Through a complicated, tumultuous series of maneuverings, including the kidnapping of one Republican legislator by the White League, the Democrats asserted control over what was supposed to be a Republican-majority legislature when it convened in New Orleans on January 4. Within an hour, however, Colonel P. Régis de Trobriand, the U.S. Army officer in charge of federal troops at the Louisiana capitol, had marched a column of bayonet-bearing soldiers onto the floor of the House of Representatives, forcibly removed five freshly seated Democratic members, and replaced them with Republicans, thus restoring the Republican majority that had been produced by Louisiana's voters.

General Sheridan had only just arrived in New Orleans, and at this point he sent a telegram to Secretary of War Belknap that quickly became public and then, almost as quickly, notorious for a particular phrase in it: "I think that the terrorism now existing in Louisiana, Mississippi, and Arkansas could be entirely removed, and confidence and fair dealing established, by the arrest and trial of the ringleaders of the armed White Leagues. If Congress would pass a bill declaring them banditti, they could be tried by a military commission. The ringleaders of this banditti, who murdered men here on the 14th of last September, and also more recently at Vicksburg, Miss., should, in justice to law and order, and the peace and prosperity of this southern part of the country, be punished. It is possible that if the President would issue a proclamation declaring them banditti, no further action need be taken except that which would devolve upon me."

The combination of Sheridan's "banditti letter," as it became known, and Colonel de Trobriand's appearance on the floor of the Louisiana House riveted the attention of the nation. People who thought of themselves as the "better element" in the North—voices of light and learning, people who had been abolitionist before the war, had loyally supported the Union cause throughout it, and until now had favored the use of federal power in the former Confederacy to ensure its proper recovery—were moved to abandon Reconstruction completely. Carl Schurz delivered a lengthy, impassioned address on the floor of the Senate, one of the most famous of his long career, decrying the "military interference in Louisiana" and conjuring up the specter of troops with drawn bayonets taking power from the leadership of the U.S. Congress itself. *The New York Times*, *The Philadelphia Inquirer*, and *The Nation*, all staunchly Republican, published horrified editorials. The legislatures of Pennsylvania and Ohio—states that had never been enthusiastic about Negro rights—passed resolutions of disapproval. In New York City, William Cullen Bryant, Peter Cooper, and other leading citizens presided over a mass meeting of protest at the Cooper Institute in Astor Place. In Boston, Charles Francis Adams, son and grandson of presidents, convened a similar meeting in Faneuil Hall; it would have passed a resolution calling for the entire removal of federal troops from the South except that the old abolitionist Wendell Phillips, who hadn't been invited to speak, stood up from the audience and summoned forth enough of his prewar fire to persuade those present not to "consign to the hands of their oppressors" the freed slaves of the former Confederacy. Even Sarah Butler wrote to her daughter, "Sheridan was a little rash in the word 'Banditti,' however truthful it might be."

President Grant, from what can be known of his thoughts, wanted to back General Sheridan and, by extension, Governor

Ames, but understanding how politically unpopular that would be, he struggled to find his way to a less definitive position. Grant's son Frederick wrote privately to Sheridan, "Mother carries her endorsement almost to an absurdity. Father is very strong in his feelings but more quiet." The Cabinet was much less sympathetic to the use of the Army to enforce Negro rights in the South. Its senior member, Secretary of State Hamilton Fish, of New York, urged Grant at a Cabinet meeting on January 9 to denounce publicly the Army's actions in Louisiana. But Grant "said 'he would certainly not denounce it' nor would he censure Sheridan," Fish wrote in his diary, though as the meeting went on "he seemed to be somewhat impressed with doubt as to the entire correctness of what had been done." Two days later Fish got a moment alone with the president, and used it to try again, urging on Grant a way of distancing himself from Sheridan: "Military interfearance with a Legislative body . . . involved a fundamental Constitutional principle on which I thought he might place himself properly on record without severely criticizing what had been done."

On January 13, Grant issued a proclamation on the Louisiana affair. In his presidential papers, those portions of it written in Grant's own hand (although Grant didn't say much, even to his closest associates, he wrote his own material, and very well) are strong for the continued enforcement of federal laws for Reconstruction. For example, he summed up the situation this way: "To say that the murder of a negro or a white republican is not considered a crime in Louisiana would probably be unjust to a great part of the people; but it is true that a great number of such murders have been committed, and no one has been punished therefore, and manifestly, as to them, the spirit of hatred and violence is stronger than law." While he acknowledged the unpopularity of troops entering the state legislature, he defended it, and Sheridan's letter as well.

But other sections of the proclamation, ones that don't appear in Grant's handwritten draft, soften his position considerably. "I have no desire to have United States troops interfere in the domestic concerns of Louisiana or any other state," the proclamation declares at one point, for example. When Grant read the text aloud to his Cabinet the day before it was issued, Hamilton Fish was pleasantly surprised. "The President read his message which . . . is much better than I had anticipated from his conversation a day or two ago," Fish wrote in his diary. "It is not all that I should wish but contains much stronger expressions of disapproval of the Military interruption than were expected and possibly stronger than the President is himself aware of."

So opponents of Reconstruction in the South—both those committed to terrorist violence and their allies who used conventional political techniques—would not have been wrong in detecting a wobble in the administration's support of General Sheridan. In Jackson, Governor Ames had convened the legislature for its regular session on January 5, the day Sheridan's letter appeared in the newspapers, and he made a strong opening statement about the Vicksburg troubles and their implications. "It cannot be possible that the people of the State will permit a few lawless, violent men to inflame the mind of a community appealing to class or race prejudices, and then by force overthrow regularly constituted authorities," he said. "To prevent such acts, and punish those who have participated in them, the whole power of the State should be invoked. The freedom of a race is at stake." Even Blanche Ames, who was in Jackson then, was finally roused to see Mississippi politics as a moral struggle. On hearing about the widespread complaints about Sheridan's recent moves, she wrote her mother, "As if a community of murderers could have any rights to be respected, and to complain of throttling when most of her citizens ought to be hung (nota bene—the colored man is not considered a citizen)."

On the very day that Mississippi's legislature convened, an all-white "taxpayers' convention" was assembling in Jackson— essentially a counter-legislature. It stated its grievances in terms not of race or violence, but of a pure-minded concern with excessive taxation and government corruption, and it resolved to establish a statewide political organization that would work to unseat the present government of Mississippi.

On February 1, Congressman L.Q.C. Lamar, who had been closely involved in orchestrating the respectable political opposition to the military intervention in Louisiana, wrote a long private letter to his protégé Edward Clark, who had helped to engineer the ouster of Peter Crosby in Vicksburg and was now trying to influence the congressional investigating committee to see the troubles from the white point of view. Lamar predicted that the committee report "will be an overwhelming vindication of your people." His letter continued with an effort to map out a political strategy for overthrowing Reconstruction. Lamar believed that the violence against Negroes in the South had been greatly exaggerated; although one couldn't prove it definitively, he had the feeling that more Negroes were being killed by other Negroes than by whites, and that more Negroes had been killed by whites in New York than in Mississippi. However, Lamar wrote, "It cannot be denied that there does exist in some of the Southern states in connection with their political affairs, a tendency to turbulence & outbreaks of a bloody character which does not exist in the Northern States nor in the other Southern states & which have been hitherto unknown in the workings of American institutions."

But did this have to present an insuperable obstacle to the cause? "Now suppose I admit this squarely," Lamar wrote, "& show 1st that it does not spring from any profession for political or race supremacy, to any disloyalty to the Government, or to any desire to disturb the settlement of the elective franchise." If he could establish these somewhat counterintuitive premises, then he could cite the propitiating parts of Grant's own recent proclamation, and conclude that the only real remedy would be "a discontinuance of Federal supervision" of the South. "Inside of this I think I can present a full expose of the terrible ordeal of plunder & oppression through which our people are passing, but out which they can never be brought as long as the present system lasts." Lamar did not spell out exactly what political moves would accompany this argument. He ended his letter by saying to Clark, "I have not given you as distinct an idea of my plan as I thought of giving when I commenced, but you can probably glimpse it."

On February 27, when the congressional investigating committee issued its report on Vicksburg, it did not turn out as Lamar had hoped, for it was a bitterly sarcastic, biting, morally outraged document.

It surely wounded the whites of Vicksburg most deeply in its accusation that their self-conception as heroic defenders of their city from a murderous Negro mob was a complete fantasy, but it went even further, claiming that what the whites preferred to see as the suppression of a Negro uprising was actually cover for a program of officially encouraged, random, unpunished violence against innocent Negroes with the overall political aim of disenfranchisement. Predictably, a minority report filed by the Democrats on the committee presented an entirely different version of the "Vicksburgh Troubles," as the report called them, but what is most striking about the minority report, at least in retrospect, is how strongly it rests its case on the supposition of Negro inferiority, not only as a natural condition but as a social and political necessity that must be firmly maintained at all costs. For example, on the question of starting Negro schools, a key part of the Reconstruction project, the Democrats wrote, "A little learning is a dangerous thing in its application to them. The educated among them are the most dangerous class in the community, as they exercise a malign and blighting influence over the future prospects of their race."

The majority report ended with a charge that couldn't have put the matter much more strongly and directly, or have set the stakes for the country much higher: "One of two things this nation must do: it must either restrain by force these violent demonstrations by the bold, fierce spirits of the whites; it must, by the exercise of all its power, if needed, secure to every man, black and white, the free exercise of the elective franchise, and punish, sternly and promptly, all who violently invade those rights; or it must say to the enfranchised voters of the South—creatures of its own word, staunch, true, and faithful to its Government—we have made you men and citizens—we have given you the right to bear arms and to vote; now work out your own salvation as others have done; fight your way up to full manhood, and prove yourselves worthy of the endowments you have received at our hands. It is for the country to decide which is the best. But the country must decide quickly."

Ames's usually taciturn father felt moved to write him from Minnesota, drawing the same conclusions about the extent to which the events in Vicksburg and New Orleans had raised the stakes for the whole country: "I fear that Congress will not give the President power to put down the White Leaguers of the South. If not, there can be nothing but a reign of terror in the South until the nation is involved in a Civil War from one end of the land to the other of which the last war is a mere trifle compared to it."

In Mississippi, the next statewide elections were set for November 1875, just eight months away. These were the elections that Ames hoped not only would affirm the principle of Negro citizenship but also might lead to his return to the Senate and from there to who knows what political eminence. But it was obvious from the taxpayers' convention that opponents would mount a stiff political challenge to the Republicans in the fall. Two things were not so clear: What was the admixture of conventional political activity and terrorism in the whites' plans? And if terrorism was part of them, would President Grant stick to his policy, in the face of the now great opposition to it, of using the Army to ensure democracy in the South? Grant was a cipher.

A few days after the Vicksburg report was published, Ben Butler, now out of public office, had another private visit with the president to discuss his son-in-law's prospects. Grant, Butler reported to Ames in a confidential letter, said "it was quite probable that you might have trouble and . . . he wished you to check in the very beginning anything that looked like a revolution . . . and to assure you that he will stand by you in every emergency to the full extent of his power." That may have sounded like a complete assurance, but it was not. The lesson of Vicksburg was that there were in fact no means by which Ames could check a revolution in the very beginning, before it became an emergency. That Grant might send troops was itself an important brake on the activities of the White Liners—they could not be completely brazen about preventing the Republican Party from organizing and Negroes from voting. But if they pursued those aims in a more shadowy manner, what Grant would do was not clear.

3

THE PEACE CONFERENCE

A delbert Ames certainly was a carpetbagger, and whites in
Mississippi certainly resented him, but he did not precisely
conform to their very detailed conception of carpetbagger
attitudes and behavior. Even his enemies did not think of him as
cynical. He was possibly a political opportunist, but he was not op-
portunistic across the broad spectrum of motives that whites as-
cribed to carpetbaggers; in particular, he had no evident interest in
money (extracted from whites) or sex (extracted from Negroes).
Ames, therefore, was not truly hated. But if one wanted to find
someone who appeared to Mississippi whites to be a carpetbagger
through and through, a true representative of the type, probably
the leading candidate in the state would be Albert T. Morgan, sheriff of Yazoo County. Hated he most definitely was.

A Union Army veteran from Wisconsin who had studied at
Oberlin College in Ohio, a hotbed of abolitionism, Morgan moved
to Mississippi after the war explicitly to seek his fortune. He arrived
in Vicksburg, and then decided to settle in Yazoo City, a drowsy
town fifty miles upriver that sat perched on the edge of the rich,
cotton-producing land of the Mississippi Delta. Along with his
brother and another partner, Morgan rented a large cotton plantation there and also opened a lumber business. Since he was an enthusiastic Radical Republican, it was unlikely that local whites
would welcome him. But any chance that they might at least have

accepted him evaporated when, first, he opened a school for colored children on the plantation, at a time when there were no
schools for Negroes in all of Yazoo County, though nearly three-
quarters of its people were black, and then, not long afterward, he
married Miss Carrie V. Highgate, originally of Syracuse, New York,
a Negro schoolmistress, churchwoman, and temperance worker.
(Whites nicknamed Morgan "Highgate Morgan," which showed
how defining a trait an interracial marriage was to them.) The 1873
sheriff's election in Yazoo County had been a miniature version of
the governor's race that same year. Morgan, who'd been up to a series of unsuccessful business ventures since he arrived in Mississippi,
ran as the equivalent of Ames—the Radical Republican and tribune
of the Negro. His opponent, and the incumbent sheriff, was the local version of James Lusk Alcorn, a former moderate Republican
named Francis P. Hilliard who had become an ally of the local
whites. In what was the only Mississippi election in the century following emancipation in which there was truly free Negro voting,
Morgan won 2,365 to 431.

County sheriffs in Mississippi exercised their law-enforcement
and tax-collecting authority in a direct, personal way. When it came
time for Morgan to take office as sheriff of Yazoo County, Hilliard
refused to vacate—meaning that he and a group of his friends literally remained, in rotation, in the sheriff's office, and kept its only
key. But in a town as small as Yazoo City, one could monitor this
situation quite closely; several weeks later, in the early morning of
January 8, 1874, Morgan learned that Hilliard had gone home,
that most of his close associates had gone out for breakfast at a local café, and that Hilliard's nephew, who was on the sheriff's office
payroll, was alone in the office. Morgan and a group of his Negro
supporters entered the sheriff's office, pulled guns, ordered the terrified nephew to leave, and took over. It was in this inglorious manner that Albert Morgan assumed office.

Hilliard's nephew ran to his house and told him what had happened, and soon word reached Morgan that Hilliard and a group of
his friends, well armed, were gathering in the street to retake the
sheriff's office. Morgan instructed his supporters to lock themselves

in the office while he walked outside to investigate. He had a brief confrontation with Hilliard, but whatever Morgan said had no effect, and Hilliard and crew rushed past him, began pounding on the locked door, and even tried to knock it down. Somebody inside fired back at the door; the bullet struck Hilliard, and soon he lay dead in the street.

Very quickly a version of the event spread among the whites in town that had Morgan himself shooting Hilliard and the Negroes in the countryside planning an uprising—with the familiar rumor (as yet never fulfilled) of plans for general rape and pillage. Morgan turned himself in. From a "damp and cold" cell in the county jail, he sent Governor Ames a detailed account of Hilliard's death and asked for his help in securing a fair trial. Ames complied—the trial was conducted in Jackson, by a judge Ames had appointed—and before long Morgan was back in Yazoo, functioning as sheriff.

"Morgan was the idol of the Yazoo negroes," a white citizen of the county later wrote. "They superstitiously looked upon him as the chosen and anointed of the Lord, sent to lead them to the land of freedom, where they were to receive forty acres, with a house on it, and a mule." What in fact Morgan undertook was to create a public education system in Yazoo County where none had existed before. This was triply upsetting to the white planters: it meant that their taxes were raised to benefit their former slaves and give them the means to cease being field hands. Like other Republican county governments in Mississippi, and the idea of Republican governance generally, Albert Morgan's administration became absolutely intolerable to the county's whites. As the white account put it, "Reason, facts, and figures made no more impression on the Negro mind than the singing of Psalms would have made on the ear of a dead horse . . . the white citizens of Yazoo county realized that their future would be fraught with ruin if they could not overthrow Radicalism. The property owners knew that they would be stripped to the skin, and with their wives and families become houseless and homeless in the future, unless these marauders were defeated."

During July and August 1874, with violence breaking out in Vicksburg, Morgan began hearing that in the part of Yazoo County that was closest to it, secret white militia companies were forming;

and as the election year of 1875 began, he heard that these groups were still in business and were being joined by similar organizations all over the county. In the summer of 1875 he went to Jackson and told Governor Ames what he'd been hearing. Ames—who this summer had decided to leave the state only for a month, and was back by July, having spent time with the Butlers in Massachusetts and then had a private, friendly audience with President Grant in Long Branch—said he was getting similar reports from all over the state. Some of these came from Republican officeholders, some from Negro farmers, and some from boastful, defiant white vigilantes. An anonymous letter received in June from "the White Leaguers" of Claiborne County, south of Yazoo and Warren counties, said, menacingly, "Our brothers in your section will look after you—Send out your negro troops & Gatlin Guns and we will wipe them from the face of The Earth which they disgrace—We have the best rifles and eager for an opportunity to use them." In August a letter arrived from Vicksburg telling Ames that his life was in danger—that the White Liners were planning to foment a "riot" in Jackson in which he would be shot and killed.

In July a Yazoo County newspaper published a supposedly genuine letter sent by two Negroes to a friend which somehow had fallen into the hands of whites elsewhere in the state. "The colored people are buyin ammonition in Yazoo City," the letter said. "The colored folks have got 1600 Army guns All prepared for Bussiness." Morgan checked around and could not find anybody in Yazoo County by the names of the letter writers, and he couldn't find evidence of any Negroes arming themselves, either. What the letter reported would have been logistically impossible anyway, because, as he later wrote, "four-fifths of the colored population were living constantly, day and night, under the eyes of white employers, or white overseers." He read the letter, accurately, as an indication that more trouble was on the way.

The Republican element in Washington that was loyal to President Grant—having in hand information on increased White Line activity all over the South and a report about the terrorism that had accompanied the fall elections in Alabama—tried to push through a new, tougher version of the Enforcement Acts in the early weeks of 1875. James G. Blaine, the presidentially ambitious Maine Republican who was Speaker of the House, arranged matters so that the House passed the bill so late in the congressional session that the Senate would not have time to vote on it. That killed it. Instead, Congress passed a federal "Civil Rights Act"—the last one until 1957—that guaranteed Negroes the right to use public accommodations in the South. The act was meant to be a fulfillment of a last wish that Charles Sumner had offered on his deathbed, but it passed in a much weaker form than Sumner would have wanted, with no enforcement provisions, so it did not have the power of law in the South.

The killing of the Enforcement Act of 1875 was partly the handiwork of Congressman Lucius Quintus Cincinnatus Lamar, who had developed a working political alliance with Blaine. After Congress adjourned, Lamar returned to Mississippi to begin building up the Democratic Party for the fall campaign. His national reputation as a Southern statesman had continued to grow because of his eloquence in public, his canny dealings in private, and his constant striking of the note of national reconciliation rather than Southern defiance. The state's leading newspaper published this poetic tribute to Lamar by an admirer, which conveys both the tenor of official political rhetoric in those days and the magnitude of Lamar's reputation:

Press where you see his white plume shine amid the ranks of war,
And be your oriflamme, to-day, the helmet of Lamar.
And on they'll burst and on they'll rush, while, like a golden star,
Amidst the thickest of the fight will blaze the helmet of Lamar.

Clearly, the days of fusionism and Liberal Republicanism were over for white Mississippians. By now they were organizing themselves as full-voiced Democrat-Conservatives, and were waging an all-out political campaign against the Republicans. At the insistence of Lamar and his associates, who had an exquisite instinct for the respectable argument, the Democrats made their platform one for tax reduction, honest government, and, most of all, the withdrawal of the federal government from Mississippi's affairs; they did not openly insist on White Line policies like Negro disenfranchisement, Negro exclusion from the Democratic Party, and resistance to the post–Civil War constitutional amendments about civil rights. That made the Democrats, officially at least, a completely respectable political party, with no connection to the White Liners who shared most of their goals.

Lamar threw himself into the "canvass," as campaigns were then known. On July 15, he went to a small railroad depot in northern Mississippi operated by Colonel William C. Falkner, a Confederate veteran, prominent anti-Reconstructionist, and grandfather and namesake of the South's greatest novelist (who changed the spelling of the family name to Faulkner), where he delivered an eloquent, enthusiastically received address of nearly three hours' duration. From there he traveled through the state speaking, and on August 3 he gave the most prominent speech, this time for a full three hours, at the state Democratic convention in Jackson.

In his speeches Lamar did not hesitate to state his view that the Negro was inherently unfit to vote. He never criticized the white vigilantes in places like Vicksburg who had tried to throw Negroes out of office by extralegal means; indeed, he blamed the bloody and unfortunate Vicksburg troubles entirely on Governor Ames. But he insisted that he was now in favor of Negro voting, as a legal principle, so long as it was not enforced by federal troops. Since every time Negroes had voted in Mississippi thus far, they had voted overwhelmingly Republican, ignoring the entreaties and promises of their former masters who ran the Democratic Party, and since Negroes were the majority of Mississippi voters, what made Lamar think that Negro voting and Democratic victory were now consistent? Given the steady increase in white violence against Negro and Republican political activity, what made him so confident that the open Negro voting he said he wanted could take place without federal protection? But Lamar's rhetoric was so powerful, his manner so forceful, and his stature as a fully reformed Confederate so solid that his speeches received an almost wholly positive reception, even in the Northern press.

Governor Ames, however, was a rare dissenter, at least in private. On the day after the Democratic convention in Jackson he wrote Blanche, "The true sentiment of the assembly was 'color line' though the platform says nothing about it. The understanding evidently is that each locality can act as it chooses, but the state convention shall put forth a platform for Northern consumption. Lamar was very bitter on me as well as on everything Republican. I am, perhaps justly, made the head and front of all Republican offending, and assaulted accordingly."

Ames differed from Lamar in another respect, and it was possibly even more important than their differing assessments of the purity of the Democrats' intentions: Ames was less committed to winning. While Lamar was knocking himself out giving speech after endless speech, Ames sat alone in the Governor's Mansion, dispirited. He read Anthony Trollope's *The Way We Live Now* and General Sherman's memoir of his war years. He toyed with two new ideas he had for inventions, one a type of ladder, the other a double-hulled sailboat. He moved from room to room seeking refuge from the mosquitoes. He wearily adjudicated disputes that had begun to break out among the Republican politicians. He thought about making a trip to Washington or Boston or Northfield in September.

In late August, Ames announced, in a letter to Blanche, "I am fully determined not to accept the Senatorship if I can get it. I do not like anything in the life I lead here, and I know we will be happier elsewhere, and elsewhere we will go. I will not commit to paper my many reasons, but that I can convince you of the correctness of my position I firmly believe." A day later he reaffirmed this decision, apologizing for the disappointment he knew it would cause Blanche's mother, who was hoping that in just six months' time the Ameses would be moving into the newly completed Butler family mansion in Washington.

Although Blanche was the furthest thing from a loyal Mississippian, she was not pleased to hear that her husband no longer

wanted to assume the role of bearer of the extended family's political aspirations that all the Butlers so much wanted him to play. Her
practical-minded father, she wrote, had felt that Ames should have
had the Mississippi legislature send him to the Senate as soon as it
convened back in January, even though he had just taken office as
governor; that he hadn't, and had felt bound to stay in Mississippi
and put through his program, had shown Ben Butler "that the
Ameses were all too honest." (Many years later Ames confided to a
historian that he had thought of having himself sent to the Senate,
but had been persuaded by fellow Republicans that if he left the
state capitol in the charge of his Negro lieutenant governor, a general race war would break out.) As for Blanche herself, she was so
concerned about the evanescence of a dream she evidently shared
with her parents that she was much more direct than usual in her
matrimonial urgings. "Of course you hate it, and long to get out of
it," she wrote Adelbert. "I have only one thing to say in regard to
it. Be sure you make no mistake . . . You do not desire to be a Senator, and tied to the State for the next six years. Well, I should like
to escape one of the two remaining years as Governor. If you can,
by all means get the Senatorship . . . Beat your enemies, take the
place, then give it up when in all respects you will be better able to
judge accurately what will be the most conducive to your contentment and happiness."

It is not clear what lay behind Adelbert's decision, or even
whether it really was a decision, rather than a preemptive renuncia-
tion of ambition born out of loneliness, frustration, and disappointment. It seems fair to surmise, though, that the reasons he did not
want to commit to paper had to do with the growing activity of the
White Liners in Mississippi and with the Republicans' inability or
unwillingness to combat it. "I have never seen such depravity
among enlightened people," he told Blanche. "Fraud is attended
by murder in all political struggles here; and what seems saddest is,
that no class of democrats, it matters not what may be their intelligence or position, frown upon these crimes, but on the other hand
the higher orders are the leaders in that which is most wicked."
Whether or not Blanche could persuade her husband to reconsider,

it remained that as the canvass began, Ames, the leader of Mississippi's Republicans, imagined himself to be fighting wholly for what was just, and not at all for what was in his personal interest, while the leader of Mississippi's Democrats, Lucius Lamar, was in the usual politician's position of fighting for what he believed to be just with the belief reinforced by its fitting so well and completely with his personal interest. If there were a new Democratic legislature, surely it would give him the U.S. Senate seat that Ames was now saying he didn't want. Ames's position was one that is, generally, the losing one in politics.

On September 1, 1875, the Republicans of Yazoo City held a public meeting in Wilson's Hall, a large second-floor room in a building on Main Street, to plan for the election canvass. Most of those present were Negroes, naturally, but several white Democrats took advantage of the open invitation and came with guns tucked inside their coats. When the meeting began and Albert Morgan rose to speak, his chief tormentor in Yazoo City, a short, aggressive white man named Henry Dixon, to whom Morgan had privately given the nickname "the human hornet," left the hall and returned a few minutes later with a black man named Philip Robinson, who had made an alliance with the Democrats. Robinson stood up and started into what Morgan remembered as "a bitter denunciation of me." Morgan asked him to sit down; Dixon, the human hornet, rose to defend Robinson's right to free speech.

Morgan had a pretty good idea of what the Democrats' game was: Robinson would go on and on, obnoxiously enough to provoke an attack by someone in the audience, and that would provide the whites with a pretext (an unwarranted attack on a Negro exercising his constitutional prerogatives) to shoot up the place. It was a quintessentially late-nineteenth-century political scene: the packed hall ringing with stem-winding oratory, just beneath which was the palpable possibility of gunplay. As Morgan later described it, he tried to speak so as to stir the political passions of the Republicans in the audience while restraining the violent proclivities of the Democrats: "As a careful surgeon seeking among the vital organs of the human frame for some murderous bullet will exercise his greatest skill and caution to not cut them, and will take care lest he cause needless pain, I endeavored with all the skill and tenderness of which I was capable, to get hold of the heart-strings of the enemy without shocking them, and thus find my way to their intellects."

This was a doomed effort. Eventually, between Morgan's endlessly unfolding speech and the audience's shouted responses to it, Henry Dixon found something that offended him enough to warrant drawing his gun and opening fire. In Morgan's version of the story, Dixon fired directly at him three times but missed, the bullets striking the wall behind him. Morgan escaped by a window near the podium and fell to the ground. But he, too, had come to the meeting armed, and he reentered Wilson's Hall and fired off a couple of shots. By this time Dixon's white friends were firing, too. Within a few minutes, one Republican, Richard Mitchell, was dead, and several others, including one Democrat, were wounded.

Somebody rang the town bell, and soon Yazoo City was in an uproar. The streets were filled with armed white patrols on horseback; the Negroes scattered to get out of range of whites with guns; Morgan managed to get to his house. Near dawn a white company headed by Henry Dixon pounded on the door and demanded to know where Morgan was. A servant of Morgan's told them he didn't know, while Morgan himself hid upstairs. By morning Yazoo City had the quality of an informal White Line military base, filled with armed men from all over the county and points more distant, who had come to defend it against the lustful and bloodthirsty Negro force they had persuaded themselves, without needing evidence, that Morgan had assembled and trained somewhere outside of town. In effect, though, this defense of Yazoo City was actually the forcible takeover of Yazoo City at gunpoint from its elected government. The Democrats were in control now.

Adelbert Ames got a report of these events that day by telegram, and the following morning before dawn Thomas Cardozo, state superintendent of education—he who had survived his arrest and release in Vicksburg the year before—turned up at the Governor's Mansion in the company of Morgan's sister-in-law, who had snuck out of Yazoo City and taken the night train to Jackson. She gave

Ames a fuller account. Morgan, who had slipped away from his house and gone to his brother's, managed to write a breathless version of the events of September 1 and have someone hand-carry it to Governor Ames. He ended with this plea: "We must have U.S. troops. Can't we get help from somewhere?"

A few days later Morgan wrote to Ames again, turning up the heat. "Can *nothing* be done? I am in great danger of losing my life," he wrote. "I do not feel like running away from here, even if I could. I might get shot in the back, or more roughly handled, even, than that. My friend, I fought four years; was wounded several times; suffered in hospitals, and as a prisoner; was in twenty-seven different engagements to free the slave and save our glorious Union—to save such a country as this! I have some love left for my country, but what is a country without it protects its defenders? . . . to be butchered here by this mob after all I have done here is too cruel."

One evening someone told Morgan that the Democrats had found out where he was. He spent the night crouching behind a fence outside his brother's house while Dixon's troops marched past him several times. Then a false rumor reached Yazoo City that federal troops were, indeed, on the way. The white patrols temporarily disbanded—it was a point in favor of the Republicans who wanted to use the Army to enforce civil rights in the South that every time troops were deployed for that purpose, the terrorists, so fearless when facing down rumored Negro uprisings, melted away and Negroes were able to organize and vote—and Morgan saw his opening. He crept away from his brother's house at twilight and walked a couple of miles to a barn where, by prearrangement, a saddled horse awaited him. He rode all night and arrived at Jackson in the morning, and, although he lived until 1922, he never saw Yazoo City again.

While Morgan was hiding out in Yazoo City, the White Liners struck again, closer to Jackson and much more severely. The Republican meeting in Yazoo City had been on a Wednesday night.

On the following Saturday afternoon, September 4, a grand Republican event took place in the small town of Clinton, Mississippi, ten miles west of Jackson and on the road to Vicksburg, home to a Baptist college, a railroad depot, and a block or two of one-story brick shops, surrounded by green rolling countryside. Just north of town, prettily situated on the crest of a hill in a wooded glen, was Moss Hill, a lovely white antebellum house surrounded by magnolia and pecan trees—just the kind of heart-swelling place where sentimental nineteenth-century Southern novels about the Civil War often began. Now it was in the hands of a Republican doctor, and on September 4 he played host to a standard political ritual of the day: a large, lengthy outdoor barbecue with generous helpings of oratory, meant to motivate voters at the start of a campaign. Governor Ames himself had been invited but had declined, and in a spirit of open political competition the Republicans had invited their opponents to send a speaker to debate their man. The Democrats accepted the offer—and in addition to their speaker, a contingent of local White Line young men carrying concealed weapons came to the barbecue.

The white people of the black-majority Southern plantation country had a deeply ingrained fear of Negro assembly, let alone Negro political organizing and free speech, so the idea of more than two thousand black men, women, and children gathered in one place for an entire day was profoundly threatening to them. The provocative character of the event and the presence of White Liners who had most likely come intending to cause trouble made it virtually inevitable that violence would break out, and it did. The Democratic speaker went first. He got through an hour's address without incident. But as soon as the Republican speaker had taken the platform and launched into what would surely have been an even longer and more extravagant response, one White Liner, in a clump of young men out in the crowd somewhere, began loudly heckling him. A witness remembered the Republican starting off with a curlicued bit of praise for the Democratic speaker: "I happily congratulate the speaker on his conservative tone. He has made a most remarkable conservative speech, and we have perfect order,

and I hope the same orderly course will be maintained at every political meeting that is held this fall." "Well, we would have peace if
you would stop telling your damned lies," the heckler shouted.

Soon the spot on Moss Hill's grounds where the heckler and his
friends were standing was in an uproar. People were shouting back
and forth and shoving each other. The band next to the podium
struck up something lively to distract the crowd. Charles Caldwell,
an ex-slave blacksmith who was the local Republican state senator,
Clinton's leading Negro citizen, and one of the organizers of the
barbecue, made his way to the trouble spot and pleaded with the
Negroes not to let themselves be goaded into a fight. But soon
guns were being fired. Most witnesses later testified that a white
man had fired the first shot, killing a Negro named Lewis Hargraves
with a bullet point-blank to the head. And the Republican witnesses,
at least, remembered the first shot being followed very quickly by a
series of coordinated volleys, such as one would hear from troops
drawn into a battle line. "The thing opened just like lightning, and
the shot rained in there just like rain from heaven," a Negro named
E. B. Welborn remembered later. Some Negroes who had brought
guns of their own fired back. Before long three white men and
seven or eight Negroes lay dead or dying on the ground, and Moss
Hill had gone from political barbecue to pandemonium. "I don't
think I ever saw the same number of men get away in a shorter time
in my life," one man remembered. Negro mothers screamed, fran-
tically gathered up their children, and ran pell-mell into the woods
or down a road that led away from the white men and their guns.
People who had brought horses or mules rode them away, or they
ran away on their own two feet. Gunfire was exchanged, but mainly
both sides beat a disorganized retreat—the Negroes because they
feared for their lives, the whites because they had substantial and
heavily armed reinforcements, companies of Democrats who had
been waiting in the nearby railroad-depot towns of Edwards and
Bolton, as well as in Jackson and Vicksburg, for a signal to come
rushing to Clinton to defend their compatriots.

As usual, whites and Negroes agreed only that there had been a
Republican barbecue outside Clinton that ended violently and dis-

agreed about almost everything else. In the Negro version, the whites had come to the barbecue explicitly to break up an impressive show of Negro political organization, and to kill a few Negroes in order to frighten the rest so much that they wouldn't vote Republican any longer—it was the same script that the Democrats had followed a few days earlier, on a smaller scale, in Yazoo City. In the white version, most of the Negro men at the barbecue were armed, they had started the trouble, they had fired the first shots, and the whole event was properly remembered as a savage and unwarranted Negro attack on white people. At the very least, the Negroes were trying to provoke the whites into doing things that would generate national sympathy for the Republican cause. This version played Clinton as a mythically heroic and successful effort by brave Confederate veterans to stand off a fearsome Negro army. One white person claimed to have seen eight hundred armed Negro men arrayed in ranks on horseback—almost certainly an impossibility, given the meager resources of the black population of Hinds County, Mississippi. Another remembered the extraordinary repulse of a well-drilled thousand-man Negro cavalry by a band of eleven white men on foot. Another, William A. Montgomery, Clinton's most prominent white citizen, testified that he and one companion had ridden out to meet a column of seventy-five mounted Negroes in full offensive charge, received forty short-range gunshots (all of which missed), and then turned the column away with a couple of deadly, well-aimed blasts from a double-barreled shotgun.

The gunfire at the barbecue had commenced a little after noon on Saturday. By late afternoon, the Negroes had disappeared into the countryside—though rumors were rife among the whites, as usual, of a Negro armed force re-forming somewhere out of sight with plans to advance on Clinton and do unspeakable things—and the town of Clinton was full of several hundred hot-blooded white militiamen. Back in the spring of 1863, Grant's army had bloodily battled its way through this area on its way from Jackson to Vicksburg. Many of the whites who were gathering now had been Confederate soldiers then, and here was their chance to fight again for the same home ground, with a better result. The respectable William

Montgomery, a former Confederate colonel who was their predesignated commander (his status would indicate that the barbecue's turning into a battle was not surprising to them), was taken aback by the size and unruliness of the gathering white force. As he testified later, "Seeing that there were so many men together, that it was bound to be a mob, as it would be in any country in the world where that number of infuriated men are gathered together—there is bound to be some lawlessness among them—I told them I would not get the credit or discredit of commanding the expedition, where I could not have full control of the men . . . and I resigned my command."

If there was ever a chance of the furies not being unleashed, Montgomery's withdrawal ended it. Also as usual, the violence at the Republican political rally was as nothing compared to the succeeding violence wrought by unopposed white posses rampaging through the countryside killing Negroes they suspected of political activity or other misdeeds, and, if the suspects were not to be found, taking or destroying their valuables. One white participant, writing with the candor that comes from the events being thirty years past and punishment out of the question, described their aims: "During the next few days there was anarchy in our county . . . [T]he question which presented itself then to the people of Hinds County was whether or not the negroes, under the reconstruction laws, should rule the county. The terrible ordeal through which we passed on that eventful fourth of September fired a determination in the minds of the white people to overthrow the negro rule at any cost. Throughout the countryside for several days the negro leaders, some white and some black, were hunted down and killed, until the negro population which had dominated the white people for so many years was whipped." A white Republican described the whites' behavior less sympathetically: "They moved around in the country, killing or destroying life, until it became one of the most sickening and heart-rending things that I have ever witnessed in my life." E. B. Welborn, the black Republican, said, "They just hunted the whole country clean out, just every man they could see they were shooting at him just the same as birds."

Very early on Sunday morning, half a dozen white men arrived at the home of a Negro Republican named Square Hodge and banged on the door. Hodge's eighteen-year-old wife, Ann, answered. One of the men asked her whether her husband had been at Clinton and where he was now. She said she didn't know. As she later remembered it, "Then he said, 'If you don't tell, I will shoot your God-damned brains out.' They . . . started to shoot under the house—mother put the children under the house; she was scared and put the children under the house . . . They had pistols pointed under the house, and I told them that nobody was under but the children." Soon the men found Square Hodge, who was hiding under a bed, and took him away. Several days later Ann Hodge heard that her husband had been killed and his body dumped in a swamp. One of the white men who had taken him away, magnanimous now that order had been restored, lent her a wagon to retrieve the body. "The buzzards had eat the entrails," she said, "but from the body down here it was as natural as ever. His shoes were tied just as I had tied them. The skull bone was on the outside of the grave, and this arm was out slightly and the other was off."

Margaret Ann Caldwell, Senator Charles Caldwell's wife, received a similar visit at about the same time that morning, but her husband had had the foresight to have left town already. On hearing this news, one of the white men at her door told her, as she remembered it, "Tell him when I saw him . . . we are going to kill him if it is two years, or one year, or six; no difference; we are going to kill him anyhow. We have orders to kill him, and we are going to do it, because he belongs to this republican party, and sticks up for these negroes . . . We are going to have the South in our own charge . . . and any man that sticks by the republican party, and he is a leader, he has got to die."

Margaret Caldwell went on to describe what else happened in Clinton that morning: "Before sun up, they went to a house where there was an old black man, a feeble old man, named Bob Beasly, and they shot him all to pieces. And they went to Mr. Willis's and took out a man, named Gamaliel Brown, and shot him all to pieces. It was early in the morning; and they went out to Sam Jackson's, president of the [Republican] club, and they shot him all to pieces. He hadn't even time to put on his clothes. And they went out to Alfred Hastings; Alfred saw them coming . . . and they shot Alfred Hastings all to pieces, another man named Ben Jackson, and then they goes out and shoots one or two further up on the Madison road; I don't know exactly; the name of one was Lewis Russell. He was shot, and Moses Hill. They were around that morning killing people before breakfast."

Later that day she encountered a young white man she knew, one of the force that had come from Vicksburg to join the fight in Clinton, and asked him, "What did it mean, their killing black people that day?" He answered, as she remembered it, "You all had a big dinner yesterday, and paraded around with your drums and flags. That was impudence to the white people. You have no right to do it. You have got to leave these damned negroes; leave them and come on to our side. You have got to join the democratic party. We are going to kill all the negroes. The negro men shall not live."

On the next morning, Monday, September 6, a large white posse of fifty or seventy-five men came to see William Haffa, a white carpetbagger who taught Negro children in a school a few miles south of Clinton. Because white Mississippians did not think black people were capable of independent action, it was widely believed in Hinds County that the Clinton barbecue had been Haffa's idea. Haffa's wife and teenage daughter pushed the door shut and screamed "Murder! Murder!" as loud as they could. A white man kicked the door down, came inside, and wrapped his hand around Alzina Haffa's throat and squeezed until she couldn't scream anymore. Her newborn baby lay on a bed squalling. Haffa himself ran to the back of the house, but another white man broke off a window shutter, caught sight of him, and fired twice. Alzina Haffa asked one of the white men to send for a doctor, but he refused, and the posse rode off. At noon a smaller delegation of several men came back to the Haffa home to make sure Haffa had died, which he had, and to search the place to see if Charles Caldwell was hiding there. Failing to find him, they rode off a short distance to a house belonging to two brothers named Stevens, Negro Republicans, made them come out of the house and stand one by one on a tree stump, and shot them dead. Because nobody was ever prosecuted for the murders that followed the barbecue at Clinton, nobody made an exact accounting of the Negro dead. Most estimates were that somewhere between thirty and fifty men had been killed.

Many Negro men left their homes and families and the cotton crops growing in their fields—which were just ready to be picked, and had to be picked soon or they would have no money for a year—because they quite rightly feared they would be killed. Traveling through the woods and swamps because the whites were patrolling the roads, they made their way, usually by night, to Jackson. That was the only place attainable on foot that felt safe, because it was the only place with a meaningful presence of the one institution that seemed able to offer protection to black people, the U.S. Army. By Monday, more than five hundred hungry and exhausted Negroes from Hinds County had congregated in Jackson near the federal courthouse and the small Army post. Senator Caldwell was the most distinguished member of the group and its natural leader; he had fled to Jackson just as hurriedly and ignominiously as anybody else. The Republican justice of the peace in Jackson moved through the rough encampment of refugees, taking testimony, which a scribe wrote down in a neat hand on lined paper. At the top of every sheet was written the witness's name, with "(colored)" after it, and at the bottom was an X—underneath which was inscribed the name again, and the notation "his mark."

Alfred Moses, one of the Negro column that William Montgomery remembered having stood down single-handedly in Clinton, testified: "Captain William Montgomery fired on me with a double-barreled shot gun and three of the shots took effect in my left leg and wounded the mule that I rode . . . I carried my mule home and staid all night and left for Jackson the next night at dark and got to Jackson Monday at dinner time. My wound is considered by the doctors a very severe one and may cause loss of the leg."

George Holmes testified: "On Sunday, September 5th, 1875, some parties came into my house while I was at church and enquired for me and they only wanted to see his shadow and they would blow his brains out on sight. My house was plundered—also went into my brother in law's house which was under the same roof—plundered his house. I left there Saturday night."

Eli Burnell testified: "On Sunday morning about 10 or 11 o'clock a squad of about 20 or 30 men come to his place and called Lewis Russell my stepfather out of the house and marched him about a quarter of a mile from the house and shot him to death—I heard the firing, and soon afterwards went in the direction and found my step-father's body riddled with bullets. I did not stop to remove the body but immediately started for Jackson on through the swamps and back fields and reached Jackson Monday evening."

Freeman Jones testified: "When I got home Dave Henderson sent for me. He asked me what I was. I told him I was a black man. Reuben Davis interposed and said, God Damn you that's not the question we asked you. The question I asked you, he said, was were you were a democrat or a Radical. I told him to come and go home with me and I would prove what I was. On the way to my house, we had to cross a large cane creek running through the field. I jumped in the cane where I got on the other side of the creek. I said to them you know what I am now—for I am a radical. They then fired several shots after me one of them taking off my hat. I fled through the woods & fields until I reached Jackson the same evening about sundown—I omitted to state that they said they intended to kill 20 Radicals for every Democrat."

John Allison testified: "My mother in law . . . told me that Widow Currie (Dave Henderson's sister) told her that if I had not left, I had better do so as they (I judge Democrats) had sworn to kill me. While we . . . were consulting as to the advisability of my leaving a white man approached on the top of the hill a quarter of a mile from the house and appeared to be watching us. He then disappeared. In the meantime having been urged by my friends and neighbors to seek safety by flight, I went into the house to change clothes . . . while I was in the house they called to me before I could change & told me that two of them were coming. I put on my boots & took to the woods and started for Jackson which place I reached about dark that evening."

Late on the afternoon of the Clinton barbecue, the Republican
speaker who had been able to get through only a sentence or two
of his remarks, Henry T. Fisher, turned up with his wife at the Governor's Mansion in Jackson, "out of breath and out of heart," as
Adelbert Ames wrote Blanche, and told Ames what had happened.
Fisher and Ames had no doubt that there had been nothing spontaneous about the deterioration of the barbecue into a shoot-out: it
was merely the latest and largest example of the White Liners' plan
to disrupt any Republican political activity and to persuade Mississippi's Negroes that any of them who actively exercised their constitutional rights were likely to wind up dead.

Every day Ames vainly hoped that things were calming down
out in the countryside, and every day more reports of horrifying
violence came in, not just from the vicinity of nearby Clinton but
from all over the state, and more Negro refugees appeared in
Jackson. Vicksburg, Ames heard, was descending into its previous
condition of outright rebellion. On Monday, September 6, the Republican sheriff of Hinds County wrote to him, "With the means
now available, I find it utterly impossible to keep the peace." After
his official report, the sheriff added a more personal postscript: "As
I write men are coming in telling of the fearful slaughter. The colored people are unarmed and defenseless. As the peace-officer of
the county, I appeal to your excellency to use what means there is at
your command to stop this slaughter of an innocent and defenseless
people. I am powerless to stop the carnage, and no man knows
where it will end if your excellency cannot give aid to a death-
stricken people."

Mississippi was in an extreme version of a condition that had
become common during the last few years in those former Confederate states that were still Republican and (not coincidentally)
had large Negro populations. The Democratic Party, functionally,
though not officially, had become as much a military as a political
organization: one wing was evidently an armed force; the other,
headed by Lucius Lamar, was a conventional political organization,

though increasingly prone to extreme rhetoric; but the link between the two was not quite provable. The only way for Republicans to ensure that Negroes would be able to organize to vote in November, and then actually do so, was through the same kind of military force the Democrats were using. But this presented an insuperable problem: no white Republicans could be found who would form a militia to oppose members of their own race, and forming a black militia was perilous in the extreme, calling forth the centuries-old and never entirely absent fear of an uprising by the majority race. Any black militia would be outnumbered and outarmed by the shadowy white force now in place all over the state; moreover, reinforcements were reportedly poised at the Alabama and Louisiana borders, ready to come to Mississippi and fight on a signal from their comrades.

For Ames and the Republicans, the concern wasn't so much that a black militia would be slaughtered, though it probably would be, as that its slaughter would set off a wider regional conflagration— and perhaps worse, renewed civil war. "You may read to your Father such portions of my letters as touch on the political situation," Ames wrote to Blanche. "Tell him that in '60 and '61 there were not such unity and such preparation against the government of the U.S. as now exist against the colored men and the government their votes have established . . . the organizing of the militia of colored men precipitates a war of races and one to be felt over the entire South." There was only one possible solution: federal troops.

The Democrats and White Liners had a challenge of their own, though it was not as severe: if they were too brazen in seizing political power at gunpoint, or too open in preventing Negro political activity, it might turn opinion in the North against them and force President Grant to deploy the Army. They were on safer ground if they made every incident look spontaneous, local, and personal, rather than like part of a planned campaign.

About five hundred members of the U.S. Army in Mississippi were stationed at the three federal posts at Jackson, Vicksburg, and Holly Springs, under the ultimate command of Brigadier General C. C. Augur, who was based in San Antonio, Texas. That was probably a sufficient force to put down the White Liners who had taken control of Yazoo City and Clinton, but, Augur told Ames by telegram on the day after the Clinton riot, "I cannot interfere with troops to quell riots in a state without orders from the President." Still, Augur did dispatch an officer to Clinton to inspect the situation.

On Tuesday, September 8, Ames telegraphed President Grant. "Domestic violence, in its most aggravated form, exists in certain parts of this State," he began, and then went on to outline the situation in Yazoo City, Clinton, and Vicksburg. "After careful examination of all reports, I find myself compelled to appeal to the general government for the means of giving that protection to which every American citizen is entitled . . . A necessity of immediate action cannot be overstated."

Grant was vacationing in Long Branch when Ames's wire arrived. He had also begun to receive plaintive letters from ordinary Mississippians about what was going on there. A few days before the Clinton riot, a black man in Macon, Mississippi, named E. C. Walker had written Ames one of the letters about White Line violence that were coming in from all over the state, reporting that White Liners from Alabama had come into his county and had killed at least one black man, that "the poor black people are lying now out in the woods afraid to come home . . . Saturday there was about 25 or 30 or 40 whites . . . with arms coming from all parts of the country to kill us poor darks." He implored Ames to do something right away. Just after violence broke out in Clinton, Walker wrote to the president himself, obviously in a state of haste and panic, because his letter was not in the same perfect English as the one to Ames. "This county is now up in Raw," he wrote, "and Pres. I have write the Hon. Governor Two (2) Letters and Pres. I know you Have it in your Powder To Stop White Peopels from Killing Black People . . . now Pres I will ask to your Hon Doant the 13 & 14 & 15 Demendments Gives the (Col'd) Peopels the Same Rights and the voice to the Balord Box as it Do the Whites."

The then-brand-new attorney general of the United States was a conservative former Democrat from New York named Edwards Pierrepont who was unkindly disposed toward Reconstruction.

Grant asked him whether the proclamation he had issued the previous December in response to the Vicksburg troubles, under which
troops could immediately be deployed in Mississippi, was still in
force. Pierrepont informed Grant that it was not, and he added his
own view, which was, "I do not think that the Constitution & the
laws now invoked were intended for a case where the State authorities were supported by a very large majority of the people and
where the State government was not found inadequate to the emergency after some effort to quell the riot. This seems to me a matter
of much gravity." On September 11, Ames telegraphed directly to
Pierrepont, renewing his plea. "The necessity which called forth my
dispatch of the 8th to the President, still exists," he began. "As the
Governor of a State, I made a demand which cannot well be refused.
Let the administration, in all its magnitude, descend upon me."

The back-and-forth among Grant, Ames, and Pierrepont took
up an entire week after the Clinton riot—a week in which Northern
papers were full of the shocking news from Mississippi and reports
on the president's evident indecisiveness in the face of it—and during that time the Democratic militia solidified its hold on the area
around Clinton. On Monday, September 13, Grant sent Pierrepont
a long handwritten letter giving his thoughts on the situation in
some detail. It was a crucial moment in which the whole fate of Reconstruction, and Negro citizenship, hung in the balance. Time was
short, and the level of civil disorder was as high as it had ever been
in American history. But Grant was anything but clear. He started
off sounding confused and annoyed: "I am somewhat perplexed to
know what directions to give in the matter. The whole public are
tired out with these annual, autumnal outbreaks in the South, and
there is so much unwholesome lying done by the press and people
in regard to the cause & extent of these breaches of the peace that
the great majority are ready now to condemn any interference on
the part of the government. I heartily wish peace and good order
might be restored without the issueing of a proclamation."

But then he seemed to reverse course. "I do not see how we are
to evade the call of the governor, if made strictly under the Constitution and acts of Congress there under," he wrote. "I think on the

whole a proclamation had better be prepared and sent to me for signature. It need not be published, nor the public made aware of its existence . . . In the mean time I would suggest the sending of a dispatch—or letter by private messenger—to Gen. Ames urging him to strengthen his position by exhausting his own resources in restoring order before he receives govt. aid." The next day Grant left Long Branch for Utica, New York, where he was to address a reunion of Union Army veterans.

With Grant away, Pierrepont showed himself to be a highly skilled practitioner of the Cabinet minister's art of steering the government in his own preferred direction without directly violating a president's instructions. He duly had drawn up, in a flowery hand by an official scribe, the presidential proclamation that was the necessary prelude to the sending of troops, as Grant had directed. He kept it in his office, undated and unsigned. On September 14, he sent Ames a letter that began with a carefully edited version of Grant's letter to him, which quoted the parts about the public's being tired of the annual autumnal outbreaks in the South and about the president's hope that Ames could solve the problem on his own, but omitted the parts where Grant had said he wanted to issue a proclamation that would lead to the sending of troops.

"You see by this the mind of the President with which I and every member of the Cabinet who has been consulted are in full accord," Pierrepont wrote, after completing his misleading summary of Grant's letter. "We cannot understand why you do not strengthen yourself in the way the President suggests . . . I suggest that you take all lawful means and all needed measures to preserve the peace by the forces in your own State and let the country see that the citizens of Miss. who are largely favorable to good order, and are largely Republican, have the courage and the manhood to *fight* for their rights, and to destroy the bloody ruffians who murder the innocent and unoffending freedmen." Pierrepont concluded his lecture by officiously assuring Ames that "if there is such resistance to your state authorities as you cannot, by all the means at your command, suppress, the President will swiftly aid you in crushing these lawless traitors to human rights."

Although Pierrepont treated Grant's letter to him as a private communication, the text of his letter to Ames was quickly published in the newspapers, presumably to reassure the outbreak-weary public that federal power would not be hastily used in Mississippi. Ames had been sitting in the Governor's Mansion, moodily waiting for news from Washington, reading English history, and writing letters to Blanche. "I threw some kisses to the moon for my sweetheart," Blanche wrote him from Lowell during this time, "which I hope he received, none the worse for having been carried to him by the man in the moon." On September 16, still not having received Pierrepont's message, Ames wrote back, "I will look to the moon tonight for the kisses you sent me by her . . . I will send them back again—no, not the same ones nor others near as *nice* but mine own—such as I have they are yours—many of them."

The next morning the Ameses' self-distracting epistolary lovemaking was interrupted by Adelbert's receiving, and Blanche's reading in the newspaper, the letter from Edwards Pierrepont. She wrote him that she was inclined to rush to Jackson—leaving the children in Massachusetts, of course—but her mother thought it would be unwise. Adelbert agreed, and instructed her to stay where she was. Ben Butler went to Washington and had a private talk with the attorney general, in which he extracted a promise that Pierrepont would at least agree to put the troops already in Mississippi at Ames's disposal, if Ames would agree not to deploy them unless it was absolutely necessary. But Pierrepont never communicated this to Ames; Ames had only the instruction to deal with the problem on his own, without federal help. He composed a long reply to Pierrepont's message, which he acknowledged had "quite exasperated me," but then decided it was too intemperate and didn't send it. He really had been given no choice but to try to organize a state militia that would take Clinton and Yazoo City back from the White Liners, and now he turned wearily to that task.

Ames had a cache of weapons in the state capitol, which federal troops were guarding so that the White Liners could not storm the building and take them away. But he was far less well equipped than the White Liners probably were, and his insufficiency in men was more severe than his insufficiency in arms. To take back Yazoo City and Clinton from the White Liners along the lines specified in Pierrepont's letter would be a daunting task. To make sure that Mississippi's Negroes had an unimpeded right to vote on Election Day in November would be even more daunting, because incidents like the ones in Yazoo City and Clinton would occur all over the state. On the day that Pierrepont was writing his chastising letter, a group of three hundred colored men in Vicksburg sent Ames a letter of their own, reporting on a resurgence of White Line activity there: "The Democrats will gain the victory. The reason why is because the colored people will be forced away from the polls and not allowed to vote for fear of being shot down. They are making preparations for it now. They are going around the streets at night dressed in soldiers clothes and making colored people run for their lives. They are drilling every night with the wharf boat guns. They have got 2 or 3 thousand stand of arms here in this city. They say they will either carry this election either by ballot or bullet and if you say much they will come to see you."

On September 22, Ames reported to Blanche that he had failed completely in his efforts to organize a state militia made up of white Republicans—"I have not been able to find even *one* man to cooperate with me." That left him no choice but to create what he knew Mississippi whites would consider the ultimate horror, a Negro militia. "I have taken steps to put all the arms I have or can possess (get) into the hands of colored people and shall demand that they fight," he wrote Blanche.

On September 30, a Democratic paper in Jackson (Mississippi's Democratic press was rhetorically what its White Liners were militarily—not much interested in the responsible tone the Democrats' political leaders used in public) published an extra edition reporting the news that a thousand breech-loading rifles, plus ammunition, had just arrived in Jackson and been signed over to the Army. By this time Ames had also transferred the state's munitions from the capitol to the Army post in Jackson. The post's adjutant general was sending almost daily requests to New Orleans and Washington for more weapons, supplies, and rations. He even ordered a hundred copies of a book called *Upton's Infantry Tactics* from a publisher in New York City. By the first week in October, there were three organized Negro militia companies in Mississippi, two in Jackson, drawn mainly from the crowd of Negro refugees who had come to town after the Clinton riot and supplied by the Army post, and the third, which was unarmed, in the railroad-depot hamlet of Edwards, a few miles to the west of Jackson, near Clinton.

Whites had a double view of Negro militias. Emotionally, they saw them as a symbol of immense power. The idea of an organized, authoritative, and potentially violent Negro force touched upon every ancient white fear about the secret malign intentions that dwelled in the Negro heart—or, perhaps more to the point, about what might happen if Negroes were able to do to whites what whites had done to them. To see, or even to think about, a Negro militia sent whites into a frenzy of fear and anticipatory violence—perhaps especially so because it was just the moment when the cotton crop had to be picked, by Negro hands. But rationally, Mississippi whites knew that if it came to an actual military encounter, the three Negro militia companies Ames had organized didn't stand a chance against the much larger, better-armed force under the rough command of the White Liners. Therefore, the rational white fear was that if a Negro militia showed itself in public, it would be massacred, and then President Grant would have no choice but to call out the Army, and the Army could defeat the White Liners just as surely as the White Liners could defeat the Negro militia. Not only that, but, once activated, the Army could and probably would guarantee a fair election in November. So the Negro militias called forth a peculiar, intense blend of fear of their strength and fear of their vulnerability.

On October 9, a militia company in Jackson under the command of Charles Caldwell marched in formation to Edwards, carrying armaments for the militia company there. Nothing could have excited white Mississippi more than the spectacle of Caldwell's small force, uniformed and bayoneted, a drummer beating out a brave rattle, leading a few wagonloads of rifles down a country road;

and it is difficult to imagine how Caldwell and his troops could have summoned the courage to march in plain sight past woods and fields that they knew concealed a much larger number of white men who wanted very badly to kill them, and had been actively trying to do so just a month earlier. Most Democrats believed that Governor Ames had sent Caldwell's company marching through the countryside as a deliberate provocation, because he could just as easily have sent the arms to Edwards by train. (Ames in fact had considered that alternative, but believed that a train carrying weapons would be stopped by the White Liners and the contents stolen; in September, just that had happened with a shipment of rifles he had sent down the Mississippi River from Greenville to Vicksburg, intending to get them into the hands of the Republicans in Yazoo City.)

The secretary of the Hinds County Democratic campaign committee, W. Calvin Wells, later wrote that many local Democrats asked him "to allow a squad of men to enter Jackson, surround the mansion at night and take Ames and hang him to a post." At around this time, Wells bumped into Lucius Lamar, who had been a professor of his at the University of Mississippi Law School, and told him about Caldwell's march and the possibility that Ames might hear that a mob was coming after him and flee northward by train, which meant he would have to pass through Lamar's hometown of Oxford. That news obliterated Lamar's customary great-souled equanimity at least for a moment. "I had never seen Colonel Lamar so indignant," Wells wrote, "nor did I ever know him to fly into such a passion. His language about Ames was decidedly more forcible than elegant," and he added, "If they will wire me when he leaves, I will organize a posse at Oxford and take him as he passes and hang the miserable scoundrel."

The chairman of the Mississippi Democratic Party was James Zachariah George, a ruddy, thickly goateed former brigadier general in the Confederate Army who was now practicing law in Jackson. Though hardly an eloquent or widely admired national statesman in the league of Lamar, George was a respectable figure, officially opposed to the use of extralegal political violence; his stated concern was with federal intrusion into Mississippi affairs, excessive taxation, and other policy matters. But when federal investigators later got hold of the copies of all the wires sent out of and received in the Western Union office in Jackson, they provided a vivid record of General George's extensive daily telegraphic contact with White Liners all over the state. (One member of George's telegraphic network was Edward Mayes, Lamar's son-in-law and future biographer.) From Edwards, William Montgomery of Clinton wired George, "We learn here that Caldwell, with 100 armed men, are marching on our town. What shall we do—submit or resist? We are able to do either. Answer immediately." The same day a Vicksburg White Liner wired George, "Caldwell's company left . . . Jackson, this morning by wagon-road guarding three wagon-loads with ordnance stores destined for Edwards; have you any information as to facts, or any instructions to give? Prompt answer." George wired back: "A difficulty should be avoided by all means. The escort is peaceable." Because George and other leading Democrats believed that Governor Ames had sent Caldwell on his march with the express purpose of getting him killed, which would become the pretext for a more successful request to the president for federal intervention, it was essential to them that the Democratic forces hold their fire. As J. S. McNeily put it, "The wire was kept hot all day to Clinton and other points on the line of march, appealing to the white men not to molest Caldwell unless outrage was attempted."

Caldwell's militia arrived in Edwards, dropped off its load of munitions, bivouacked for the night, and marched back to Jackson the next day. A rumor quickly spread all through white Mississippi that now that he had successfully accomplished one mission, Caldwell would be sent on another: his militia would travel by train to Vaughn's Station, the railway depot in Yazoo County, and march overland to Yazoo City to restore the exiled Albert T. Morgan to the sheriff's office. More than a thousand white men formed themselves into military companies and stationed themselves at locations all over Yazoo County, waiting to capture and publicly hang Morgan, and slaughter Caldwell and his Negro troops.

It was during this period, with Jackson alive with alarms and rumors and militiamen of both parties drilling in the streets, that a man from New York named George K. Chase arrived in town as the personal emissary of Attorney General Pierrepont. Chase was a friend of Pierrepont's, a gentleman and a businessman, though he had gone bankrupt a few years earlier and was not currently engaged in business. Pierrepont, he said later, had sent him because he knew "that I had some capacity for managing men and things." Chase obviously had instructions to inspect the situation in Mississippi, report on it privately to Pierrepont, and try to do what he could to make peace during the election canvass. Pierrepont had given him a modest budget to hire secret agents around the state to keep him informed.

Chase adopted the role of neutral broker between Governor Ames and General George, as if he and Pierrepont regarded the two parties in Mississippi as equally legitimate entities caught up in an unfortunate misunderstanding. He checked into a hotel room and traveled back and forth between the Governor's Mansion, where he would meet with Ames, and the Democratic Party headquarters, where he would meet with George and his chief associate, Ethelbert Barksdale, editor of an incendiary Democratic newspaper called *The Clarion* and brother of a Confederate brigadier general who had been killed in the Battle of Gettysburg. Possibly excepting Barksdale, Chase found all the principals to be honorable, temperate, and impressive men.

The reports about a coming confrontation between the Negro militia and the white force gathering in Yazoo County disturbed Chase greatly. If it occurred, Mississippi would unquestionably descend into a state of general insurrection, and that would make sending federal troops unavoidable and so set off another consuming national controversy, the greatest since the end of the Civil War. General George was equally disturbed. The anticipated march of the militia from Vaughn's Station to Yazoo City would be so provocative that bloodshed would be unavoidable, and nothing was more urgent than to prevent it from happening.

With prodding from George and Barksdale, Chase conceived of a plan. He would convene a peace conference in the Governor's

Mansion between Ames and the state's leading white citizens, summoned by George and Barksdale. The two sides would strike a bargain, in which Ames would promise not to send Charles Caldwell, Albert Morgan, and the Negro militia to Yazoo City—indeed, to disband the Negro militias entirely—and the white citizens would promise to ensure that the quickly approaching election would be free and fair, without violence or intimidation of Negro voters. On October 12, as plans for the conference were coming together, George wired a white militiaman in Yazoo County: "It is possible that the purpose to send militia to Yazoo will be abandoned. Will keep you advised. Private."

Ames's command of the state militia was an open matter—he had been ordered to assemble it by the president of the United States. The unstated premise of the peace conference was that General George was just as surely in command of the covert white militias as Governor Ames was in command of the Negro ones. How else would it be possible for them to negotiate a truce? George presented himself, at least publicly and to Chase, as a law-abiding political leader who was not in control of the bloodthirsty Confederate veterans who were roaming all over Mississippi with guns and no legal authority, meting out violent retribution to politically active Negroes whenever they pleased. He agreed, perhaps, with their goals, but he disapproved of their means. If they were, however, entirely beyond the reach of the Democratic Party and the state's leading white citizens, then how could George, Barksdale, and their allies deliver on their side of the proposed bargain? Chase was so caught up in the heady business of playing the role of peacemaker— as, to be grand about it, the man who could save hundreds of Negro lives in Mississippi and ward off a national crisis that might lead to a second civil war—that he did not spend much time, at least then, puzzling over that question.

The peace conference took place on October 13, 1875, three weeks before the election, at the Governor's Mansion. Judging by the accounts of participants, it went almost eerily well, with no acrimony or even argument. One participant remembered that Chase said not a single word, Ames said very little, and General George dominated. Ames promised not to send the militia to restore Albert

Morgan to power in Yazoo City or to ship any more guns around the state. The only mild resistance he offered was that he would not agree to George's request that he disband the Negro militias entirely; instead, he would collect their weapons and put them in the safe keeping of the Army, and ask the militia members to return to their homes. The Democrats, in return, would guarantee full Negro voting rights in November. The conference was over in little more than two hours. As George Chase remembered it, displaying a broker's self-congratulation, "The citizens expressed themselves well-satisfied with the governor, and regretted very much that they had not known him personally before. They were happy to find him so much of a gentleman, and they all expressed themselves as very favorably impressed with him. General Wharton, one of the prominent men, said he was never more surprised in his life, and that it was hard to tell whether they had captured the governor or the governor had captured them. They said they were delighted with the turn events had taken, and that there would be no more killing, but there would be peace and quiet, and everybody would have a chance to vote."

Before the peace conference, Ames had been gloomy about the election. He occupied the curious zone of stillness that sometimes descends around the person at the center of a great controversy. He read the letters from Negroes pouring in from all over Mississippi with their reports of fresh outrages and their pleas for protection, and he met with visitors who had firsthand accounts, but he still had plenty of time to read his English history, to write Blanche, and to brood, with the absolute clarity of a condemned man, on the approaching end of Republican rule in Mississippi, of Negro citizenship, and of his own political career. On September 24 he wrote to Blanche, "The programme of the Democracy now is to remain passive till two or three days before the election, when it will be too brief a time for Grant to issue his proclamation—he needs five days—at least that seems to be the minimum time to make his proclamation generally known—and on the day of election or two or three days preceding—bring forth their guns, rifles and pistols for slaughter."

On the day before the peace conference, Ames, still gloomy and astute, had written to Blanche that the game was actually over, because it was already too late for enough federal troops to ensure fair elections to get to Mississippi and disperse themselves all over the state. He ran through the logistics of impossibility: "My demand must be made in writing—not by telegraph. Four days will thus be consumed. A number of days will be taken by the President for consideration, and when he decides to act, five days must be given . . . Ten days at most would be all the time allowed in which the troops could act. Of course they would have to be moved from where they are now to points of action. The result would be that hardly a day would be left for them to act in."

Ames knew exactly how enormous the effect of the Mississippi election would be, and what the larger result would be: "Yes, a *revolution* has taken place—by force of arms—and a race are disfranchised—they are to be returned to a condition of serfdom— an era of second slavery . . . The nation should have acted but *it* was '*tired* of the annual autumnal outbreaks in the South'—see Grant's and Pierrepont's letter to me. The political death of the Negro will forever release the nation from the weariness from such 'political outbreaks.' You may think I exaggerate. Time will show you how accurate my statements are." He told Blanche he had privately decided to resign after the election.

As soon as the peace conference had been successfully concluded, however, and the happy result instantly communicated, by telegraph and newspaper, to an eagerly curious nation, Ames's mood changed. First he was defensive about the criticism that was sure to come, from Negroes in Mississippi and from such Radical Republicans as there still were outside the state. As he put it, "My dread is that I fear somebody will think I have 'sold out.'" He told Blanche that the deal he had made wasn't actually as favorable to the Democrats as most people believed. He still had the weapons (now stored in armories), and he could still call up the Negro militias in the event of new troubles. And Albert Morgan, though publicly the most forceful possible advocate of confrontation (*"No Compromise,"* he had written Ames on the day of the peace conference), had privately come to Ames and said he would not return to Yazoo City with the Negro militia because he would surely be killed—hardly an unreasonable expectation. So Ames could not order the action that the Democrats were most eager for him not to undertake.

Ames believed it possible that somebody might be opening and reading his letters to his wife, so he occasionally hinted to Blanche that he knew things he couldn't commit to paper. One early hint had been about his knowledge of a plan for a general massacre of the Negro militias, of Albert Morgan, and of himself that was to take place if the peace conference was not successful. Ames had bravely faced death many times before, and had regularly received death threats while governor, but he may have felt that his superiors had now lost their right to presume upon his courage. In any case, the peace conference took him momentarily from being unerringly bleak in his perception of the situation in Mississippi to being gauzily optimistic. On October 16 he wrote to Pierrepont, "Through the timely and skillful intervention of Mr. G. K. Chase, a bloody revolution has been averted . . . I write this letter chiefly to thank you for sending here a gentleman who has succeeded in inspiring us all with confidence, and who by his wisdom and tact has saved the state from a catastrophe of blood." Even to Blanche he wrote, "The indications now are that we will have a fair election."

In the wake of the peace conference, the incidents of White Line violence around the state abated. Mississippi's Negroes returned to the fields and brought in the cotton crop. A letter from Attorney General Pierrepont reported that the president and the entire Cabinet were gratified at the news of the wise and judicious course Ames had chosen to pursue, and that he himself thought it would be admired in the North. "You may feel assured that this Department will be always ready to aid you in any lawful way to preserve order, and to give the right to every citizen to vote as he pleases."

Just after the peace conference, George Chase, his mission accomplished and his requirement to be scrupulously neutral therefore no longer in force, moved into an unoccupied children's room in the Governor's Mansion. He and Ames, who were only one year apart in age, discovered that they had a good deal in common, including mutual friends in Maine and a shared interest in the flour business. Chase was a "talker," Ames wrote Blanche, and the lonely Ames was grateful for a garrulous companion. They began taking breakfast and supper together—"Do not get jealous," Ames playfully ordered Blanche. They played games of croquet on the lawn of the mansion. Chase titillated Ames—who, for all the eventfulness of his career, had never lived in a big city—with stories about life in New York. "A more immoral picture thereof I have never heard presented," Ames gasped. He managed to find a woman in Jackson named Mrs. Rhodes who secretly worked as a spiritualist, an avocation much in vogue at the time, and they conducted nighttime sessions in the Governor's Mansion during which Ames communicated with Abraham Lincoln and, under Mrs. Rhodes's direction, was able to write out a message, containing some advice about his difficult situation, from Napoleon Bonaparte.

On October 19, two weeks before Election Day, the two new friends, who were understandably feeling worn out, left Jackson for a brief pleasure trip to New Orleans.

4

REVOLUTION

With so much at stake, why hadn't President Grant responded more forcefully to Governor Ames's request for federal troops after the Clinton riot on September 4? Why did he temporize and allow his anti-Reconstruction attorney general to handle the matter for him?

Mississippi in 1875 had two Negro members of Congress, Senator Blanche Kelso Bruce and Representative John Roy Lynch, who represented a district whose largest town was Natchez. Bruce was a stolid, well-dressed burgher who operated skillfully in private. Lynch was Mississippi's most renowned Negro orator; he aroused some jealousy on Ames's part whenever they appeared on a platform together. Both men were supporters of Negro rights. Neither was especially radical. Bruce cared about keeping his relations with his white political colleagues in good order, which he did by not grandstanding or asking them for more than they were prepared to give; and Lynch, the illegitimate son of a white plantation owner, had an unaccountably romantic idea of the nobility of the Southern planter class's intentions toward colored people.

In late November 1875, with the Mississippi elections over, Congressman Lynch went to the White House for a private interview with President Grant. He was there mainly on a standard political mission of the time, which was to persuade Grant to fire a local postmaster. A man named Pursell in the small town of Summit,

Mississippi, although he was "a good, capable, and efficient post-master," had refused to help the Republican Party during the fall canvass—not even contributing money to the party. Grant didn't need much persuading. He agreed right away to dismiss Pursell and replace him with another man Lynch recommended, who could be counted on to work for the party as well as to deliver the mail.

His business concluded, Lynch used the time remaining in his appointment to ask Grant why he had not sent troops to Mississippi. For many years Lynch kept this conversation with the president to himself, but in 1913, when he was an old man living in Chicago, his account of what Grant had said to him was finally published. Given that this was a conversation with the president of the United States on the subject of a major turning point in American history with enormous consequences for Lynch personally, it is likely that Lynch remembered accurately the thrust of Grant's answer; but that he remembered it word for word, after all those years, as he indicated in his memoir, is a stretch.

According to Lynch, Grant told him that as soon as Ames's request for troops had arrived, he had prepared the proclamation that would lead to their being deployed in Mississippi. He was all set to sign and issue it. But then a delegation of Ohio Republicans called on him at the White House. In those days of nonuniform election schedules, Ohio's state elections were set for October 13. If Grant sent troops to Mississippi in September, the Ohio Republicans told him, it would be so unpopular in Ohio, which had voted by a wide margin against ratification of the Fifteenth Amendment, that the Democrats would surely capture the governorship. So, calculating that it would be better to hold Ohio for the Republicans and lose Mississippi than the other way around, Grant changed his mind and did not issue his proclamation.

"I should not have yielded," Lynch quoted Grant as telling him. "I believed at the time I was making a grave mistake. But as presented, it was duty on one side, and party obligation on the other. Between the two I hesitated, but finally yielded to what I believed was my party obligation. If a mistake was made, it was one of the head and not of the heart. That my heart was right and my intentions good, no one who knows me will question."

Grant went on, Lynch wrote, to give his view of the legacy of the Civil War, in light of the recent events in Mississippi. The war had abolished slavery and established the authority of the national government over the state governments. But now even many leading Republicans were retreating from the idea of national sovereignty. "Whatever their motives may be," Lynch remembered Grant telling him, "future mischief of a very serious nature is bound to be the result. It requires no prophet to foresee that the national government will soon be at a great disadvantage and that the results of the war of the rebellion will have been in a large measure lost . . . What you have just passed through in the state of Mississippi is only the beginning of what is sure to follow. I do not wish to create unnecessary alarm, nor to be looked upon as a prophet of evil, but it is impossible for me to close my eyes in the face of things that are as plain to me as the noonday sun."

The planning of George Chase's much-publicized peace conference in Mississippi coincided exactly with the final stage of the Ohio campaign; the conference took place on the very day of the Ohio election, which the Republicans did indeed win. Governor Ames had had a strong suspicion, which he expressed several times in letters to Blanche, that Grant and Pierrepont withheld help in Mississippi because of the election in Ohio. If it was for Ohio's sake that Grant did not send troops to Mississippi, then the chief beneficiary of his decision was the man who succeeded him in the White House, Rutherford B. Hayes, who surely would not have become president if he had not been reelected as governor of Ohio in 1875.

Less than a week after Adelbert Ames and George Chase returned to Jackson from their trip to New Orleans—and also less than a week before Mississippi's Election Day—Chase wrote a letter to his friend and superior in Washington, the attorney general, that began: "I deem it my duty to give you facts relative to the situation in Mississippi to-day. It is impossible to have a fair election on November 2nd without the aid of U.S. troops."

Chase later described the process that had brought him to this complete and rapid change in his assessment of the situation, so soon after the successful peace conference. Now that he was living in the Governor's Mansion, he saw at first hand the daily Negro visitors who brought Ames their alarming stories about White Line activity all over the state, which had renewed after the brief lull that followed the peace conference. The visitors would meet with the governor; Ames would then pass their reports on to Chase; Chase would go see his Democratic friends James George and Ethelbert Barksdale, and ask them why the agreement they had made seemed to be crumbling; and George and Barksdale would promise to investigate. Soon they would give Chase a sheaf of evidence proving that the violent incident he had inquired about had been personal, not political, in nature. Chase said, "I was met every time in that way; if there was an outrage or any disturbance, they reported it a personal quarrel; they had so many ways to prove the democratic side of it; a dozen affidavits or statements to prove that no such thing occurred, or if it did occur that the party killed or the party outraged was the aggressor." Before long—though too late—Chase concluded that the peace conference had been a sham.

Setting up the peace conference in the first place had required Chase to turn a blind eye to what was going on around Mississippi when he first arrived there. The worst of the incidents of early October 1875 was in Friars Point, a settlement on the Mississippi River that was the seat of Coahoma County, upriver from Vicksburg and Greenville. Like the rest of Mississippi's cotton plantation country, Friars Point had a heavy black population majority, and it was home to James Lusk Alcorn. In 1873 a Negro ally of Ames's, John Milton Brown, a schoolteacher from Oberlin, Ohio, had been elected sheriff of Coahoma County on a nearly unanimous Negro vote, over Alcorn's nephew. As Election Day approached in 1875, the familiar story line played out: respectable local whites became increasingly concerned, to the point of alarm, about excessive taxation and government corruption. At the same time, Ames was getting reports from local Republicans that well-armed Confederate veterans, whose political objection was more bluntly to Negroes holding government power and whose methods were less refined, were coming to Coahoma County from other parts of Mississippi and from neighboring Tennessee and Arkansas.

On October 2, a Saturday, Coahoma County's Republicans nominated an interracial slate of candidates, headed by Sheriff Brown and also including Senator Alcorn's rebellious son, who was running for treasurer. On Monday, October 4, both parties scheduled political rallies, the Democrats' to be held first and then the Republicans'. A rumor circulated that L.Q.C. Lamar was going to address the Democratic rally and that Negroes were going to come and try to prevent him from speaking; neither prospect, Lamar's visit or the Negro disruption, materialized, but the rumor alone was enough to generate a bellicose mood among the whites. Before the Republican meeting, scheduled for the evening so that the Negro field hands would have time to come in to Friars Point from the countryside, a spy brought Sheriff Brown an alarming report. "The colored people were to come in," Brown remembered a few years later, "and I was informed that the Democrats had the names of all the leading Republicans on their dead-list, and that my name was at the head of it; and that when we met they were to come and take us out and hang or shoot us." Brown sent word to the plantations that the meeting was canceled and everyone should stay home. But the whites who had planned on disrupting the Republican meeting—by the same routine as at Yazoo City and Clinton—came anyway, and they took control of Friars Point, including the sheriff's office.

The next day the Negroes who had intended to be at the Republican meeting decided to return to Friars Point and try to reestablish the elected Republican government there; in the town, a force of several hundred heavily armed whites assembled, under the command of Senator Alcorn (who was armed with a double-barreled shotgun) and a former Confederate general named James R. Chalmers. As always in these situations, the whites persuaded themselves that the Negroes were more numerous and better armed than they, and that their intention was not only to reestablish their political rights but, as Alcorn later put it, "to sack and burn the town." John Brown attempted, unsuccessfully, to persuade both sides to disperse. General Chalmers then led his main force out to a bridge a mile south of town where the Negroes were assembled, and secretly sent a smaller group on a flanking maneuver to a spot south of the bridge, so that when his militia opened fire, the Negroes saw that they were surrounded and quickly scattered.

The familiar pattern in what whites called "Negro riots," but to the Negroes looked like well-organized armed disruptions of Republican political activity, played itself out in Friars Point as it had in Clinton and Yazoo City. The worst violence came not during the battle itself, which ended in a Negro rout after only a few minutes, but afterward, when remnants of the white force, out of the direct control of their official commanders, roamed the countryside killing politically active Negroes. John Brown, who seems to have felt that if he was to be stripped of political office he could at least function as a repository of the memory of specific acts of terrorism, gave this account of what happened after the battle at Friars Point:

"The colored men scattered all over the county, threw away their guns that they had with them, and some of them ran as far away as Shufordsville, where they were followed by white men. On the way, they met up with a preacher, an old colored man named Nelson Bright, and they shot him. He was hunting his mules and had no gun with him at the time. They went farther and killed another colored man, as I understand . . . There were others who came by way of Hopson's Bayou. They stopped at Helena [just across the Mississippi River in Arkansas] and captured Monroe Lewis there. They had heard of him, and they tied a rope around his neck. I didn't see this, but I heard of it. They took that man a distance of eight miles, leading him with his rope, and treated him very cruelly, as I was told. They had him say his prayers and hold up his hands, and they discharged two barrels of a shot-gun through him. That is the way they murdered him, as I heard from the people who saw it near by; they killed him in that way."

Brown continued: "They went to Black's Bayou and found William Alcorn and took him out and killed him. They went on to Governor Alcorn's place and stopped overnight . . . They staid there and had their cooking done by Charles Green, and after cooking for them all night until the next morning he was tired, and the governor was not there, and he was lying down after breakfast. One of the men said that he must try his gun this morning, and he turned and shot this old man on the porch. I was told this by Governor Alcorn's son and others who saw it, that that was the way in which it was done. There was one man that was named Robert Simmonds whom they overtook when they were away up in Jonestown . . . These colored people and Robert Simmonds had been to the town and heard of the riot and were talking about it. They were captured by these men, who took them by their homes, and their wives begged for them to have their lives spared. D. F. Alcorn went and begged for them, but they took them within three miles and a half of Friar's Point, and there they were shot and left lying on the ground. Their bodies were there, I heard, from the 5th of October to the 1st of December. They were found and identified by their clothing and things in their pockets. These are all the cases that I know of personally of men that were killed. I heard of others, but these were the men that I knew."

Brown himself slipped away through the woods, leaving behind a sick wife and a newborn baby, and got across the Mississippi to Helena, which was the nearest place that had a Western Union operator. On October 7 he wired Ames, "I have been driven from my county by an armed force. I am utterly powerless to enforce law or to restore order—answer immediately." The following day Brown somehow, via his wife, got a longer message to Ames. "A perfect state of terror reigns supreme throughout the country," he wrote. "If there is any protection for the People of Coahoma let us have it at once. They are going to God & humanity for protection." Three times during the month of October, Brown surreptitiously returned to Friars Point to see whether he could restore himself as sheriff; each time he quickly concluded that if the Democrats found him, he would be killed, and he returned to Helena. So Coahoma was another county where the Democrats had seized control, before the election, by force of arms, and Ames was unable to dislodge them.

General James Z. George was in telegraphic communication with the Coahoma Democratic militia, as he was with white militias all over the state, and the Democrats almost immediately got their version of events into the national press. On the day of the riot, two

Democratic leaders wired the Associated Press via Helena: "The sheriff of Coahoma County caused our town to be invaded this morning by an armed mob of negroes. We drove them back. We are fully organized for defense, with Senator Alcorn and General Chalmers in command. The sheriff has fled the county. Send us aid immediately." A week later a much longer and detailed account written by Senator Alcorn himself appeared in the *New-York Tribune*, Horace Greeley's paper, under the headline "THE FRIARS POINT WAR." The subtitle—lengthy, in the nineteenth-century style—read: "SHERIFF BROWN THE AUTHOR OF ALL THE MISCHIEF— THE STRUGGLES OF A CORRUPT RING FOR CONTROL—A MAN WHO HOLDS THREE OFFICES AT ONCE—BROWN'S INCENDIARY HARANGUES— PARTICULARS OF THE FIGHTING." This, not Brown's account, was what most Americans knew about the events in Coahoma County: that an informal army of Negroes, whipped up into a murderous passion by their unscrupulous leaders, had been repelled and prevented from committing who knew what horrible misdeeds by a heroic, outnumbered band of self-defending whites.

To the ousted county sheriffs Albert Morgan and John Brown, and to Congressman John Lynch, and, increasingly, to Governor Ames, and even, finally, to the conciliatory George K. Chase, it began to appear that the White Liners in Mississippi were at the very least a tightly controlled statewide organization, and quite possibly a regional or even a national one, with indeterminate but real ties to the Democratic Party. Every local incident was too similar in its particulars to every other one, and the timing of them too coincident, for it to be otherwise. Republicans regularly heard about large shipments of expensive and high-quality rifles coming into Mississippi and winding up in the hands of supposedly local and unofficial self-defense organizations. And the young men in those organizations, most of them Confederate veterans, seemed to be arriving from Alabama and Tennessee and Texas and Louisiana to help out their racial brethren in confrontations with Negroes. Were they just wandering to Mississippi on their own? Democratic newspapers, many

of which were operated by White Liners (the Arkansas reinforcements who came to the aid of the whites in Friars Point, for example, were organized and led by the editor of the newspaper in
Helena), had quite similar things to say about the rapidly unfolding
political events. Were they operating individually? By the eve of the
election, Mississippi felt to the Republicans awfully like a state that
was being taken over by a relentless conquering army.

A company in New York whose guns were ubiquitous in Mississippi then, Remington, had just begun producing a mechanical
product it called a "type-writer." In Washington, D.C., Alexander
Graham Bell was just a few months away from filing a patent on the
telephone, a machine that carried human speech across telegraph
wires. But in Mississippi in 1875, people communicated over dis-
tances by handwritten letter—especially Republicans, since the local
operations of the Western Union telegraph company (and its jour-
nalistic partner, the Associated Press) were, Ames suspected, under
Democratic control. That meant there was a lag between information and action. During the late October days when Ames and his
friend George Chase were making their peace treaty with the Democrats, disbanding the state militia, and vacationing in New Orleans,
Mississippi Republicans were sending handwritten letters to the
governor's office, sometimes neat and patient and addressed to
"Your Excellency," sometimes rushed and palpably terrified, sometimes elegantly literate, often not, telling Ames about incidents of
violent intimidation of prospective voters.

"Lawless bodies of armed men, mounted, are riding rough-
shod over defenceless citizens," a man from Natchez wrote. "Are
such aggressions to be tolerated in times of peace? Has the citizen
no constitutional rights that are to be protected from lawless violence?" From Liberty, a petition arrived from "we of the collorde
voters of Amite," pleading for protection from the Democrats. The
Republican sheriff of the same county wrote, "Everything here is
exceedingly warm, and every trick is resorted to, by the blood-
letting 'God and morality' democracy . . . They do beat the devil,
though, in their low, mean, murderous tricks, and it seems a mystery to me that 'Providence' does not remove them 'root & branch,'

as the preachers say to sinners." From Hernando, a man named William Canly wrote, "We, as Republicans of the State of Mississippi, do ask you to tell us whether we are to be murdered by the whites of the State or not, without any protection at all? Dear sir, did not the 14th Article and first section of the Constitution of the United States say that no person shall be deprived of life or property without due process of law? It said all persons shall have equal protection of the laws. But I say we colored men don't get it at all."

From Shannon, W. F. Simonton wrote, "It is utterly impossible for us to have anything like a fair election here. A great many of the colored people fear they will be murdered if they vote for the Republican ticket." From Jasper County, N. R. Blackman wrote that he had overheard "a rank old Demicrit" remark to one of his former slaves "that the democratic party was agoing to carry this election, and he said with threght of vilance interdation, that if they failed they intended to have blood—blood." From Vicksburg, an anonymous correspondent reported, "Ever since Saturday the democrat party has been like roaring lions; they have sworn to not let no colored militia organize in this city, and been going around since Saturday night with their guns, going around to halls to see if any of them are gathered together, to break them up, and making their threats what they intend to do with the governor." A man named Abraham Burriss wrote, "We are poor and cannot afford to buy guns, and except derive some protection *they will* killed nearly every one of us. But give us guns and we will show the scoundrels that the colored people *will fight* . . . Arm us; let us protect ourselves, and show the scoundrels, assasans, that we have men of valior to come in contact with."

Back in Massachusetts, Blanche Ames, who also hadn't received word of the peace treaty, was imploring her father, in Washington, to go to President Grant and ask that federal troops be made ready to report to Governor Ames right away, because the ordinary cycle of Ames making a new request to Grant and Grant then responding would take too long to prevent a disaster on Election Day. Ben Butler sent word back to his daughter that (as she reported to her husband) "he saw Grant and he had half written the telegram ordering the troops to report to you, when your telegram arrived saying that you had effected a temporary compromise, but could not tell how long it would last. Then Father went to Pierrepont and they looked up all the laws in the case and decided that as Governor you were the senior officer in command in the state, and Grant again agreed to send troops to you." It would be far too easy to conclude from this that Grant and Pierrepont had actually been prepared to send troops to Mississippi—Grant had been anything but resolute, and Pierrepont was actively skeptical about Reconstruction and suspicious of Ames, else he would not have sent a representative down to Jackson to keep an eye on him—but what is indisputable is that the October peace treaty was helpful to the Democrats, and that its central premise was a sham.

When Blanche finally got the letter from her husband reporting on the peace treaty and the prospect of a fair election in November, she was skeptical. She urged him to resign the governorship immediately and, while he still had a compliant Republican legislature at his disposal, have himself sent to the U.S. Senate. But Ames had sunk into a strange state: alternately brooding and almost frivolous, at those moments when he was able to persuade himself that what was clearly inevitable was not really going to happen, and, at the times when he was being realistic, fiercely passionate in his bitterness at the betrayal of democracy in Mississippi and its inevitable lasting consequences for the colored people of the South. Blanche, as usual, had fewer illusions than her husband. She never believed his weary assurances that the election could be fair, and she never shared his recurrent inclinations to bow to the cruel fate that seemed to be ordained for him and leave politics. "Success is the only thing the world appreciates or respects," she wrote Adelbert, by way of trying to persuade him to make himself a senator while there was still time.

By now the election was less than a week away. On October 28, Attorney General Pierrepont, having received Chase's ominous report about Democratic activity since the peace treaty, wired Ames that the federal government would, after all, deploy troops to ensure a free election. Ames also received a telegram from Brigadier

General Augur, the commander of the Army's Department of the Gulf, saying he had ordered the troops in Mississippi to be held in readiness to intervene in case of disorder on Election Day, and had dispatched a junior officer to Jackson to see Ames and assess the situation. Chase called upon the Democratic leaders, James George and Ethelbert Barksdale, to ensure that they were prepared to honor their promise of peace. From Washington, Ben Butler reported to Blanche that both President Grant and Attorney General Pierrepont had assured him they were now ready to use force in Mississippi to ensure a free election.

But this was all absurd, because the time when federal intervention could have made a difference had passed. Governor Ames was left to read his increasingly alarming mail, to greet the Republican refugees arriving in Jackson from the countryside for protection, to play croquet on the lawn of the Governor's Mansion, and to write despairing letters to Blanche. "The election ceases to have any interest for us," he wrote on October 30. "It is lost. Gone forever. The republican candidate for the presidency next year may want this state, but he as well might want the moon for a toy. In this sad plight, I can but think that I have conscientiously done my duty, and also predicted consequences." The next day was Ames's fortieth birthday—the occasion for a grim reflection on the simultaneous evanescence of his young manhood and his political promise. "This day has not been a happy one," he wrote Blanche. "I lay awake not a few hours last night as miserable as one cares to be, thinking over the defeat which will befall us the day after tomorrow—Tuesday, the 2ⁿᵈ. As I thought—pondered—I fell into bad humor with all the world, and with a will to avenge my many wrongs, finally, in all my helplessness, went to sleep with an aching head."

The Democratic Party–White Line alliance was not stupid enough to stage any one incident before the election that would be so dramatic as to demand the attention of President Grant, but it was certainly active all over the state (and so were Mississippi's Negro voters, who campaigned aggressively where they could). One technique, the most benign, was to bribe Negro voters to vote

Democratic. A rougher, more common tactic was later explained by George Chase: "Their object was to destroy the leaders or drive them out. One smart nigger in some localities would control the votes of two or three hundred niggers, and the democrats wanted to get those recognized leaders out of the way; or they would not scare him out, they would kill him." Even this was relatively restrained compared with some of the Democrats' other activities as the election drew nearer and the likelihood of federal intervention decreased. Chase had placed an agent in Yazoo County, who reported to him that a man named Sublit "had a band of his own of about 100 armed men, that they went about the county scaring the niggers; that they would start out on a raid with a rope hitched to each saddle, and would ride over the country firing their guns and scaring the niggers, and that when the niggers would see the ropes tied to their saddle, that was enough for them, they did not want anything more."

In Hinds County, home of the state capital, Charles Caldwell, possibly the Mississippi Negro whom whites most feared and hated, wrote (with a political associate) a long letter to Ames including this summary of the situation: "The intimidation and threatening of colored voters continues uninterrupted, and with as much system, determined purpose, as if it were a legitimate means of canvassing and the chief one to be relied on in controlling the colored element . . . the peace agreement is held in utter contempt, and only serves as a cover for perpetrating the very wrongs upon the freedom of the elective franchise which it was intended to prevent."

By the time he got Caldwell's letter, Ames no longer had to rely on reports from the field for his sense of what the Democrats were up to. In Jackson itself, an Army captain—part of the detachment of troops supposedly waiting to pounce on any sign of election fraud—lent the Democratic Party a cannon for use in a pre-election political parade. The Democrats mounted it on a caisson, hitched it to a team of mules, and marched through the streets in broad daylight. As they passed the Governor's Mansion, they stopped to jeer and gesticulate, and a few rowdy young men took out their pistols and fired at the windows.

That night the same group, better lubricated and less cautious, held a second parade by torchlight. Long after midnight, they returned to the Governor's Mansion and began firing again—not just pistols, but also the cannon, while Governor Ames, George Chase, and various servants and staff members huddled inside trying to decide what to do. One of Ames's servants later testified that when he had slipped out to the mansion's stable, near the back gate, he overheard a couple of Democrats debating whether to go in and kill Ames and the others. They decided not to and, after a while, moved on to the offices of the Republican Party newspaper in Jackson, the *Pilot*—which in those days, when not much distinction was made between journalism and politics, was a gathering place for Republican refugees from the countryside—where they smashed all the windows.

On November 1, the day before the election, Ames wrote to Blanche, "The reports which come to me almost hourly are truly sickening. Violence, threats of murder, and consequent intimidation are co-extensive with the limits of the state. Republican leaders in many localities are hiding in the swamps or have sought refuge beyond the borders of their own counties. The government of the U.S. does not interfere, and will not, unless to prevent actual bloodshed."

The worst incidents took place in the parts of Mississippi that had the heaviest black population majorities. (And there were no incidents, either of political violence or of "Negro uprisings," in areas that already had secure Democratic voting majorities.) In Lowndes County, on the Alabama border, the Democrats acquired another cannon, which, as in Jackson, they paraded around and fired in connection with political rallies. In adjoining Colfax County, they had two cannons. The Democratic rallies were heavily populated by boisterous, drunken armed young white men, who loudly issued boasts and threats about what would befall those who dared to vote Republican on Election Day. In the Negro communities, word spread that many of these young men had come across the border from Alabama and that there were many more like them waiting to cross into Mississippi if the call came. The night before the election, in the Lowndes County seat, Columbus, the standard rumors of a Negro uprising reached white ears, and somebody—never identified, suspected by the Republicans to be white ruffians, believed by the Democrats to be bad Negroes—set a series of fires on the edge of town. A white posse was formed which, in the course of putting down the Negro uprising, killed four black people and wounded three, including an elderly woman.

On Election Day, James George, in Jackson, sent a wire to the Lowndes Democrats asking for a report. "Town fired last night in fourteen places," George's man in Columbus wired back. "All quiet to-day, General Harp in command." At the county courthouse, a Democratic mob was on hand to greet those black voters who, after the terrors of the night before, dared to show up. As one black Republican officeholder in Lowndes County described the scene to Ames, "The voters did not get to vote, & them that did not voted at the point of gun & piostol of the dimmacte party. My life was throatent at the ballot-box in Columbus as one of the registers or judges of the election."

Claiborne County, at the other end of the state—just below Vicksburg, on the Mississippi River—had been in a condition of high White Line excitement for more than a year, ever since a Negro legislator had married the daughter of a local plantation owner. On the Saturday before the election, the Republicans held a rally—which, the White Liners told themselves, was properly understood as an attempt by a thousand armed, inflamed Negroes to march to the county seat, Port Gibson, and burn it to the ground. So, as usual, they decided to defend themselves. Several hundred heavily armed whites, some on horseback, some on foot, assembled to greet the Republicans. The inevitable row began, and the Republicans fled before the speeches had even begun; the White Liners stayed behind to feast on the uneaten Republican barbecue, and then formed themselves into smaller patrols that roamed the back roads of the county at night. The Republicans dispatched a courier to Governor Ames with an urgent request for troops to restore order before Election Day; the courier managed to evade the White Line patrols by riding through open fields, and arrived in Jackson the next morning, but of course the request went unfulfilled.

On Election Day, a substantial party of Negro voters led by a man carrying a white flag came to the polling place in Port Gibson. They were met by armed, quarrelsome White Liners (who by some accounts had a cannon, yet another of the cannons appearing all over Mississippi in connection with the Democratic election campaign), and soon there was firing. One witness later gave this written account: "On the day of the election eighty men armed with Remington breach loader rifles who marked in double file military steps out of the empty store room . . . on main street Port Gibson at the sound of the bugle . . . within a few feet of the polls. Immediately after the firing commenced." The Negroes ran for their lives; one of them, an old man named John Morris, was killed, and six others were wounded. A white Republican witness later testified that "the moment the first pistol was fired," James George's man in Port Gibson, J. D. Vertner, "ran for the telegraph-office with his pistol in his hand, and telegraphed to General George that everything was all right there; that there was nothing that amounted to anything; that all was peace; and that they would resume the voting, &c." George wired back: "Your dispatch satisfactory. Push on the column, but keep quiet. News from all parts show immense gains. We are sure to carry the State."

At another Claiborne County polling place, in Peytona, not a single Republican vote was cast. At another, in Bethel, the same Republican testified, "the democrats, just as they were commencing to count out the votes . . . came in, burst open the door suddenly, and rushed in and put out the lights, knocked the clerk over, and jerked up the ballot-box, and away they went with it." The only polling place where there was a substantial Republican vote was in the town of Grand Gulf, where the Negro voters had decided to come armed. The Republican vote total in the county as a whole went from 1,844, in the 1873 election, to 496 in this one.

Probably the most extreme case of White Line election activity, or at least the best organized, was in Monroe County, just north of Lowndes on the Alabama border, which had an almost two-to-one black population majority. Just after the peace treaty of mid-October, Lucius Lamar came to Monroe County and gave a speech in which, according to the Democratic paper in Vicksburg, "in manly and ringing tones he declared that the contest involved 'the supremacy of the unconquered and unconquerable Saxon race'"— which was not what he said in his speeches on the floor of the House in Washington. The *Examiner*, the Democratic paper in Aberdeen, the county seat, editorialized in early October, "The present contest is rather a revolution than a political campaign—it is the rebellion, if you see fit to apply that term, of a downtrodden people against an absolutism imposed by their own hirelings, and by the grace of God we will cast it off next November, or cast off the willfully and maliciously ignorant tools who eat our bread, live in our houses, attend schools that we support, come to us for aid and succor in their hour of need, and yet are deaf to our appeals when we entreat them to assist us in throwing off a galling yoke that has been borne until further endurance is but the basest cowardice."

The *Examiner* approvingly quoted this statement by the Democratic candidate for state senator: "Whoever eats the white man's meat must vote with the white man, or refrain from voting at all." The Democrats put this policy into practice through either bribery (from a kitty, rumored to amount to seventy-five hundred dollars, reserved for this purpose) or intimidation. A man named Miles Walker later testified that the owner of the plantation where he worked had asked him how he was going to vote and, when Walker said Republican, had said, "I won't give you meat and bread if you go against us . . . we will hang you up between the sky and the ground." George Cook, a Negro Republican officeholder, received an anonymous letter that began, "You are known to be a vile, corrupt, and thieving scoundrel, unworthy to live in any community," and that went on to order him to leave the county by October 15. A group of Democrats armed with rifles rode up to the home of Howard Settle, a Negro deputy sheriff, but he saw them coming and ran away and hid in the woods.

The county sheriff, James W. Lee, implored Governor Ames to send troops—"Things are getting in an awful condition here," he wrote—but Ames could not. The Democrats, for their part, had a strong political organization with a militia-like aspect: it had many aggressive young male recruits, with more rumored to be poised across the Alabama border waiting for the call; a cannon that had been rigged to be loaded with buckshot; and a fresh supply of Prussian needle guns, rapid-firing weapons that had been introduced since the Civil War. In late October, Republican political rallies in two rural hamlets in Monroe County, Sulphur Springs and Paine's Chapel, were broken up by Democrats in what had become the standard manner: young rowdies came and flung around enough insults and threats to draw a response they could choose to see as provocative, and then routed the assembled Negroes.

Black Republicans had a custom of bringing drums to political rallies and banging on them to underscore the drama of the best lines of rhetoric—standard practice in American politics at the time. But in Southern plantation country drums carried a special charge, since for Negroes they represented an importation of African culture and were also useful as a potential means of communication between plantations. Therefore, for whites drums conjured up the possibility of insurrection by the Negro majority. "Stop that; you cannot beat that drum here," a Republican remembered a Democrat saying at a rally. "This is a white man's country, and we don't allow that." The Democrats made a special point of cutting the heads out of the Republicans' drums. In the days before the election, White Line militiamen rode through the county with folded drumheads stuck into their hatbands, where Negro voters could easily see them.

On Election Day, the Democrats posted armed sentries at two fords on the Tombigbee River, which bisected Monroe County, so that the large population of rural Negro voters living on the other side of the river could not get to their polling places, and drew up a drawbridge at another spot. At the polling place in Spring Hill, whites with guns, knives, and clubs started another disturbance, and drove dozens of Negro would-be voters away.

At the most important polling place in the county, the courthouse in Aberdeen, arriving Negroes encountered the cannon, placed on the courthouse lawn, and a complement of more than a hundred armed and mounted soldiers, wearing makeshift uniforms, under the command of a former Confederate general and local plantation owner named Reuben Davis, whose picture-book white-columned mansion is still a local tourist attraction. The whites of Aberdeen had, as usual, heard rumors that the Negroes were planning to come to town, not to vote but to burn the place down and murder its white citizens, including the women and children; they also had heard that there was a fresh shipment of needle guns meant for the Negroes secreted in the county jail. In the whites' accounts, the Negroes arrived at the courthouse early in the morning in a military-style column, carrying fresh-cut wooden clubs (each made from an entire sapling), intending to form themselves into a cordon and prevent whites from voting.

Just before the polls were to open, a prominent Democrat named Tom Sykes told James Lee, the Republican sheriff, that if the waiting Negroes—waiting, depending on which account you believed, either to vote or to arm themselves, keep whites away from the polls, and rampage through the town—did not disperse immediately, he and his allies would "cover the yard with dead niggers in fifteen minutes," according to testimony by two Negro eyewitnesses. The cannon was aimed directly at the waiting Negroes, and the situation quickly deteriorated. As James Lee remembered it, "Several hundred colored men were knocked down during the time with pistols and sticks; and they fled in wild disorder and confusion from the courthouse in every direction." Lee had been counting on fourteen hundred Republican votes in Aberdeen; he got ninety, and the Democrats carried Monroe County.

Months later, Reuben Davis, after giving his account of the incident as a simple matter of self-defense, offered this view of relations between the races: "I think the world is made up of various grades of life. I think the negro is about two degrees below the white man. I think that God put the white man at the last link in the chain. I think that the negro is by nature dishonest; I think the negro is by nature destitute of all ideas of virtue, and I think the negro is capable of being induced to commit any crime whatever, however violent, especially if he was encouraged by bad white men. That is my opinion of the negro. I don't think he is the equal of the white man intellectually or morally. I don't think he can ever be civilized to the extent that the white man has been civilized."

White Mississippi chose to believe things about Negro plans and activities for which there was no hard evidence, but which conformed to everything they thought they knew about Negroes' nature and the proper order of the world. Believing these things permitted them to do whatever it took to take back political power in Mississippi—and in the fall of 1875 that is what they did. All over the state, Republican vote totals were down significantly from what they had been in the 1873 elections. In Yazoo County, the most extreme case, with a Negro population of more than twelve thousand, there were only seven Republican votes. The Democrats swept back into control of the state legislature.

The passing of Election Day did not bring peace to Mississippi, however. The Democratic Party, by now quite obviously equipped with both a conventional political organization and a terrorist one, had demonstrated that the federal government was not going to challenge its activities in any meaningful way. Not a single murder of a Negro during Ames's governorship had been legally treated as a crime, and not a single perpetrator of anti-Negro violence had been punished. Now there was no brake on the behavior of anyone with brutal inclinations. All over the state, parties of vigilantes "waited upon" (as they liked to put it) politically active Republicans of both races and demanded that they leave Mississippi immediately or be killed.

A man named Amos Sanders, in the town of Macon, received a note from an anonymous "Committee of Thirteen," which had a small picture of a coffin with his name on it and the legend "The Grave is not dug but can be easily done as it will not take much of a hole for you," telling him he'd better have left the county by the day after the election, "for the writers are determined not to be ruled by a damn Carpet Bagger as you are." In De Kalb, a Republican official wrote to Ames that he and his political allies had gone into hiding from a Democratic mob. In Aberdeen, the Democratic paper, two days after the election, published a "Monroe County farmers' pledge of honor," with forty signatories who promised not to hire any Negro laborer who had voted Republican, or any dismissed from another plantation for that reason. Once again Republican refugees made their way to Jackson, often traveling at night through the swamps and fields, in the hope of finding safety, and once again Democratic vigilantes paraded through the streets at night, firing their guns. At three in the morning on the Sunday after the election, Governor Ames and his friend George Chase slipped out of Jackson by train, headed back north.

In Issaquena County, in the black-majority Delta just north of Vicksburg, there had been relatively little White Line activity before the election, and as a result the Republicans had voted freely and won. That alarmed the county's whites; conversely, the election results elsewhere in the state emboldened them. In mid-November, in a country store, a group of Negroes got into a quarrel with a white salesclerk, and the salesclerk pulled out a knife and stabbed one of them. Local whites took the salesclerk into custody to protect him from being (depending on which race was telling the story) either properly prosecuted for his crime or brutally murdered by Negro vigilantes. In any case, when a group of Negro Republicans tried to capture the salesclerk, they ended by wounding him in an inconclusive scuffle; the Democrats retaliated by going out, arresting some Negroes, and imprisoning them in a pharmacy. When they tried to escape, there was another scuffle, and shots were exchanged.

Over the next few days, Issaquena County went into a state of high alarm. The whites, who imagined that Negro Republican politics and government were the institutional prelude to the carrying out of long-cherished plans for general marauding, believed that another Negro militia was forming, just out of their view, which would soon rampage through the county unless harsh measures were taken right away. The Negroes were rumored to be in possession of a large supply of top-quality armaments that had recently been shipped to them from the North. "We barricaded our doors, and kept armed for two or three weeks; for two or three weeks we were vigilant and watchful; some nights we did not go to bed at all," a white later testified. The cotton harvest was in by now; the whites heard that the Negroes planned to burn all the cotton gins and so, with a few well-placed fires, destroy the entire year's economic output of the county in an instant.

And the Negroes—with more reason, given the events of the past couple of years in Mississippi and Louisiana—feared that whites were using these rumors as a pretext to come and kill them. A white man later testified that a black man named Derry Brown, who had a reputation as the worst of all the "bad Negroes" in Issaquena County, had been overheard saying to other Negroes, "To arms, to arms! We cannot stand this thing; we have got to kill out the white people in this county." A black man, on the other hand, testified, "I heerd the white people say they wanted to get all the negroes that had an education—all of them that knowed anything—they intended to get hold of them, and they wanted to kill all of them that could read and write and all the brave men."

In the countryside surrounding the town of Rolling Fork—a rich plantation land where there was a black population majority of nine hundred to forty, and where, forty years after these events, the great blues musician Muddy Waters was born—groups of ten or twelve whites began riding the back roads and waiting upon Negroes they considered to be troublemakers. On the afternoon of Sunday, December 5, they went to six Negro homes and took the men away from their families at gunpoint. Sometime between then and the next morning, the six men were executed out in the cotton fields. A Republican election judge, Bowie Foreman, found some of the bodies. "It was a fearful sight," he testified. "They were lying there butchered like hogs."

On Tuesday white leaders in Rolling Fork met with a delegation of "good Negroes" from the plantations, and this resulted in a formal, signed, published agreement in which the Negroes promised to "do their utmost to arrest and deliver" to the whites everyone on a list of fourteen "turbulent" Negroes, some of whom were Republican officeholders. At the head of the list was Derry Brown.

There were no more killings, but more parties of armed whites— one of them led by William S. Farrish, a former captain in the Confederate Army whose son became one of the first rich Texas oilmen, and whose grandson served as U.S. ambassador to the Court of St. James's under President George H. W. Bush—rode through the plantations waiting on people. Most of the leading Republicans in Issaquena County wound up leaving. Derry Brown was arrested and sent to Vicksburg, where he was put in prison while his cotton crop went to ruin.

The whites did not bother to deny what had happened, or to pretend they had operated within the range of conventional legal procedures. They explained their actions as a simple matter of self-defense, having nothing to do with the question of which party or race held political power in Issaquena County. When asked whether his compatriots had murdered six unarmed, never formally accused, unresisting Negroes in cold blood, one white man said, "If they did that, if it was not in a pitched fight, it was done to strike terror to the hearts of these negro men, with a view of their own preservation. It was anticipated, from the threats that had been made and which they intended to carry into execution, to burn houses and kill women and children. You cannot imagine the horrible state of feeling that existed over there at this time."

In Mississippi, after the cotton harvest had been gathered and ginned, a long and convivial holiday season ensued that people called "the Christmas." One Thursday afternoon in the town of Clinton, during the early days of the Christmas in 1875, a Negro teenager named David Washington wandered into the main street and encountered a group of rowdy white men who began taunting him. Washington, who lived in another town in Mississippi, was the nephew of the notorious Charles Caldwell, whose family he was visiting for a few days. The whites asked Washington how many white people he'd killed on the day of the Clinton riot, and whether he'd come back to town now to kill more white people. Washington hurried back to the Caldwells' house.

Charles Caldwell had been out hunting all day. On his way back home, he heard what had happened, and he walked into town to see if he needed to defend his nephew. He found things peaceful, returned home for an early dinner, and then went back to town just as dusk was falling. A white man named Buck Cabell, who had a reputation for being friendly to Negroes and who hadn't been visibly involved in political violence, came up to him, greeted him warmly, and asked him to come have a Christmas drink. They went into the basement of one of the stores in town, where a table and chairs were set up and a few white men were sitting around. Cabell ushered Caldwell into a chair, poured him a whiskey, and touched his glass to Caldwell's.

Somebody standing outside the store and looking in the basement window fired a single shot into Charles Caldwell's back. Caldwell's minister heard Caldwell's screams of agony and came rushing over; according to him, Caldwell asked the white men in the basement to take him outside because he wanted to die in the open air, not closed up like a dog. They accommodated that request, but not Caldwell's next one, that he be carried back the short distance to his house so he could say goodbye to his wife. He was sitting in the street outside the store. According to the minister, he pulled his coat around himself for warmth and said, "Remember when you kill me you kill a gentleman and a brave man. Never say you killed a coward. I want you to remember it when I am gone."

Caldwell tried to stagger to his feet. A white man shouted, "We'll save him while we got him; dead men tell no tales," and—again according to the minister—they fired thirty or forty shots into him from close range, which amounted more to a frenzied mutilation of a corpse than to a murder. This was a crystallized version of what had been happening all over Mississippi for more than a year: the enactment of a white fantasy of courage and self-protection against an unimaginably horrible Negro threat, which took the form of executing an unarmed, unaccused man for the crime of being an active American citizen.

Margaret Ann Caldwell began her story of that evening as follows: "I was at my room until just nearly dark.

"The moon was quite young, and the chapel bell rang.

"We live right by it. I knew the minute the bell tolled what it all meant.

"And the young men that lived right across the street, when the bell tolled, they rushed right out; they went through the door and some slid down the window and over they sprang; some went over the fence. They all ran to the chapel and got their guns. There was 150 guns there to my own knowing; had been there since the riot, at the Baptist chapel. They all got their guns."

Margaret Caldwell ventured out of her house, hiding her face. It was getting dark, and white men with guns were everywhere. Approaching the store where her husband had been shot—the one place in town that was lit up—she stepped over a body lying in the street, not knowing whose it was. A white man she knew, who was holding a gun, told her to go away, or else "they would make it very damned hot for me."

So she went back home. As she put it, "I went on over to the house, and went up stairs and back to my room and laid down a widow."

Charles Caldwell's brother Sam, who had also heard the commotion, mounted his horse and rode into town to see what was going on. He was killed by the white men, too, with a single gunshot to the head. When the Caldwells' minister came over to their house and called out to Margaret Caldwell, who was hiding upstairs, "Answer; don't be afraid; nobody will hurt you," she didn't say anything, for she was afraid. The minister called out again, and this time she asked him what he wanted. "I have come to tell you the news, and it is sad news to you," he said. "Your husband is dead. He is killed, and your brother, too, Sam." The minister rode off.

After some time—as Margaret Caldwell, now joined by Sam Caldwell's widow and three children, cowered in the house against the sound of the white mob in the town—two of Clinton's leading Negroes arrived bearing the dead bodies of the Caldwell brothers. They brought them up to the bedroom and laid them out, so that they could be prepared for a decent burial. "Those who have seen Caldwell's corpse," Blanche Ames wrote her mother, "report that the body had to be tied together, while on his head and neck there was not a space where one could lay a hand."

At one o'clock in the morning, the train from Vicksburg to Jackson stopped in Clinton, and a load of young men who called themselves Modocs—Confederate veterans who made themselves available to travel anywhere that white-on-black political violence was under way, so that they could enthusiastically participate in it, operating on the collective fantasy that they were a tribe of wild Indians—alighted and walked over to the Caldwell house. "They all marched up to my house and went into where the two dead bodies laid," Margaret Caldwell remembered, "and they cursed them, those dead bodies, there, and they danced and threw open the window, and sung all their songs, and challenged the dead body to get up and meet them, and carried on there like a parcel of wild Indians over those dead bodies." Such was Margaret Caldwell's first night as a widow.

Adelbert Ames may have fallen into a condition of utter despair about Mississippi and about his own career as a politician, but his wife and in-laws, who were less idealistic but more determined than he, had not. On December 8 the entire Ames family returned to Jackson—perhaps an indication that Blanche felt her presence was necessary to prevent her husband's being drawn back into the passivity of the pre-election period. The Butlers, at least, had a clear program in mind: to stabilize Adelbert's governorship so that he could soon ascend to the Senate. Since Mississippi had just elected a Democratic legislature that hated Ames, this was going to take some work. "This is your time of political effort," Blanche's mother, who was dying of throat cancer but nonetheless was intensely focused on Adelbert's political future, wrote from Lowell. "Do the work bravely and well, and have no fears of the result. For my own part, I should be grateful to get you back to Washington. But for all that, a Governor is a power, and it must not be lightly yielded. My idea is not to give up an inch of power while you possess it, unless compelled."

At the same time, Congressman L.Q.C. Lamar, having spent

Election Day in Washington, safely insulated from what his party had done to win in Mississippi, had returned to the state. He wanted the same Senate seat that Ames (or Ames's wife and her family, anyway) did. Now that the election was over, he could devote himself to maneuvering, with his usual subtle touch, to get it. The selection of Mississippi's next senator would occur before the end of Ames's term as governor, which had another two years to run. Ames in the governorship would definitely be an impediment, even with the legislature being Democratic; but now there was talk in Jackson about removing Ames from office right away, through impeachment, on grounds ranging from corruption to (incredibly) having incited the political violence that had engulfed the state.

In Washington, Ben Butler got to work. "Be not cast down or worried," he wrote to Ames. He went to see President Grant, who indicated that in the event of an impeachment, he was inclined to offer a strong public defense of Ames. The Army instituted court-martial proceedings against the young officer who had lent a cannon to the Democrats, and George Chase returned to Mississippi to testify. Butler urged Ames to make a major speech presenting his case, and promised to make sure that leading national newspapers published it afterward. Senator Oliver P. Morton of Indiana, one of the remaining strong Republican supporters of Reconstruction, introduced a bill proposing a federal investigation of the Democrats' tactics during the campaign, whose findings, it was obvious, could serve as a pretext for invalidating the election results and for the Senate's refusing to seat anybody the new Mississippi legislature elected to it. If Morton's bill passed, and if the Mississippi legislature did impeach Ames, it meant that each side would be launching its own elaborate inquiry into the last few years of Mississippi politics, in the hope of building an evidentiary case strong enough to determine who would hold the state's highest offices.

The atmosphere in Jackson was such that impeachment was definitely not the worst fate for Ames—assassination was. "At night in the town here, the crack of the pistol or gun is as frequent as the barking of the dogs," Blanche wrote to her mother. "Night before last they gave us a few shots as they passed the Mansion yard, by way of a reminder. I do not think they fired at the windows, only discharged the guns to disturb our slumbers." A member of the white mob that had killed Charles Caldwell in Clinton—a respectable Republican judge who was suffering pangs of conscience—came to the mansion and gave the Ameses a detailed account of that evening, which roused even Blanche into a state of moral horror. Butler, the Ameses' four-year-old son, began asking her constantly how the angels take people to heaven after they die. "His last idea is that they put a chain around the neck and pull them up," Blanche wrote.

In January 1876, the new legislature convened, and Ames gave a long, eloquent, carefully prepared address, focusing primarily on the horrors of the election campaign, and secondarily on the healthy financial condition of the state government. In February, a legislative committee produced a thirteen-count bill of impeachment against Ames. Buried deep within the bill was evidence of a real policy dispute: Should the main goal of the Mississippi state government be educating Negroes, the Republicans' principal project, or subsidizing the railroad companies to build more lines, which was the Democrats'? But most of the stated accusations in the articles of impeachment had to do with minor official thievery by men Ames had appointed. One article asserted that Ames's having put Charles Caldwell in charge of a state militia company was an impeachable offense; another accused Ames of misconduct during the Vicksburg troubles of late 1874.

As soon as he got the news, Ben Butler, through intermediaries, set up a line of communication in Washington to Congressman Lamar, who sent him assurances that he was surprised and disappointed that Mississippi's legislature was moving in this direction and that he would do what he could to stop Ames from being impeached. (Or anyway this was Butler's version; Lamar wrote a friend in Mississippi that Butler had promised he would persuade Ames to resign and squelch the Senate investigation of the Mississippi campaign.) Butler had the impression that Lamar was going to dispatch a messenger to Jackson and put a halt to the proceedings right away, but within a few days one house of the state legislature had already voted for impeachment. The state's highest-ranking

Negro officials, A. K. Davis, the lieutenant governor, and Thomas Cardozo, the commissioner of education, were impeached, too.

Lamar urged Butler to hire a lawyer friend of his in Jackson to defend Ames, but by that time the Butlers had lost faith in Lamar— "a double dealer upon whom no dependence can be placed, as it is well known that in all matters political he does not hesitate to be false," as Blanche put it—and Ben Butler engaged a different lawyer, from Washington, and sent him to Jackson to defend his son-in-law. Meanwhile, the removal of Ames's state government moved steadily forward in Jackson. A. K. Davis resigned and left Mississippi, which opened the way for the removal of Ames—the Democrats would never have gotten rid of Ames first and left a Negro as governor. Blanche reported to her mother, "Of the principal men in Jackson, there is hardly one who has not, by counsel or action, taken some part in the Negro murders. These murderers, and I use the term advisedly, thinking that Father ought to be or might be interested in Gen'l. Ames' case and come here to lend assistance, have arranged a plan to assassinate him."

Matters came to a head in late March when, within a matter of days, Ames's lawyer arrived in Jackson; the U.S. Senate approved a resolution appointing five of its members as a select committee to investigate the Mississippi elections of 1875; and the U.S. Supreme Court handed down its decision in the case of *United States v. Cruikshank et al.*, arising from the Colfax massacre in Louisiana in 1873. The decision dealt a heavy blow to Reconstruction, as if it needed another one, by ruling that enforcement of the post–Civil War constitutional amendments guaranteeing the civil rights of the former slaves was a matter properly left to state governments, not the federal government. President Grant, who had not so long ago been thinking about trying to run for a third term and who was in immediate political trouble again because his secretary of war had just been forced to resign in a bribery scandal, had fallen into one of his public silences about Reconstruction. He said nothing about these momentous developments. Grant's annual message at the beginning of 1875 had been substantially devoted to condemning events in the South; his message in 1876 didn't mention the South at all.

Very soon, Ames would go on trial in Mississippi, and almost certainly be convicted. If there was any hope that he still might get to the Senate with the help of the results of the new select committee's investigation, an impeachment conviction would hardly improve his chances. Anyway he was weary. On March 28, he made a deal with the Mississippi legislature: he would resign as governor if the impeachment charges against him were dropped.

Ames's decision to stop fighting came as an unpleasant surprise to Ben Butler—"I will not conceal from you that the matter strikes the public mind unfavorably," he wrote his son-in-law. "I will, however, keep my own mind open until I hear the circumstances"—and even to Ames's new lawyer, who dashed off a letter as soon as he heard the news, imploring Ames to reconsider. Ames's reply—which it's hard to imagine that his lawyer, having just traveled across the country to defend Ames, didn't find infuriating—was that he had already decided to resign back in November, that it was only because charges had been brought against him that he stayed on, to defend his honor, that if the charges were dropped, nothing stood in the way of his original desire.

The Ameses quickly left Mississippi. In Washington, the new Senate select committee on the Mississippi elections began its work, chaired by Senator George Boutwell of Massachusetts. It hired as its staff director a Scottish-born journalist, lecturer, and political activist named James Redpath, one of the few prominent white abolitionists who remained strongly committed to Negro rights. All through the spring of 1876, Redpath sought out potential witnesses and received terrifying handwritten eyewitness accounts of conditions in Mississippi, both before and after the elections. "Oh, if only I could see you, or some one, to put out my wrongs too, so the world could know the deadly prejudice these men have against a northern man," a carpetbagger named William Pitt, from Arkabutla, wrote. "I have been to Andersonville"—the notoriously brutal Confederate prison in Georgia for captured Union soldiers—"and have seen men eat the excrement from other prisoners, but that is an old tale. I would rather be at Andersonville than here."

One writer, a white man, warned the committee to beware of Southern hospitality once it got to Mississippi. "These people expect to *capture* the Senatorial Committee," he wrote. "They will be met, promptly; they will be *received, welcomed*; houses & parlors, & society will be thrown open; facilities will be afforded for obtaining *truth*; in this latter, they will be *officious*; the committee will be assured that their doors are always open to *gentlemen!*" Black writers, on the other hand, often expressed fear about what would happen to them if they testified. An informant from Port Gibson—who, despite his bravado, signed his name and then scratched it out—wrote, "A great many colored are intimidated & fear (as I think unnecessary) that they would be shot down if it was known they were going to testify." And, indeed, one witness who did testify reported to the committee that he had been met afterward in the street by an armed mob, which forced him to say that everything he had told the committee had been a lie.

Adelbert Ames came to Washington in late April to testify himself. Occupational categories were not as strict then as now; James Redpath, in addition to his work for the Senate committee, also served as a correspondent for *The New York Times*, which had recently become, under a new editor, one of the Northern newspapers sympathetic to Reconstruction. After Ames had finished testifying, he and Redpath repaired to the Butler family mansion in Washington, where Redpath interviewed Ames (along with Albert T. Morgan, George Chase, and other Mississippi dramatis personae who were in town) for the *Times*. Thus a long article published on May 2, 1876, gave Ames's version of the election: that the Democrats had won it "due wholly to fraud, violence, and murder to such an extent and degree that the Northern mind seems incapable of comprehending it."

In the month since his resignation, Ames had shaken off the almost paralyzed quality he'd had during the awful period of campaign, electoral defeat, and impeachment; now, at a distance of time and space from the events, he spoke in a clear, passionate voice. He attacked Lamar as a two-faced fraud whose dignified self-presentation outside of Mississippi was nothing but a convenient pose, and he dismissed all the Mississippi Democrats' arguments about government corruption and excessive taxation. It was obvious what the election was really about, he said: "In one phrase—hostility to the negro as a citizen. The South cares for no other question. Everything gives way to it. They support or oppose men, advocate or denounce policies, flatter or murder, just as such action will help them as far as possible to recover their old power over the negro. Everything that stands in the line of their march to this end is overthrown."

Just a few days later, bad trouble broke out in an area along the border between Mississippi and Louisiana south of Natchez. In adjoining Wilkinson County, Mississippi, and West Feliciana Parish, Louisiana—heavily black plantation country, a Republican stronghold for the past few years, and therefore a region with unusually good Negro schools—a group calling itself the Regulators, or sometimes the Bulldozers, made up mainly of Confederate veterans, had been patrolling the area with increasing brazenness. They would wait upon Republican officeholders and other Negroes deemed to be troublesome (meaning, usually, politically active) and threaten them, and it was easy for them to avoid the remote risk of an encounter with legal authorities simply by slipping back and forth across the state line. "These Regulators in our section of the country . . . are better armed to-day than they were in confederate times, and they are more violent," the Republican tax collector of West Feliciana Parish, E. L. Weber, told the select committee.

One evening in May two Negroes murdered a shopkeeper named Aaronson, a Jew recently arrived from Germany whose store was just on the Mississippi side of the line. The Regulators found the perpetrators, extracted confessions, and hanged them—without recourse to the law, of course. Or so the Democrats' version of the story went; the Republicans' was quite different. It was that Aaronson had actually been murdered by white men in blackface—partly because local whites suspected him of selling stolen seed cotton, but mainly as a way of providing a pretext for killing Negroes. The retaliatory hangings set off the familiar drama that began with widespread and allegedly persuasive rumors of a never quite visible Negro uprising: unspeakably horrible in its intentions, impressively armed, and impeccably organized, with its hundreds of foot soldiers whipped into a bloodthirsty emotional frenzy by their leaders. The whites, once again, resolved to defend themselves, and a killing spree began, on both sides of the state line.

At one plantation, Regulators rode up and unceremoniously shot six black men. "One was in bed and said he was sick," a Negro eyewitness named Kenner James testified, "and they said to him to turn over and take a pill, and they shot him right in the mouth." Another group of Regulators freely entered a U.S. Army post, whose commander was sympathetic to their cause and the regular recipient of gifts from them, and delivered a severe beating to a Negro soldier. A Negro named Alfred Black gave this account of his visit from the Regulators: "These men told me that my republicanism was played out, and I was going to be put back in my place, and they said that they had killed fifty, that they had shot them; that they had hung twelve, and I could go to the forks of the road and see them, some with their tongues hanging out, as black as the tarbucket." A dispatch from E. L. Weber in Louisiana, which made its way to the offices of the select committee in Washington, put the number of Negroes who had been shot and hanged at thirty-eight. "Will the country stand by with folded arms, and see us murdered without cause?" Weber asked. "Is there no remedy?"

During the summer the Senate select committee came to Mississippi and took testimony all over the state. By that time a new round of political terrorism had already begun in connection with the 1876 presidential election, now just a few months away. The committee confined its investigation to the previous campaign, and the man who had worried that its sympathies would be captured by charming white Southerners need not have. As Senator Boutwell put it a quarter century later in his memoirs, "For myself I had no doubt that the election of 1875 was carried by the Democrats by a preconceived plan of riots and assassinations." The two Democratic senators on the committee issued a minority report that stated the familiar Democratic arguments about the horrors of Reconstruction, but the majority report—and, more important, the copious printed evidentiary record that accompanied it, amounting to more than two thousand pages of small type—provide an amazingly complete and vivid record of what went on. It was issued on August 7, 1876, in plenty of time for use in the campaign and, if the occasion arose, in an official challenge to the seating of L.Q.C. Lamar as a U.S. senator.

In his memoirs, Boutwell told this story, which was not in the report:

"While I was conducting the investigation at Jackson, a stout negro from the plantation sought an interview with me after he had been examined by the committee. He was a mulatto of unusual sense, but he was under a strong feeling in regard to the outrages that had been perpetrated upon the negro race.

"Finally he said: 'Had we not better take off the leaders? We can do it in a night.'

"I said: 'No. It would end in the sacrifice of the black population. It would be as wrong on your part as is their conduct towards you. Moreover, we intend to protect you, and in the end you will be placed on good ground.'"

By the time the Boutwell Report was released, Adelbert Ames was in the Midwest, helping his father and brother manage the family's flour mills in Northfield, Minnesota, and Fort Atkinson, Iowa. One day in early September, when he was at the mill in Northfield, he was surprised to hear gunfire coming from the center of the town. He hurried over, and encountered a battle between the townspeople and a band of bank robbers. They were the Jesse James–Cole Younger gang, later much memorialized in dime novels and Hollywood Westerns, and Ames had happened upon the most famous incident of their careers as outlaws. In this case the James gang was no match for the townspeople of Northfield—they, including Ames, fought back, and the robbery ended with the robbers fleeing, having killed a bank clerk, gotten no money, and lost two of their own crew, who lay dead in the street for a day while people from the countryside rode into town on their wagons to have a look. Ames wrote Blanche that it reminded him of the past fall's campaign in

Mississippi: "Is it not strange that Mississippi should come up here to visit me."

It may have been strange, but it was not happenstance. Cole Younger, who was soon captured and imprisoned but lived long enough to be released, to tour the country in Wild West shows, and to write his memoirs, said that the gang had come to Northfield— all the way from Missouri—because they'd heard that the bank there held deposits from Ames and from Ben Butler. The robbers were former Confederate soldiers, the Missouri version of the young veterans in Mississippi who roamed around serving as an informal White Line terrorist militia. For them the Civil War had never ended.

5

THE MISSISSIPPI PLAN

A s the 1876 presidential election drew near, Democrats had begun to talk about the possibility of other Southern states implementing the "Mississippi plan." The post–Civil War constitutional amendments had seemed to promise the Republicans an unbeatable majority in national politics, because they added the freed slaves living in the former Confederate states, who overwhelmingly voted Republican, to the electorate. Even if white Southerners bitterly opposed Reconstruction and the Republican Party, the most heavily black Southern states, like Mississippi and Louisiana, would still join the Republicans' base in the Northeast and Midwest to create a bloc big enough to win presidential elections. That was how Grant had won reelection in 1872.

For Democrats, and especially for white Southern Democrats, this was a problem to which the Mississippi plan offered a solution. Using violence and intimidation to suppress the black vote—but subtly enough so that the federal government would not be forced to use federal troops to enforce Negro rights—the Democrats could sweep the entire South. James George and Ethelbert Barksdale, the Confederate general and the newspaper editor who ran Democratic politics in Mississippi in 1875, were the inventors of the Mississippi plan. They had been sufficiently respectable to be able to maintain contact with Lucius Lamar and other elected Democrats in Washington, and even with leading Republicans, but sufficiently ruthless to keep within their range of communication the White Liners, Bulldozers, Regulators, and free-roaming ex-Confederate soldiers who were ready, willing, and able to murder and terrorize to an extent unknown before or since in American politics. The 1876 election would be, among other things, a test of the Mississippi plan.

In Mississippi itself, of course, the plan was already in place. There was hardly a cessation of political violence between the end of 1875's campaign and the beginning of 1876's. In late July 1876, more than three months before Election Day, a Republican from Macon, Mississippi, wrote to James Redpath, "The Negroes are now almost ready to take to the swamps, and unless the Government sends troops here at least a month before the Election, the Negroes will not go to the polls. We look for the Government to stand by us and if it does not it can take these Southern States and do what it pleases with them. And the prair of every Northern man that has fought for ten years like I have for the Government will be that these Southern men will clean them up like Sitting Bull and Custer." As Election Day drew near, those Mississippi Republicans who still dared to hold open political rallies found them disrupted by armed White Liners according to what was by now a well-rehearsed routine. The Democrats also adopted a couple of new tactics. One was issuing "certificates of loyalty" to Negroes who promised to vote Democratic, which protected them and their families from violence and loss of employment. Another was a registration system made state law by the new legislature, under which voters were required to tell a Democratic Party appointee where they were employed and which election district they lived in, or they would not be allowed to vote. Any Negro voter who didn't want to take, or couldn't pass, this quiz—who was not, in other words, willing to have his voting behavior reported to his employer—could not vote.

On Election Day, Samuel Tilden, governor of New York and the Democratic presidential nominee, carried Mississippi by more than fifty-five thousand votes. Democrats swept almost all the other races. In Yazoo County, only two people cast Republican votes; in Tallahatchie County, only one; in Lowndes County, only thirteen.

The Republican presidential nominee was Rutherford B. Hayes, governor of Ohio, whose reelection campaign the year before had been helped by Grant's decision to ignore Governor Ames's pleas for federal troops to ensure a free election in Mississippi. If that decision had saved Hayes and doomed Ames, it was a harbinger of the future of the Republican Party. The nomination of Hayes—a hard-money man at a time when currency policy, which pitted farmers against bankers, was becoming the dominant issue in national politics—was a sign that the Republicans were now the party of business, not the party of Reconstruction. So it should not be surprising that the party's leaders chose not to use the hundreds of pages of shocking testimony in the Boutwell Report about the previous year's depredations in Mississippi as campaign material. Reconstruction had become a negative item for Democrats to emphasize as a way of attacking Republicans, rather than a positive one for Republicans to use in rallying Southern Negroes and Northern veterans of the Union Army to their side.

After the Mississippi election of 1875, only three Southern states remained in Republican hands: South Carolina (the state with proportionally the highest black population), Florida, and Louisiana. A Democratic newspaper in South Carolina, *The Spartanburg Herald,* had sent a correspondent to Mississippi to cover the 1875 campaign, and in December it published an article called "What Was Done in Mississippi." "I would not have believed that so many colored people could have been got to vote the Democratic ticket as I have seen do it here today," it said.

On July 4, 1876, the day the United States celebrated its centennial, a company of the South Carolina state militia (which whites called the Negro militia), parading in the town of Hamburg, had an unpleasant confrontation with two whites in a buggy who claimed the militia was not letting them pass. Soon the militia leaders were arrested for obstructing a public highway and put in jail. Over the next few days, well-armed white men from all over South Carolina and Georgia descended on Hamburg, supposedly to protect the whites there from the threat of a Negro riot. When the whites demanded that the members of the state militia surrender their weapons, they refused, and barricaded themselves inside a building for protection.

As at Colfax three years earlier, the whites arrayed themselves outside. On July 8 came an exchange of gunfire in which a white man was shot and killed. The whites produced a cannon and began firing it at the building, and this quickly turned the exchange into a rout. One Negro was shot as he ran out of the building. The rest were captured, and five of them, "regarded as ringleaders in bringing on the difficulty," as one white historian later put it, "were singly shot to death by their infuriated captors." As at Colfax, the bodies of the murdered Negroes lay out in the sun for days because their families feared to claim them. One had his tongue cut off. Another had his hip hacked away with an ax.

The Hamburg massacre was big news, and in the North it generated a certain amount of the old outrage over violence and Confederate bitter-endism. "I cannot help waving the bloody shirt when men are being murdered," Ben Butler wrote to a political associate. South Carolina's governor, Daniel Chamberlain—like Ames, an idealistic white New Englander—asked President Grant to send federal troops. Hamburg, he wrote, "foreshadows a campaign of blood and violence, such a campaign as is popularly known as a campaign conducted on the 'Mississippi plan.'" In his reply, Grant railed against what was happening in South Carolina and had happened before in Mississippi. "The scene in Hamburgh, as cruel, bloodythirsty, wanton, unprovoked, and uncalled for as it was, is only a repetition of the course which has been pursued in other Southern States within the last few years, notably in Mississippi and Louisiana," he wrote. "Mississippi is governed today by officials chosen through fraud and violence, such as would scarcely be accredited to savages, much less to a civilized and Christian people." But then he offered Chamberlain nothing but encouragement to solve the problem on his own, "without aid from the Federal Government."

In September a second, worse massacre occurred in and around the town of Ellenton, not far from Hamburg. A large party of armed whites (in South Carolina, these organizations called themselves "rifle clubs") rode through the countryside threatening people and disrupting Republican political activity. An incident in which two black robbers entered the home of a white woman and one of them hit her with a stick set off a protracted killing spree by the local rifle club. A careful accounting by U.S. marshals produced a list of seventeen Negroes murdered during a weeklong white rampage. One was a ninety-year-old man. One was a teenage boy whose ear was cut off after he was killed. A Negro state legislator named Simon Coker, whom some whites came upon sitting at a railway station with his wife and a schoolteacher friend of hers, was forced into a boxcar, taken to the next town, and executed in an open field in full view of the passengers on the train. Then the white men took his money, his watch, his shirt studs, and his wedding ring and rode away. A little later the rifle club came upon a group of terrified and lightly armed Negroes, and was preparing for battle—or slaughter—when, providentially, federal troops arrived and restored order.

Finally, but not until October 17, President Grant issued a proclamation ordering the rifle clubs to disperse, the necessary legal prelude to sending troops to South Carolina should they fail to obey. About a thousand soldiers arrived in the last days of the campaign—enough to produce an election result that was more Republican than it would have been otherwise, but less Republican than if Grant had made it clear after Hamburg that terrorizing black voters would not be tolerated. An anti-Reconstruction historian later estimated that 150 Negroes were murdered in South Carolina during the campaign, while the Democrats' official leader (as in Mississippi, a patrician former Confederate general, Wade Hampton) was campaigning as a statesman.

In Florida, a Republican newspaper warned at the outset of the campaign that the Democrats would adopt "the shot-gun policy pursued in Mississippi," and this wasn't far off, although Florida Democrats were much more hesitant to resort to murder than their brethren in Mississippi. Nonetheless, armed Democratic Party–affiliated Regulators rode through rural Florida warning Negroes not to vote Republican. Some Florida Negroes testified afterward that the Regulators had forced them at gunpoint to swear they would vote Democratic. At least one local Democratic organization published a pledge that had been signed by local farmers and merchants that they would discriminate economically against anyone who voted Republican, and many individual plantation owners told the Negroes who worked for them that they would be out of jobs unless they voted Democratic. "The substance of it was about like this: that all colored people who voted the Republican ticket were to be starved out next year," one Florida Republican testified after the election. Jefferson County's Negro state senator was "waited upon" and shot at by two armed gunmen a week before the election. In Levy County, shots were fired into the house of a white man who taught at a school for Negroes, and, when he went to vote on Election Day, he got so many threats from Democrats who were hanging around at the polling place that he and his family fled the county.

In Columbia County, the Negro state senator, E. G. Johnson, had been assassinated during the summer of 1875, and this broke a tie between the two parties in the state Senate in favor of the Democrats. During the 1876 campaign, a group of Regulators murdered a black man named Moses Smith who was actively campaigning for the Republicans, while his wife pleaded for mercy. In another notorious incident, Regulators abducted a group of local Republican leaders, took them out into the woods, and put nooses around their necks. A U.S. Senate investigating committee later reported, "The colored men had been marched from the road several miles into the deep woods, where all chances of rescue by passing persons was removed. They begged hard for their lives, and were finally told that they might be spared if they would agree to vote the democratic ticket and induce a number of other colored men to do the same." After that there was no Republican activity in Columbia County.

President Grant sent a small complement of troops to Florida; they arrived just a few days before the election and dispersed in groups of ten to the polling places where there had been the worst reports of trouble, and wherever they went, there was no election violence. But the Regulators were far more numerous than the soldiers and were reinforced by allies from Georgia who came to join the fight. During the final days of the campaign, they broke up Republican rallies using the methods developed in Mississippi— starting altercations and choosing to treat the rallies as Negro uprisings that had to be put down lest those assembled work their will on the local whites. In one town, a Democrat who worked for the railroad sent a large Negro work crew to Alabama, promising that he would bring them back to vote, but their train home was made to break down in a remote rural area in Alabama, and it didn't move again until the polls had closed.

On Election Day, all over Florida, Regulators on horseback stood out on the roads leading to polling places, rifles slung across their saddles, and kept Negroes from voting. In the town of Monticello, five hundred white armed horsemen paraded through the streets. In several locations, the Democrats printed "galvanized" sample ballots for illiterate Negroes, with the names of Democratic candidates printed beneath Republican insignia. In one location in Key West, according to the Senate report, "a boisterous and pressing crowd kept republicans from getting access to the polling place, so that many were forced away." An anti-Reconstruction historian reluctantly summed up the Democratic campaign this way: "They were not over-scrupulous about means. They sought results primarily. The key-note of their campaign was not persuasion. That had failed. The key-note was threatened violence and economic coercion."

Louisiana's switch from the Republican to the Democratic Party in the initial returns from the 1876 election was best understood, a Senate subcommittee report said, as belonging to this historical continuum: "The atrocities of Saint Bartholomew and the threats of Charles IX forced Henry of Navarre and his cousin the Prince of Condé to abjure the Protestant faith; Galileo, through fear, was made to promise that he would never again teach the truth of the earth's motion; and a great apostle was made, through fear, to swear that he never knew the Master whom he had followed, that Saviour to whom we all now make believe we know." But Grant, though he had had plenty of warnings, including one delivered in person in the White House by T. Morris Chester, the Negro journalist turned Louisiana politician, made no effort in advance to prevent political violence in Louisiana.

Democratic terrorist activity was most heavily concentrated in two parts of the state, Ouachita Parish, in the northeastern part of Louisiana, and three parishes in the southeast that bordered Mississippi; the locations made it easier for Democratic militiamen to slip in and out of the state. In Ouachita, a Republican named Dr. B. H. Dinkgrave was murdered two months before Election Day, and two others were wounded. In October, according to the subcommittee, "Primus Johnson, a colored republican, was shot to death while holding his infant child in his arms, before his own house. His brother-in-law, Eaton Logwood, was shot at the same time, at the same place, and died of his wounds while the committee was in New Orleans." (An Army lieutenant who came upon the wounded Johnson and Logwood reported, "Upon arriving at Logwood's the scene was indeed appalling, one which will never be erased from my mind; helpless women, frightened men and children all huddled together in groups, looking terror-stricken as though about to be slaughtered; a few more surrounding a camp fire, which was burning to keep them warm.") The subcommittee report went on: "Another republican, by the name of Ferdinand Bynum, was killed. The precise date of that murder is not known. His body was found in the Ouachita River sometime after the election. George Shelton, Spencer Dickerson, H. W. Burrill, and William Lewis were shot and wounded by two different parties about two weeks before the election."

On the Saturday night before Election Day, "the rifle-clubs took the field. They visited the house of Abram Williams, an old colored republican, sixty years of age. He was taken from his house, stripped, and severely whipped. They visited the house of Willis Frazier, took him also from his bed and brutally whipped him. They visited the house of a son of Abram Williams. He had taken the precaution to spend the night in the cotton-field. Not finding him at home, they whipped his wife, and committed another outrage upon her person. Merrimon Rhodes, on that night, was killed. A few days later his body, disemboweled, was found in the bayou and was buried. They visited the house of Randall Driver. They took him from his bed and from his house and brutally whipped him. They visited the house of Henry Pinkston. He was taken from his bed, from his house, and shot to death. His infant child was killed. His wife was cut in different places; she was shot and nearly slain."

In West Feliciana Parish, where dozens of Negroes had been murdered in the spring of 1876, two prominent black Republicans were killed during the fall campaign season, and there were many incidents of armed intimidation. In East Feliciana, the Bulldozers got an early start; they killed a dozen politically active Negroes, including a former state legislator named John Gair, in the fall of 1875 (Gair "was literally shot to pieces"), and on Election Day 1876 not a single Republican vote was cast in the parish. In East Baton Rouge Parish, another Senate investigating committee reported that "more than sixty colored republicans were killed in the parish on account of their politics within the eight months preceding the November election." The committee provided a partial roster, which begins this way:

> April 13, 1876. Jerry Myers, hung, Tenth ward, on Joors
> Road, twelve miles from Baton Rouge.
> April 13, 1876. Samuel Myers, shot, Tenth ward, on Joors
> road, twelve miles from Baton Rouge.
> January 5, 1876. Taylor Hawkins, shot. Fourth ward, ten
> miles from Baton Rouge.
> February 16, 1876. George Washington (alias Christmas,)
> Tenth or Eleventh ward, shot on Greenwell Springs road,
> and then burned with coal oil.

The committee reported that a few weeks before Election Day, the parish coroner received a letter from someone signing himself "the captain of the regulators" that said if he continued to perform inquiries into the cause of death of black Republicans, "he would be sent where the bodies of those whom he had holden inquests upon had been sent." It was no surprise that "thenceforward he took no further inquests as coroner out of fear of his life."

Southern politics in those days didn't have many good-government reformers, but when the Republicans cheated, they usually did so in traditional ways, not through terrorism. In South Carolina, Florida, and Louisiana, where they were still in power, their chief weapon was control of the local "returning boards" in charge of counting the votes after the polls had closed. These returning boards tried— but it is difficult to determine just how much—to counterbalance the effects of the violent organizations on the Democratic side by rigging the count so as to produce higher Republican and lower Democratic totals; they then picked slates of Republicans to send to the electoral college. Such techniques are useful only in close elections, which the 1876 election would not have been if the Democrats had not used the Mississippi plan. There was a clear causal chain, from Grant's deciding in 1875 not to do what was needed to have a free election in Mississippi, to the Democrats' taking that state, to the Mississippi events emboldening Democrats in South Carolina, Florida, and Louisiana to try to win in the same way the Mississippi Democrats had, to the campaigns in those three states ending in very close calls, with both sides claiming to have been cheated out of their rightful victories.

Nationally, it was the closest presidential election the United States had ever had. The electoral vote count was so tight that the switch of any one of the disputed Southern states would give the presidency to Tilden. As they had a year earlier right after the Mississippi elections, the Republicans in the Senate quickly launched detailed investigations of the campaigns in South Carolina, Florida, and Louisiana, expecting to show evidence of the Democrats' violent tactics that would support keeping the three states in the Republican column. A complicated, shadowy bargaining session in Washington ensued that took up the whole winter of 1876–77 and ended with the Compromise of 1877, the traditional midpoint of American history, in which the Democrats agreed to let Hayes become president and the Republicans agreed in return to remove the remaining federal troops from the South. Reconstruction, which had wound up producing a lower-intensity continuation of the

Civil War, was over. The South had won. And the events in Mississippi in 1875 had been the decisive battle.

On the day of President Hayes's inauguration, March 5, 1877, L.Q.C. Lamar walked into the U.S. Senate chamber and presented his credentials for membership. The Mississippi legislature had elected Lamar to the Senate back in 1875 as soon as it convened as a Democratic Party–controlled body, but Lamar hadn't been able to get himself seated. First Governor Ames had refused to sign Lamar's certificate of election. Then, after Ames's impeachment and resignation, Lamar obtained the certificate, but the Senate, still under Republican control, would not seat him because of the violent provenance of the legislature that elected him.

Lamar was one of two new Southern senators with questionable credentials; the other was William Pitt Kellogg, the Republican former governor of Louisiana, whom the Democrats did not want to seat. James Blaine, Republican of Maine, the former Speaker of the House who was newly elected to the Senate, got himself put in charge of Kellogg's case, on the understanding that he'd help his party get Kellogg seated. But Blaine double-crossed his fellow Republicans by rising not to admit Kellogg but to yield the floor to a Democratic senator who offered a resolution to admit Lamar. The speculation in Washington was that Blaine was repaying a favor: both he and Lamar were very close to the railroad interests, and in the House of Representatives Lamar had quashed what would have been a career-ruining investigation into Blaine's railroad activities. As a delaying tactic, one of the betrayed, stunned Republican senators read out the report of the Boutwell Committee on the Mississippi elections on the floor, and then there was a debate, but it was no use: Lamar, with the support of all the Democrats and of those Republicans controlled by Blaine, was seated.

Just a few days later, Mississippi's other U.S. senator, Blanche K. Bruce, paid a call on Lamar, who was at home sick. It was still a few years before the advent of the federal civil service system, so senators had much greater power than they do now to distribute jobs with the federal government, at a time when such jobs were highly prized, especially in a state like Mississippi where there were no substantial private employers. Democrats in Mississippi could finally satisfy their tremendous pent-up demand for federal jobs, now that Lamar was a senator. The most immediate case at hand was the postmastership of Vicksburg.

Senator Bruce, ever the accommodationist, had ignored the entreaties of the Radical Republicans and voted for Lamar's admission to the Senate without Lamar's even having to ask. Lamar liked him; they had worked together successfully over the past few years. "I believe him to be a noble negro," Lamar wrote a Mississippi friend. He gave this account of their meeting, in a letter marked "Private & Confidential": "I told him that I regarded him as the legitimate representative of the colored people of Miss. And myself as that of the whites; that however distinct the two races unquestionably were, they were one indivisible community; that in my opinion the happiness & prosperity of his race were just as important as the happiness and prosperity of the whites; that I had no desire to ignore, disregard or subordinate the interests or rights of the colored people of Mississippi; that of course in case of conflict for mastery or power between the two my feelings & actions would be for the white race; but that true patriotism & statesmanship would aim to prevent such conflict & seek to bring about a harmonious cooperation & development of their social forces, & that he & I might by unselfishly acting in concert do great good for our state."

Lamar and Bruce struck a deal: Bruce would assent to the removal of all white Republicans from federal office, and Lamar would permit the appointment of some Negro Republicans, so long as they were "acceptable to the white community." That way Lamar and Bruce could cooperate on patronage matters, rather than squabbling, and each man could build up his own political machinery back home. For example, Vicksburg could have two postmasters, one white and one black. Lamar reported this to his friend in Mississippi and obviously received a disappointed reply asking why all offices couldn't go to white Democrats, because his next letter was somewhat defensive: "You are right in your view that boldness is needed by our public men from the South. But the boldness that is needed is that of a wise good man. I know well the end I have in view, but I am not equally confident of my means."

So Lamar would proceed more cautiously than his supporters back home would have liked. He sketched out the problems he confronted in Washington: President Hayes, whom he had seen recently, and his closest political allies "are not *en rapport* with us on a single sentiment." He went on: "Hayes does not strike me as a man of much strength in public affairs . . . He is well meaning, but is very ignorant of the South. His ideas of the negro are what he gets from Whittier"—John Greenleaf Whittier, the sentimental poet— "& Uncle Tom's Cabin," although, on the positive side of the ledger, Hayes, unlike Grant, "is full of the idea of being a great Pacificator." The only member of the Cabinet who was truly sympathetic to the Southern cause was Carl Schurz, now secretary of the interior.

Most difficult of all for Lamar's Mississippi allies to grasp, perhaps, was that in the North, incredible though it might seem, the Republicans were the Bourbon party. As Lamar put it, "The intellect, courage, literature, moral ideas (I mean convictions on ethical questions) and aggregations of wealth are represented by banks, shipping, manufacturers & railroads, at the North, are arrayed against the Democrats." Hence Republicans did not merit, and were too powerful to tolerate, the sort of complete dismissal that white Southerners thought they deserved. There was no choice but to cooperate with them.

For some years, Lamar's arrangement with Blanche Bruce held. White Republicans, especially if they had come to Mississippi during Reconstruction, were dealt with mercilessly. Black Republicans, if they knew their place, were dealt into the political game.

Not long after Lamar was seated in the Senate, a particularly brutal incident occurred of White Line revenge being taken against a white Republican. It began when, in Kemper County, on the Alabama border, a White Liner was found murdered on a country road. The Republican county sheriff, a former judge named W. W. Chisolm—a white Southerner and former Confederate who had thrown in with the Republicans after the war and had testified before the Boutwell Committee—was charged with the crime, and a large mob of white men, some of them from Alabama, assembled to take him to jail. The scene quickly turned into something much closer to vigilantism than criminal justice, with the mob massed outside the jail drinking, shouting, and firing guns. A few men went to Chisolm's house and killed another white Republican who was there. A gun battle broke out at the jail, which a friend of Chisolm's later described as "a scene to have equaled in horror Milton or Dante's most extravagant conceptions of hell itself." Chisolm's teenage son and daughter had come to the jail because they feared for their father's life; the boy was killed and the girl was badly wounded, as was Chisolm himself. When the battle died down, friends carried the Chisolms back home, where the sheriff and his daughter lingered for a couple of weeks and then died.

Nearly a year later, in March 1878, Chisolm's survivors, his widow and another son, traveled to Washington and called upon President Hayes to ask for federal employment. Afterward, Chisolm's son saw Adelbert Ames, who happened to be in town, and gave him an account of the meeting, which Ames passed along to Blanche in a letter:

"Mrs. C.—'You know about my husband, Judge Chisolm, who was murdered in Miss. I will spare you a recitation of the facts. We cannot live there and my son here wishes a place under your government.' Mr. Hayes (kind of laughing) 'What are your politics, young man?' Young Chisolm, 'Republican, of course. I supposed you knew that.' Mr. Hayes (kind of laughing) 'Well, you know that I only give appointments to Democrats in the South.' Young C.— 'In that case, as a Republican, I stand no chance.' Mr. Hayes—'I do not say it is true, but I have no doubt you can get a place.'

"Thus ended the interview and Mrs. C. and her son left the White House indignant and outraged. Of course Hayes has not aided him nor will he, nor has it been his purpose to. The feeling of contempt for Hayes is universal here. It is deep and bitter. Even those holding office under him despise him."

Mississippi's Negro Republicans remained figures of distinct, though carefully limited, influence in politics, even as white Republicans were killed, were driven away, or fled. But that wound up being a temporary circumstance. Blanche Bruce served only one full term in the Senate; in 1881 he was replaced by James Z. George, the architect of the Democratic Party victory in the 1875 election. (George's political partner in 1875, Ethelbert Barksdale, served two terms in the House of Representatives in the 1880s.) Bruce stayed on in Washington, working in a succession of federal jobs, and continued to play a part in distributing patronage to Mississippi Negroes. John R. Lynch lost his seat in Congress in the 1876 election; he won it back for one term, then lost it again. He was chair of the Mississippi Republican Party through the 1880s. One year he gave the keynote address at the Republican National Convention.

In the late 1880s, the former Confederate states began passing Jim Crow laws, which replaced the thus far informal and violent nullification of Negro rights with a formal, highly detailed legal system. Mississippi's first Jim Crow law, passed in 1888, required separated seating for black and white passengers on trains. By the early twentieth century, all the Southern states had elaborate Jim Crow structures mandating separate education, employment, and public accommodations for the two races. Mississippi's system was noteworthy for the harsh penalties it gave for minor thievery, which produced a large black prison population of men who were then leased to landowners as hired labor.

The most important feature of the Jim Crow system, though not the most obvious, was Negro disenfranchisement. In a democracy, people who vote can get themselves treated decently; people who can't are powerless against others' malign impulses. Once the federal government had made it plain, most dramatically in Mississippi in 1875, that it would not enforce black people's constitutional right to vote, it left the way clear for the Southern states, after a time, to take that right away explicitly. All the Southern states found legal means of restricting Negro voting rights. In Mississippi a new state constitution ratified in 1890 required that all voters be able to read and interpret any portion of Mississippi's charter, if asked. This amounted to giving local registrars of voters, by this time all white Democrats, the power to strike any Negro from the rolls. Those few who could read well could be disqualified on grounds of faulty interpretation. Naturally, the number of Negro registered voters dropped severely, especially Republican voters, which made it safe for the Democratic Party to ignore Mississippi's black politicians. Soon they had all disappeared, as the white Republicans had a few years earlier. The original brokers of the deal for black political participation after Reconstruction were by then out of Mississippi politics, Bruce because he had lost his seat, Lamar because, in 1888, he had become a justice of the United States Supreme Court. (Bruce named his son after a white politician, Roscoe Conkling, and sent him to Harvard; it shows the direction in which the country moved that Roscoe Conkling Bruce, Jr., in the 1920s, was not allowed to live in the Harvard freshman dormitories because of his race.) John Lynch, though he owned a plantation in Mississippi and was a member of its bar, joined the Army and left Mississippi in 1898. Later he settled in Chicago.

"Need I tell you I hold the state has gone beyond redemption," Adelbert Ames wrote to his wife, from the depths of his emptiness, two days after the Mississippi election of 1875. Among the seemingly endless cruelties the South visited upon Ames was one of nomenclature: "Redemption" was just the word that white Southerners chose to denote the bloody events of the mid-1870s; and the leaders of the successful campaign of political violence, defiance of the national government, and local repeal of part of the Constitution called themselves "Redeemers." The name implied a divine sanction for the retaking of the authority the whites had lost in the Civil War, and a heavenly quality to the reestablishment of white supremacy in the post-Reconstruction South. "Reconstruction," the North's word, was sturdy, purposeful, and optimistic. "Redemption," the South's, was empyrean.

In the heat of battle in 1875, respectable white Mississippians were uncomfortable about the particulars of how they were winning back political control of their state. Lamar, for example, regularly condemned racial violence even as he was extolling (for Mississippi audiences) white supremacy. But as time passed and the goals of the Redeemers were enshrined in law, the political risk of offending public opinion in the North disappeared, and the South became much more unapologetic. The Redemption story became a durable, emotionally stirring defining myth, informally passed along on front porches and, later, openly celebrated with monuments and commemorations. For at least three-quarters of a century, it was an important part of what white Southerners knew about themselves. It was how they explained the system they lived in.

The Redemption story was woven together from threads that were visible in white Southern culture during the events themselves: the humiliation and ruination of the white South, especially the plantation South, during the Civil War; the horrors of "Negro rule" during Reconstruction; the cynical scheming of carpetbaggers and scalawags along with their radical allies in Washington; the gallery of familiar Negro types, loyal and insolent and addled by radical promises; the oppressive taxation and corruption of Republican state governments in the South; most of all, the ever-imminent "Negro uprisings," bent on rape and pillage, repulsed in the nick of time by brave and weary Confederate veterans forced once again to take up arms. These elements took on a purer, more orderly form, the clean lines of a stock plot, over time. The story had a political aspect, but one of its features was that it took what had been essentially political events and transmogrified them into a string of local incidents of heroic self-protection.

As Reconstruction ended, modern industrial America began. With it came the advent of a national popular culture, in which faster and better printing presses and cameras and trains enabled the whole country to get at the same time cultural products that had previously been much more local. Reconstruction, like the Wild West, was a standard topic in the new national entertainments, and it was usually presented from the Southern point of view, because that matched the country's prejudices at the time and because the story of Redemption, as Southerners had worked it out over the years, had it all—sex and violence and good and evil and a natural three-act structure.

The person most responsible for making the Redemption story

into a staple of American popular culture was Thomas Dixon, a Baptist minister, lawyer, politician, and prolific novelist. Dixon was born in North Carolina in 1864, so he experienced Reconstruction through hearing the endless stories about it after it was over rather than as a mature eyewitness to the events themselves. In 1902 his novel *The Leopard's Spots* appeared, a distillation of the mythology he'd been raised on. He meant *The Leopard's Spots* to be as influential (in the opposite direction) as *Uncle Tom's Cabin* had been. He may have succeeded, although *The Leopard's Spots* is not at the same level of literary accomplishment—it's crudely schematic, and employs all the conventions of late-Victorian commercial fiction in the most mechanical way possible. But to drive home the comparison, Dixon imported Simon Legree, the fictional plantation overseer from the Red River valley of Louisiana who is the leading villain of *Uncle Tom's Cabin*, to postwar small-town North Carolina, where *The Leopard's Spots* is set, and made him into a no less villainous white native Southern (that is, "scalawag") Republican.

Dixon's point in appropriating Simon Legree, the national symbol of oppression of the Negro, was to portray white Reconstructionists as exploiters of black people, in the cause of their own political power and enrichment, not liberators. Conversely, in Dixon's work, white Southerners who were Democrats were the Negro's true friends. In this and most other respects, Dixon was expressing the standard views of white Southerners of his generation and class—and he couldn't have made it plainer that his warmth and good intentions toward black people were contingent on the firm understanding that they were inferior in every way, economically, politically, socially, even biologically. Without that condition, the warmth turns steely and cruel. *The Leopard's Spots*—like its two successors in Dixon's "Reconstruction trilogy," *The Clansman* (1905) and *The Traitor* (1907)—is the relatively rare example of a book brought out by a leading American publisher that, rather than being subtly racist or implicitly racist or unconsciously racist or racist-in-passing, is, simply and directly, racist. Its core concern is to make clear the superiority of one race over another, and its central emotion is a violent, obsessive fear and hatred of the race deemed inferior. The passage from which the book's title is drawn reads this way:

> The Ethiopian can not change his skin, or the leopard his spots . . . If a man really believes in equality, let him prove it by giving his daughter to a Negro in marriage. That is the test. When she sinks with her mulatto children into the black abyss of a Negro life, then ask him! Your scheme of education is humbug . . . Education! Can you change the color of his skin, the kink of his hair, the bulge of his lips, the spread of his nose, or the beat of his heart, with a spelling book? The Negro is the human donkey. You can train him, but you can't make of him a horse . . . What is called our race prejudice is simply God's first law of nature—the instinct of self-preservation.

The plot line of *The Leopard's Spots* roughly follows the true story of the recapture of the South by the Democratic Party. Dixon splits the redemption story in two. The first redemption comes not long after the end of the Civil War, courtesy of the Ku Klux Klan. Later, a biracial, economically populist government comes to power in North Carolina, which necessitates a second redemption on the Mississippi model, in which a paramilitary organization called the Red Shirts restores white rule by parading around on horseback carrying rifles and frightening Negro voters away from the polls. In both cases, the familiar "Negro uprising," with elements of social insolence, economic indolence, rapacious intentions toward beautiful, innocent young white women, and rumored military operations, triggers the redemption story. In both there is a salaciously rendered lynching scene, one involving hanging, the other burning alive. All the ungovernable impulses that white people feel toward Negroes are relocated in the Negroes' hearts, so as to give whites a pretext for enacting them, and for effacing the line between politics and violence.

Dixon candidly rejects all the respectable arguments against Reconstruction that Southern members of Congress liked to use—about corruption, federal intrusion, and excessive taxation—and insists that the real aim of the Southern Redeemers was to nullify the Fourteenth and Fifteenth amendments, disenfranchise the Negro, and reestablish a political order whose primary feature was white racial superiority. In describing the first redemption, he sums up the question at hand this way: "Henceforth there could be but one issue: Are you a White Man or a Negro? . . . These determined impassioned men believed that this question was more important than any theory of tariff or finance and that it was larger than the South, or even the nation, and held in its solution the brightest hopes of the progress of the human race. And they believed that they were ordained of God in this crisis to give this question its first authoritative answer."

Uncle Tom's Cabin's influence over American public opinion had come not just through its being read but also through the touring theatrical versions that were staples of American culture for decades. Thomas Dixon, aiming to emulate *Uncle Tom's Cabin* in this way, too, wrote a stage version of his second Reconstruction novel, *The Clansman*, which played all over the country. *The Clansman* uses the same well-established mythological structure as *The Leopard's Spots*—Reconstruction horrors, Negro uprising, attempted rape, white violence, redemption—but it has more material set in Washington. Ben Butler ("whose name was enough to start a riot in any assembly in America") makes a brief appearance. And it ends, less realistically than *The Leopard's Spots*, with the one event that never actually happened during Reconstruction: President Grant dispatching troops to the South and local white paramilitary forces triumphing anyway.

The motion-picture industry was beginning, and Dixon wanted to have his play of *The Clansman* made into a movie. In the early teens he made an alliance with David Wark Griffith, the Kentuckian son of a Confederate veteran, who had become one of the first generation of film directors. Griffith made Dixon's play into *The Birth of a Nation*, the first American film masterpiece—the work that showed the country the immense power that the new medium possessed. It was *The Birth of a Nation*, rather than Dixon's novels or his play, that had an impact and a staying power commensurate with

Uncle Tom's Cabin. Its plot combines elements of *The Clansman* and *The Leopard's Spots*, plus Civil War battle scenes that were in neither novel; nonetheless, it is thematically faithful to Dixon's work. The most unforgettable scene is the attempted rape of a white girl by a black man, which she escapes only by throwing herself off a cliff; the South is redeemed when Klansmen on horseback stand in the way of Negro voters on Election Day.

Dixon had an acquaintanceship with Woodrow Wilson, another son of the Reconstruction South, because they had both been students at The Johns Hopkins University at the same time. D. W. Griffith and Dixon had used Wilson's academic work as source material for their film, and when it was ready to open in 1915, Dixon persuaded Wilson, who by now was president of the United States, to hold the first-ever White House movie screening for *The Birth of a Nation.* According to Dixon, Wilson turned to him when the film was over and said, "It is like writing history with lightning, and my only regret is that it is all so terribly true." Dixon held a second screening in a Washington hotel, attended by dignitaries, including the chief justice of the United States, Edward Douglass White, of Louisiana, who had been a Confederate soldier and later a member of the white militia that fought the U.S. Army in the streets of New Orleans during Reconstruction. The implied endorsement from the highest officials of the American government helped put to rest whatever incipient unease with *The Birth of a Nation* may have been stirring, and so made its long, prosperous, and influential commercial and cultural life possible.

Reconstruction is a vivid, even eerie example of the way in which history (as the unfolding of actual events), popular mythology, entertainment, history (as an academic endeavor), and politics can all become intertwined and begin to influence each other. During Reconstruction itself, the story of the repulse of the Negro uprising was almost completely a fantasy, yet it was so deeply and firmly implanted in the heads of white Southerners that it gave their political project of using organized violence to take away Negroes' right to vote an important psychological undergirding; that they believed in it enhanced their ability to influence the distribution of money and power in the South. After Reconstruction was over, the story kept gaining force, partly because of its great dramatic power for white audiences all over the country, partly because, now that it was safely located in the past, it offered a far more comfortable explanation for why Reconstruction had come to an end than what had actually happened. Politicians, writers, and scholars who had been raised on the story used it as the basis for activities outside the realm of folklore and entertainment: political strategy, government policy, and serious academic work.

Another aspect of the new America that emerged after Reconstruction, besides a more organized national popular culture, was the great research university, and academics as a structured profession. Reconstruction was a major subject for the first generation of American professors who had been formally trained in graduate schools (often in Germany), who had graduate students themselves, and who thought of scholarly publication as their central project. They almost universally presented Reconstruction as having failed because full Negro citizenship was a bad idea. They were dispassionate enough not to traffic in the romantic and quasi-religious concept of redemption; instead, they showed the end of Reconstruction as something more practical, though not much less noble: as reunion, as the knitting together, after fifteen years of tribal and sectional horrors, of a great modern nation.

In 1902, *Reconstruction and the Constitution* appeared, a book by John W. Burgess, the founder and dean of the faculty of political science at Columbia University—arguably the founder of the discipline of political science in the United States. It began with the assertion that although the South had been wrong to resist the authority of the national government, the authors of Reconstruction had been equally wrong in enfranchising the Negro. Men of enlightenment in the North were becoming more sympathetic with traditional Southern white racial attitudes as immigrants who looked strange to them poured into the Northern cities, as the United States, with the successful conclusion of the Spanish-American War, began acquiring overseas colonies, and as advanced scientific opinion began positing an inherent biological rank-ordering of the races. The recent history of the South seemed to Burgess to demonstrate the success of a policy of codified white supremacy. He wrote that "the North is learning every day by valuable experiences that there are vast differences in political capacity between the races, and that it is the white man's mission, his duty and his right, to hold the reins of political power in his own hand for the civilization of the world and the welfare of mankind."

Of the brief period when the Fourteenth and Fifteenth amendments had the force of law in the South, Burgess wrote: "It was the most soul-sickening spectacle that Americans had ever been called upon to behold . . . In place of government by the most intelligent and virtuous part of the people for the benefit of the governed, here was government by the most ignorant and vicious part of the population for the benefit, the vulgar, materialistic, brutal benefit of the governing set." So the climactic events in Mississippi in 1875, though undoubtedly unattractive in ways that did not merit specification, were, to Burgess, necessary, and salutary in their effects. For the redeemers, "it was now a choice between complete destruction and the employment of any means necessary to escape from it. There was no use in talking about observing the letter of the law at such a moment. The law was iniquitous and it was rapidly destroying all that was left of prosperity, civilization, morality, and decency. If it would not yield, it had to be broken. The movement was successful. It was really a revolution."

A figure of an importance equivalent to Burgess's in the field of American history was James Ford Rhodes, a rich and politically well connected Ohio businessman who retired young and spent nineteen years producing a seven-volume history of the United States from 1850 to 1877. Rhodes's final volume, published in 1906, covered the end of Reconstruction, and because it represented the completion of an ambitious masterwork of American history, a great honoring of the author followed, which gave special authority to his view of Reconstruction.

Rather than romanticizing the South and trafficking in Thomas Dixon–style mythology, Rhodes wrote as a Progressive, a bearer of the political tradition that had begun with the failed Liberal Republican movement of 1872. He believed in a unified, modern, industrial, internationally powerful United States, with free trade, stable currency, and clean government. He therefore saw the Civil War as having been fundamentally about the establishment of national authority, not the abolition of slavery, and he treated the idea of legal equality of the races as unworthy of serious consideration. So although Rhodes worked in the manner of a professional historian, carefully reading and citing the archival record, he generally ignored the enormous body of sworn testimony about Reconstruction from Republicans, and never once quoted from a Negro witness. Rhodes wrote in a sweeping, authoritative narrative prose, and he took pains to be fair-minded. In writing about the events in Mississippi, for example, he presented Adelbert Ames as an honest man and John R. Lynch as "a credit to his race." He did not give credence to the ubiquitous rumors of Negro uprisings. He did not present the Republican state government as a kleptocracy. He treated the worst of the violence against Negroes as unfortunate and regrettable, insisting that the leading white men of the state would never have sanctioned it.

Still, Rhodes saw the redemption of Mississippi as a wholly salutary development. He alluded only very lightly to the campaign of murder and terror against Negroes and white Republicans, emphasizing instead the peace agreement between Governor Ames and General George; he treated the new era that redemption ushered in as one of prosperity, progress, and racial harmony; and, mainly, he presented the basic idea of Reconstruction as absurd on its face. About Ames, Rhodes wrote, "Like the men who had enacted Congressional reconstruction, he did not appreciate the great fact of race, that between none of the important races of mankind was there a difference so wide as between the Caucasian and the Negro." The redeemers, because they definitely did appreciate that great fact, had right on their side.

A few years before Rhodes's final volume appeared, Woodrow Wilson—then newly installed as president of Princeton University, and so already one of the nation's most admired and respectable figures—completed his own five-volume *History of the American People* with a treatment of Reconstruction and its aftermath. Wilson, a Southerner and the son of a Confederate veteran, was more dramatic, less careful about citing sources, and more passionate in his dislike of Reconstruction than Rhodes. Without being specific about what the South's redemption entailed, he admired its aims and understood its means, even if he did not celebrate them: "The white men of the South were aroused by the mere instinct of self-preservation to rid themselves, by fair means or foul, of the intolerable burden of governments sustained by the votes of ignorant negroes and conducted in the interests of adventurers; governments whose incredible debts were incurred that thieves might be enriched, whose increasing loans and taxes went to no public use but into the pockets of party managers and corrupt contractors . . . They could act only by private combination, by private means, as a force outside the government, hostile to it, proscribed by it, of whom opposition and bitter resistance was expected, and expected with defiance."

The leading historian specifically of Reconstruction was William Archibald Dunning, a colleague of Burgess's at Columbia University. Dunning was especially influential because he encouraged his graduate students to write dissertations that were medium-scale studies of specific subtopics of Reconstruction history; these were published as books and wound up forming a sizable shelf that was for at least half a century the authoritative record of the period. Dunning's own one-volume summary of all the work he and his students had done, *Reconstruction, Political and Economic*, appeared in 1907.

Like other leading academic writers on Reconstruction, Dunning treated the period of "Radical Reconstruction" after 1868 as a nightmarish mistake whose horrors exceeded those of the Civil War; for him the South's redemption was entirely salutary, even heroic. Like the others, he explicitly identified the granting of full Negro citizenship as Reconstruction's terrible central flaw. In his preface, he wrote that the entire period is best understood as "the struggle through which the southern whites, subjugated by adversaries of their own race, thwarted the scheme which threatened permanent subjection to another race." After the passage and enforcement of the Fourteenth and Fifteenth amendments, "all the

forces that made for civilization were dominated by a mass of bar-
barous freedmen," and this was a problem that went far beyond the
realm of state government: "The demoralization of the South was
less political than social in its essence . . . the antithesis and antipa-
thy of race and color were crucial and ineradicable. Intelligence and
capacity were almost exclusively in one race." Political equality was
merely a prelude to the much more serious threat, social equality:
"A more intimate association with the other race than that which
business and politics involved was the end toward which the ambition of the blacks tended consciously or unconsciously to direct itself." And the ultimate expression of this urge was "the hideous
crimes against white womanhood which now assumed new meaning in the annals of outrage."

This all sounds like Thomas Dixon, but Dunning's version of
Reconstruction was different in important ways that greatly enhanced its influence. He mainly wrote in the calm analytic voice of
a modern scholar, eschewing the trafficking in heroes and villains
that characterizes the work of Dixon and other popular writers.
While Dixon depicted the Ku Klux Klan and other terrorist organizations as leaders of white resistance to Reconstruction, Dunning
played down their role—they were "extremists," whose motives
were understandable (even if one could not entirely approve of
their activities), but the real work was done by men of the better
sort, who operated within the bounds of the political system. Dunning also played down what he called "the picturesque details" of
the period in favor of broad thematic material, which permitted him
to ignore the copious evidentiary record of violence contained in
congressional reports. His version of events is, indeed, so fuzzy and
generalized as to verge on intentional misrepresentation. About
Mississippi in the fall of 1875, for example, he wrote: "The aggressive and violent element among the whites entered early and with
ardor into the work of the contest . . . by boisterous parades, miscellaneous firing, and other demonstrations, half sportive and half
serious, they impressed the blacks with a sense of impending danger. Actual violence was rare."

When Reconstruction was actually ending and its supporters were rapidly losing political power, they did at least have enough influence left to be able to conduct a public argument about it. But within a generation, the combination of legal and political developments like the Jim Crow system (which seemed at the time to demonstrate the practicality of a white-supremacy regime), the new academic work on Reconstruction (which soon became the basis for the treatment of the period in all the standard American history and civics textbooks), and the sturdy popular mythology of the period had created a much more airtight consensus than had existed at the time. In the early years of the twentieth century, Reconstruction was more vividly inscribed in American memory than the Civil War. It was believed to have been a horrible failure. The Radical Republicans had been a destructive force in American life. Reconstruction's end had been a relief, which blessedly closed a chapter in American history and made a great new national life possible. The contemporaneous understanding of how Reconstruction had ended—the disturbing story contained in volume after volume of testimony and documents collected by congressional investigators—was in effect erased, even though it still sat on the shelves of libraries.

As time passed, opponents of Reconstruction usually said that what was wrong with it was its political corruption, not its goal of establishing the ex-slaves' rights, which had been their real objection; and they more and more often claimed that what had ended Reconstruction was statesmanship, as opposed to the real cause, a successful campaign of political terrorism in defiance of the U.S. government. The more pervasive this understanding of the past became, the less Americans were inclined to think of the South's refusal to obey the Fourteenth and Fifteenth amendments as a problem. So, in America's mainstream political and intellectual life, for three-quarters of a century, it wasn't.

For decades, defense of Reconstruction, and telling the true story of how it ended, went on only in obscure corners of the national discourse. Most of the defenders were participants who had been expelled from the South after redemption, and those defenders who were not participants were almost always black.

Pinckney Benton Stewart Pinchback, the most prominent Negro politician in Louisiana during Reconstruction—an outsized figure: newspaper publisher, gambler, orator, speculator, dandy, mountebank—served for a few months as the state's governor and claimed seats in both houses of Congress following disputed elections but could not persuade the members of either to seat him. During the 1876 presidential campaign, when his hopes of being a senator had just evaporated, so he was free to speak incautiously, he gave an eloquently angry speech to a Northern audience about what was going on in the South: "Here, under the protecting care of a stable government, with an enlightened public opinion and a powerful public press to rebuke outrage and wrong, to hold up to public scorn the murderers and assassins, to urge and insist upon the prosecution of criminals and the maintenance of law, of course the people are happy and prosperous, and I do not marvel that you regard the stories of outrages, arson, and murder that come almost daily from the South as gross exaggerations. But gentlemen, as disagreeable as it may be to you to hear and as unpleasant as it is, there is no denying the fact that the bloody shirt is no mythical garment . . . to-day, in that vast area of country lying south of Mason and Dixon's line . . . neither free speech, free press, peaceable assembly, not the right to keep and bear arms, or security for persons and property, are enjoyed by Republicans."

He went on: "I am frequently asked how it is that in localities where the colored largely outnumber the whites, in conflicts between the races, the colored people are always the sufferers . . . The colored, as a class, are poor, without experience, unarmed, no channel of communication or transportation open to them, naturally docile and peaceable, utterly without organization, they scatter at the first appearance of danger. With a war of races certain to end in their extermination, if once begun, continually held up before them by both democrats and Republicans, with the terrible examples of New Orleans, Colfax, Coushatta, Vicksburg, Clinton, Yazoo, East Feliciana, and Hamburg, with the certainty that their murderers will be regarded as heroes instead of criminals, do you wonder, can the country marvel, that they do not fight? Under like circumstances, what people would fight?"

Pinchback remained in Louisiana for some years after the end of

Reconstruction, continuing to play the part of Negro power broker. In 1893, as the Jim Crow period was beginning, he moved to Washington, D.C., where he spent the rest of his life. In 1903, the Union League Club of New York City, established during the Civil War to support the Northern cause, celebrated its fortieth anniversary by inviting one of America's most prominent Republicans, Elihu Root, to come to its grand clubhouse and give an address. Root—at the time, secretary of war; soon, secretary of state—said, regarding the three postwar amendments to the Constitution, "I fear that we will have to face the conclusion that the experiment has failed. The suffrage has been taken away from the negro, and, in many of the Southern States, the black man no longer has the right to suffrage." Root was saying this not in a celebratory way, but in order to prod his audience to take on the issue of Negro rights again. And the baldness of his statement moved Pinchback, by now in his sixties, to make another of his passionate speeches.

Bitterly, he reviewed the events of the previous quarter century in the South: the capitulation to whites by Rutherford Hayes and the Republican Party; the consequent advent of legal segregation, with all its degradations and dangers for colored people; and the abolition of democracy and adherence to the Constitution where Southern Negroes were concerned. He noted, too, the whole nation's sense not of outrage but of willed unawareness at best, and at worst of relief or even rejoicing about these developments. Pinchback summed up his feelings, as a witness to and a mainly helpless participant in the sickening progression: "Of late it has become quite fashionable to charge every negro who attempts to make a manly defense of his race with 'incendiarism' . . . Southern white men in the halls of Congress, in the press and on the rostrum, either South or North, speak with impunity of how they cheated and killed 'niggers' to obtain possession of the Southern state governments, and how they will continue to do it if necessary to retain control. But no cry of incendiarism is raised against them. On the contrary, their friends and sympathizers applaud their utterances and they are hailed as champions of white supremacy and valiant defenders of American civilization. 'O Shame! Where is thy blush?'"

John Roy Lynch, the former Mississippi congressman (who, along with James Lynch, another celebrated black Mississippi politican of the day, was possibly the inspiration for the Negro villain in Thomas Dixon's novel *The Clansman*, an oratorically gifted preacher-politician named Silas Lynch), like Pinchback remained in the South until the advent of Jim Crow. Also like Pinchback, during the 1876 presidential campaign he accurately predicted what was going to happen in the South, in both the long run (the disenfranchisement of Negroes) and the short (a Republican defeat). On August 12 of that year, Lynch stood on the floor of the House of Representatives and offered a response to Lucius Lamar's rosy vision, just presented, of the gathering of reformist energy that would produce a Democratic victory. Southern Democrats, *pace* Lamar, did not care about civil service reform or free trade, Lynch said. They cared only about one thing, firmly redrawing the color line. "Now, sir, let me say that the South is proposed to be carried by the democratic party," he went on. "Every Southern state they propose to carry as they carried Mississippi last year; a State with 30,000 republican majority reversed by giving 30,000 democratic majority nominally. They propose to carry all the others the same way, not by the power of the ballot, but by an organized system of terrorism and violence. That is the way they propose to do it."

In 1913, when Lynch's memoir, *The Facts of Reconstruction*, appeared, it was as obscure as the works of Rhodes and Dunning were celebrated—although Adelbert Ames ordered six copies, for a total of $9.61. In 1917 Lynch contributed a long article on "Some Historical Errors of James Ford Rhodes" to *The Journal of Negro History*, which had been founded the previous year by the black historian Carter G. Woodson. He also wrote an autobiography, which remained unpublished until long after his death. All these works repeat each other substantially; Lynch did not do original research, and his style is more a speaker's than a writer's, with the main energy going into the answering of charges, in great flourishes of rhetoric, rather than into storytelling or analysis.

What disturbed Lynch most of all was the by now standard description of his fellow Negro Mississippi officeholders as, at best, illiterates and incompetents. He defended them at some length. He also argued persuasively against the idea that the Republicans had nearly sunk Mississippi under a crushing load of taxation and debt. His own theory, repeated in all his works, was that it was the Democrats who had robbed the state treasury, not in any metaphoric way but in the exact amount of $315,612.19, which money they used to furnish the party's militias with their rifles and cannons during the 1875 campaign. The only statewide officeholder elected in 1875 was the treasurer, a Democrat named William L. Hemingway. He had won by the same means as the local Democrats had won in 1875, and soon afterward he was removed from office because he could not account for a large sum of money; Lynch believed the party had elected him so that he could take the fall for its campaign-season thefts to arm the White Liners.

Lynch did not dwell on the Democrats' tactics in the 1875 campaign, but he certainly had no use for the idea that conditions in Mississippi had become so intolerable as to excuse those tactics, or for the idea that the state had been redeemed. His version of what had happened was simply this: "The democrats, together with the radical element in charge of the party machinery, determined to seize the State Government vi et armis; not because it was at all necessary for any special reason, but simply because conditions at that time seemed to indicate that it could be safely done."

W.E.B. Du Bois, one of the first black Americans to earn a Ph.D., had written about Reconstruction here and there for years, always favorably. *The Atlantic Monthly* published an article of his about it in 1901, and he gave a pro-Reconstruction paper at the 1909 convention of the American Historical Association, with William Archibald Dunning in the audience. In 1935 his massive work *Black Reconstruction in America* appeared; it was the first full-length serious refutation of the prevailing view of Reconstruction. *Black Reconstruction in America* is only incidentally concerned with telling the story of the end of Reconstruction from a different perspective; its primary mission is to give Reconstruction a Marxian interpretation, as a regime that was brought to a close by moneyed interests because it had empowered the "black proletariat."

Today Du Bois's book stands as a classic, tide-turning work of revisionism, but in 1935 it did not change most Americans' minds about Reconstruction. Even professional historians did not begin to reexamine the period intensively until decades later; even liberal politicians did not dare to question the Jim Crow system in the South. At the time that *Black Reconstruction in America* was published, the book on the subject that was probably most familiar to white readers was *The Tragic Era: The Revolution After Lincoln*, a 1929 bestseller by Claude Bowers, former U.S. ambassador to Spain and Chile and a prolific popular author, in comparison to which Dunning's and Rhodes's versions of Reconstruction are positively judicious. Bowers presents Adelbert Ames as "deadly dull," lacking in "the courage or capacity to cope with the criminals around him," "arrogant, insolent, tyrannical," and as the possessor of a "dull brain." He gives us the climactic period of the 1875 campaign in this way:

"Great masses moving from place to place with dash, daring, determination. Old men rising with trembling voices to pledge life, fortune, and sacred honor to the winning of the fight. Youths turning politicians, grandsires urging them to battle for constitutional liberty. 'What a marvelous uprising!' said one man to another. 'Uprising? It is no uprising; it is an insurrection.' Immense crowds moving in orderly procession with bands and banners, pausing on every hilltop to fire cannon. Prancing cavalry on the highways, all homes thrown open for the entertainment of visiting clubs, a people impoverishing themselves for hospitality. Women joyously cooking for multitudes everywhere. The brilliant Lamar, literally inspired, rushing from meeting to meeting to meeting, arousing the wildest enthusiasm, without striking a demagogic note." And so on.

Benjamin Butler died in 1893, and Adelbert and Blanche Ames, who had moved to New Jersey for a few years and by now had six children, took over the Butler family homestead in Lowell. They oversaw the various Ames and Butler business interests from there, and became ever more prosperous and well established, so that the idea of Ames and Butler as two of the most hated men in America began to seem like a distant memory from some colorful period of conflict now safely located far back in the national past.

In 1895, Ames encountered an article in *Scribner's* magazine by E. Benjamin Andrews, the president of Brown University—an excerpt from a book Andrews was writing called *The History of the Last Quarter-Century in the United States.* Like other authority figures in the early years of the Jim Crow system and of the emergence of the United States as an industrial world power, Andrews believed, more by virtue of absorption than of inquiry, that Reconstruction had been a horrible failure. One illustration for Andrews's article was a picture of Ames, with the caption "How baneful the doings of such law-makers were in the South is partly revealed by the accompanying table"—which showed Mississippi's public debt increasing from zero to $20 million during Reconstruction.

Ames wrote Andrews a long letter—eighteen handwritten pages—that sternly objected to this charge. First he pointed out that the debt Mississippi acquired during Reconstruction was not $20 million but $500,000, and for legitimate purposes; then he offered a detailed summary of the state budget during his governorship. But a good part of the letter was taken up with his succinct account of what the real issue had been: "There was no 'corruption' as the statistics prove. Even corruption could not justify the taking of human life. The most violent periods were those before there was any public debt and later when the state finances were in a most flourishing condition. When you picture, to our imagination, a mob of howling negroes in quest of white men's gore you give us something as unreal as the mythical sea-serpent. And yet, it is true that such mythical negro mobs have been utilized to justify many crimes. The real fact is—it would be an insult to any community of white men in Mississippi to suggest it had ever feared or ever could fear a negro mob.

"There was a time when policy made it advisable for the white men of Mississippi to advance 'corruption,' 'negro mobs,' anything and everything but the real reason for their conduct. That time has long since passed. There is no good reason why the truth should not be stated in plain terms. It is that they are white men, Anglo-Saxons—a dominant race—educated to believe in negro slavery. To perpetuate their existing order of things they ventured everything and lost. An unjust and tyrannical power (from their standpoint) had filled their state with mourning, beggared them, freed their slaves and as a last insult and injury made the ex-slave a political equal. They resisted by intimidation violence and murder. Excuses by the way of justification were given while the powerful hand of the national government was to be feared. Soon the national government and public opinion ceased to be dreaded. Then they announced boldly that this is a white man's government and that the negro and ex-slave should forever form no part of it."

Five months later Andrews finally responded, rather sheepishly admitting that he had picked up the statistic about Mississippi's debt from a wildly partisan Southern author, who had taken it from a speech given on the floor of the House of Representatives, many years after the fact, by a Democrat from Virginia. This was a typical means of transmission of misinformation about Reconstruction, especially by people who were too busy to examine the copious record: the Southern redeemers had built up a great library of unproven assertions—about "Negro uprisings" and the excesses of "Negro rule"—which, with repetition, acquired the patina of demonstrated fact. "I shall ascertain and fairly state the truth in this matter if I can," Andrews promised. Ames replied at great length; finally, this time, Andrews admitted that he had obtained the official records "and am pained to find that my statement, so far as Mississippi was concerned, was without foundation." (Andrews did indeed correct his account, and quote from Ames's letters, in his book.)

In 1899, Ames, who was just back from having served as a volunteer, at the age of sixty-three, in the Spanish-American War, began a long correspondence with James Wilford Garner, a young historian of the Dunning school who was writing his dissertation on Reconstruction in Mississippi. The two men struck up the cordial but wary relationship that historians and their subjects often have. Each had something to gain from the transaction—Garner, Ames's papers and his reminiscences; Ames, restoration of his reputation—but didn't want to surrender too much in order to get it. Garner's book, which Du Bois called the fairest of the works of the Dunning school, was published in 1901. It treated Reconstruction as (to use a word Garner chose in one of his letters to Ames) unwise, and most of Ames's Negro political associates as "millstones about the neck of your administration," but it absolved Ames personally of the charges of corruption and fiscally ruinous governance that had been in the air since the days of his impeachment proceedings. It meant the world to Ames to be given back his reputation for personal honor and integrity.

Ames tried to persuade Garner to accept his view of the 1875 campaign—not as the redemption of Mississippi but as a shameful event "which trampled the State government literally under foot by armed resistance and wholesale riot and murder, with the end, as followed, of open defiance of the constitutional amendments, the wholesale disfranchisement of the colored man, and his denial of all political rights practically, and quite as practically of his civil rights where the government cares to touch him, and all making a chapter of the most disgraceful character." This Garner did not do. Indeed, the retrospective tide was running strongly the other way: not only did the idea that Mississippi had been redeemed in 1875 (and the entire South the following year, reuniting the nation) acquire quasi-official status from its repeated prominent endorsements, but the idea that Ames had been personally corrupt kept reappearing.

Ames lived a very long life. Over the years, he had occasion to express his views privately about what had happened in Mississippi. In 1913, at the age of seventy-eight, he wrote to John R. Lynch, who had sent him a copy of *The Facts of Reconstruction*, "He who was a slave is now at best but a serf. His road to life, liberty, and the pursuit of happiness seems endless—thanks to the attitude of our Christian nation of this day and generation." In 1929, at age ninety-three, he wrote the director of Mississippi's Department of Archives and History, "The days are many before Christ's Sermon on the Mount will be our national religion. Mississippi like other states has a weary task before it."

By that time, Ames, having been forgotten by the public for years, had become a minor national celebrity because he was the last surviving Civil War general. Through a friendship with Henry Flagler, the Standard Oil partner who had retired to Florida and devoted himself to building a railroad and hotels there, he began to spend winters in the beach resort of Ormond, Florida. There he became a companion and golf partner of the elderly John D. Rockefeller. In the public mind, the two spry old men, who had both long survived the great controversies of their lives, stood not for Reconstruction and industrial monopoly but for the quaintness of the nineteenth century. Ames died in 1933, when he was ninety-seven.

In 1956, a book written by Senator John Fitzgerald Kennedy, the ambitious young Democrat from Massachusetts, appeared called *Profiles in Courage*. It comprised a series of small portraits of especially admirable U.S. senators throughout American history. Its merits as a book aside (it was a bestseller, and won the Pulitzer Prize), *Profiles in Courage* helped to position Kennedy as a national political figure. It lent him gravity, it demonstrated that he had steeped himself in the national tradition, and it presented the work of politicians in a positive light. Kennedy aspired to lead a party that could not succeed in a national election without carrying the South, which had had its loyalty since the days of secession, war, and Reconstruction, and the Senate where he served was dominated by Reconstruction-hating Southern Democrats. One subject of a lionizing chapter in *Profiles in Courage* was Lucius Quintus Cincinnatus Lamar of Mississippi.

At that same time, finally and it seemed miraculously, the great thick ice-cap freeze on civil rights in the South was beginning to soften. In 1954, the U.S. Supreme Court had unanimously declared segregated public schools to be unconstitutional. As Kennedy was writing *Profiles in Courage*, Martin Luther King, Jr., and the Southern Christian Leadership Conference were leading their boycott of the municipal bus system in Montgomery, Alabama, challenging one local instance of the Jim Crow system of racial separation in public facilities. The year following the publication of *Profiles in Courage*, President Dwight Eisenhower, the first military commander since Grant to serve in the White House, sent federal troops to Little Rock, Arkansas, to ensure that its Central High School would be integrated, and Congress passed the first civil rights legislation since 1875. Each of these represented the accomplishment, almost a century later, of one of the goals of Reconstruction.

It must not have been clear to Kennedy, however, that a systemic change was on the way. He voted for the 1957 federal civil rights act, but only after it had been substantially weakened through an amendment proposed by Southerners, which he also voted for. And in his book he treated Lucius Lamar as a hero, in a way that involved his fully absorbing what was still the conventional wisdom about Reconstruction. Reconstruction had been "a black nightmare the South could never forget." Its advocates were interested only in the base pursuit of political power. The 1875 election result was produced by "a wave of popularity" for the Democrats. The end of Reconstruction meant the "restitution of normal Federal-state relations and the withdrawal of military rule." Kennedy simply didn't mention the issue of Negro rights and white violence, as if the presence of federal troops in the South had been just for the purpose of oppression for its own sake. In his bibliography, he cited two worshipful biographies of Lamar, Claude Bowers's *The Tragic Era*, and one report by anti-Reconstruction House Democrats; he did not refer to the most complete record of the end of Reconstruction in Mississippi, the two-thousand-page Senate report compiled under the supervision of George Boutwell, former holder of Kennedy's own seat.

Kennedy devoted one paragraph to Adelbert Ames. "No state suffered more from carpetbag rule than Mississippi," he wrote. "Adelbert Ames, first Senator and then Governor, was a native of Maine, a son-in-law of the notorious 'butcher of New Orleans,' Ben Butler . . . He was chosen Governor by a majority composed of freed slaves and radical Republicans, sustained and nourished by Federal bayonets . . . Vast areas of northern Mississippi lay in ruins. Taxes increased to a level fourteen times as high as normal in order to support the extravagance of the reconstruction government and heavy state and national war debts."

Ames's fourth child, Blanche—born in 1878, the first of the three post-Reconstruction Ames children—was a botanical artist, married to a professor of botany at Harvard named Oakes Ames (who was the grandson of the unrelated congressman Oakes Ames, the central figure in the Crédit Mobilier scandal, another much-reviled figure of Reconstruction times from Massachusetts). She was also a passionately loyal family member. She sent Senator Kennedy a long letter objecting to his treatment of her father and asking for corrections in subsequent editions of *Profiles in Courage*. "Imagine—if *you* were called upon to implement and enforce the 'Pious Wish' of the Supreme Court decision on desegregation in the Southern schools"; she wrote, "you would be subject to the same kind of calumny and slander as that slung at General Ames. Perhaps you could bear it with the same fortitude he showed and gentle charity." Kennedy responded promptly, politely, and blandly. "It is not anticipated that *Profiles in Courage* will go through another printing and thus there will be no opportunity to make changes in the text," he wrote. "However, your letter has succeeded in stimulating me to further research with respect to the matters you mention."

There were many more printings of *Profiles in Courage*, but no changes. Not long after Kennedy became president of the United States, the rising force and moral reach of the civil rights movement in the South pushed him to do exactly what Adelbert Ames had unsuccessfully begged Grant to do in the fall of 1875—send federal troops to Mississippi to enforce civil rights and social order, specifically to Lucius Lamar's hometown, Oxford, in connection with the contested integration of the University of Mississippi. In June 1963, Kennedy proposed the most ambitious piece of federal civil rights legislation since the end of Reconstruction, which went much further than he had been willing to go just a few years earlier in the direction of overturning the Jim Crow laws and enforcing it with federal power.

That same month the National Broadcasting Company announced that it was planning to produce a documentary version of *Profiles in Courage*, whose chapter on Lamar still stood unchanged. Blanche Ames wrote to Kennedy, reminding him of his earlier promise to look into the history of Reconstruction more deeply and asking him to correct the treatment of her father. Though an octogenarian by now, she was tireless, and this had become the great cause of her late life. She had begun writing a book about Ames and Reconstruction, she was in touch with several prominent historians, and good luck had brought her another weapon in the battle to restore her father's reputation: her grandson George Ames Plimpton, a charming young man who published a literary magazine called *The Paris Review* and who seemed to know everybody, was a friend of the Kennedys. She enlisted him as an adviser and lobbyist.

"Dear Grandma," Plimpton wrote to Blanche Ames. "You are to be congratulated heartily for your letter to the Junior Senator from Massachusetts . . . I will, of course, let you know, should I see him or his wife, what his reaction to it was, though I should presume you've already heard from him yourself. I am setting off for Europe this Friday on the invitation of Mr. Vanderbilt . . . I've planned to go down to the Villa on the 5ᵗʰ for two days"—that was the eighteenth-century Villa del Balbianello, on Lake Como, owned by Blanche's older brother, Butler Ames, where Jacqueline Kennedy had been a visitor—"the first to entertain the Vanderbilts for dinner, the second to do the same for Sadro Khan and journey with him to the South of France for a short visit before heading back to Paris." He promised to be in touch after these peregrinations.

Blanche Ames never heard back from President Kennedy. In August 1963 she received a polite off-putting letter from Kennedy's assistant Theodore Sorensen, who reminded her of how busy the president was. She wrote Sorensen back, insisting again on a correction, and heard nothing further. George Plimpton, during this period, was invited to a state dinner at the White House. After the meal, President Kennedy pulled aside a small group of people, including Plimpton, and asked them if they'd like a private tour of the White House. When the group was in the Oval Office, Kennedy asked Plimpton if there was any way he could get his grandmother to "cease and desist"—her incessant letters were cutting into the work of the White House. Plimpton said he would see what he could do.

It was not clear at that point whether Kennedy could get his civil rights bill passed, or how much effort he was willing to expend on it. Those are still unanswerable questions. Within a few months he was dead, and within a year the bill was law, thanks to the continuing success of the civil rights movement, to the legislative skill of Kennedy's successor as president, Lyndon Johnson, and to the bill's having gotten the reputation of being Kennedy's legacy. On that evening in the White House, after he'd made his request of Plimpton, Kennedy asked him, "How much do you know about your great-grandfather Ames?" Plimpton said he remembered Ames as a very old man when he was a very little boy. Kennedy said he'd been studying up, and he'd found out what Ames liked to say to his troops during the Civil War, when he detected any laxness of purpose. Assuming an erect posture and loud voice meant to evoke his idea of Ames, Kennedy said (to himself? to Plimpton? to entertain the others?): "For God's sake, draw up your bowels!"

NOTES

A NOTE TO THE READER

ix *"The problem of the twentieth century"*: W.E.B. Du Bois, *The Souls of Black Folk* (1903, repr., New York: Library of America, 1986), 372.

ix *"They came at night"*: Ibid., 373.

x *"Guerrilla raiding"*: Ibid., 382.

x *"So the Freedmen's Bureau died"*: Ibid., 390.

PROLOGUE

3 For a basic sequence of the month's events, from the white point of view, see J. A. Williams, "Judge Williams Writes Interesting Review of Colfax Riot-White Supremacy, 1873," Vol. 1, and an unidentified newspaper clipping titled "Colfax Riot," in the Cammie G. Henry Research Center, Ruby & Woodrow Hughes Collection, Folder 3, Watson Library, Northwestern State University, Natchitoches, Louisiana; O. W. Watson, "An Incident of My Boyhood Days," Cammie G. Henry Research Center, Robert DeBlieux Collection, Folder 3; John I. McCain, "An interesting review of Reconstruction days in Colfax" and "Looking Backward," Cammie G. Henry Research Center, Judge Jones Collection, Folders 32–33; E. E. Davis Jr., "The Colfax Riot" (1873) and Milton Dunn, "Christopher Columbus Nash: A Tribute," Cammie G. Henry Research Center, Judge Jones Collection, Folder 32; Kate Grant, "From Blue to Gray," Layssard Papers, Louisiana State University Libraries, Special Collections; Committee of Seventy, "History of the Riot at Colfax" (Clark & Hofeline, 1874); Mannie White Johnson, "The Colfax Riot of April, 1873" (master's thesis, Southern Methodist University, 1929) (a copy can be found in the local history collection, Colfax public library).

3 For the black point of view, see "Horrible Massacre in Grant Parish, Louisiana. Two Hundred Men Killed. Details of the Occurrence. Meeting of Colored Men in New Orleans. Addresses and Speeches" (Louisiana Republican Party, 1873); *Condition of the South*, House Report 101, 43rd Cong., 2nd Sess.; Ulysses S. Grant, "Message of the President of the United States, Jan-

uary 13, 1875"; T. W. DeKlyne, "Report of T. W. DeKlyne, Colonel and Assistant Adjutant General," *New Orleans Republic*, April 18, 1873; Joel M.
Sipress, "The Triumph of Reaction: Political Struggle in a New South Community, 1865–1898" (PhD diss., University of North Carolina, 1993).

3 *Deeply lodged in the consciousness of the South:* Watson, "An Incident," 1: Mc-
Cain, "An interesting review," 1–2.

4 *Colfax, Louisiana, was not really a town:* Committee of Seventy, "History of
the Riot at Colfax," 1.

4 *Local legend had it that Simon Legree:* Johnson, "The Colfax Riot," 39.

5 *"If it were in my power":* McCain, "Looking Backward," 4.

5 *Louisiana had a close and corrupt election: Condition of the South*, 21–25;
Davis, "The Colfax Riot," 1; Eric Foner, *Reconstruction: America's Unfinished Revolution, 1863–1877* (New York: HarperCollins, 1988), 550.

5 *"In his face he bears":* Committee of Seventy, "History of the Riot at Colfax," 3.

6 *one surviving photograph of Nash:* Dunn, "Christopher Columbus Nash."

6 *Both men had had long, harsh experiences:* Sipress, "Triumph of Reaction," 75;
Dunn, "Christopher Columbus Nash," 3–4.

6 *One evening in 1871 Columbus Nash:* Sipress, "Triumph of Reaction," 79–80.

6 *William Ward was said to have killed a white man:* Committee of Seventy,
"History of the Riot at Colfax," 3.

6 *The Republican governor, William Pitt Kellogg:* McCain, "Looking Backward," 2.

7 *Nash himself:* Grant, "From Blue to Gray."

8 *"When the political fever has spent its force":* Ibid., 68.

8 *"[S]trange white men appeared":* Ibid., 72.

8 *"the negroes quit work":* Ibid., 130.

9 *nightmare quite literally:* Williams, "Judge Williams Writes," Vol. 1, part 8.

9 *in the other side's version, it was merely a break-in:* "Horrible Massacre," 6.

9 *"Dey picked dat pore little body outer hits coffin":* Grant, "From Blue to Gray,"
172.

9 *"They laid their destructive hands on the casket":* Williams, "Judge Williams
Writes," Vol. 1, part 8.

9 *"Subsequently, a plot was discovered":* Grant, "From Blue to Gray," 135.

10 *"look into affairs": Report and Testimony of the Select Committee of the United
States Senate to Investigate the Causes of the Removal of the Negroes from the
Southern States to the Northern States*, Senate Report 693, part 2, 46th Cong.,
2nd Sess., 101.

10 *Adams's list:* Ibid., 198.

11 *2,141 Negroes had been killed: Condition of the South*, 10.

11 *"Now, in a great many parts of that country": Causes of the Removal of the Negroes*, 111.

12 *fueled by reliable-sounding intelligence reports:* Committee of Seventy, "History of the Riot at Colfax," 9–10.

12 *And the whites believed that the Negroes in Colfax:* Davis, "The Colfax
Riot," 1.

12 *A white Republican planter named William Calhoun:* McCain, "Looking
Backward," 2.

12 *a Negro named Louis Meekin: Louisiana Democrat*, April 23, 1873.

12 *a black man named Jesse McKinney: Condition of the South*, 9.

12 *"cried like a pig"*: Trial transcript published in *New Orleans Republican*, May 23, 1874.

13 *"One of our boys rideing in advance"*: Watson, "An Incident," 3.

13 *the only injury reported was that a white man had his thumb shot off*: Ibid., 2.

13 *"You will most probably say why dident you fight"*: Ibid.

13 *"The sight of those panic stricken youth"*: Grant, "From Blue to Gray," 155.

14 *For one day, the courthouse actually opened*: *Condition of the South*, 9.

14 *"Hour Pepel are in troubel"*: William Ward, letter to Rev. Jacob Johnson, April 5, 1873. In the case records of *United States v. C.C. Nash et al.*, Record Group 21, National Archives, Southwest District, Fort Worth, Texas.

14 *"'Arm yourselves!'"*: Grant, "From Blue to Gray," 151.

15 *Some of the Negroes said later*: *New Orleans Republican*, May 29, 1874.

15 *"They were informed"*: Davis, "The Colfax Riot," 2.

15 *Across the Red River*: Williams, "Judge Williams Writes," Vol. 1, part 4.

16 *Steve Kimbrell*: McCain, "Looking Backward," 6–7.

16 *the man who had replaced Ward*: Committee of Seventy, "History of the Riot at Colfax," 10.

16 *"was reminded that it did not look much like [mercy]"*: "Horrible Massacre," 8.

16 *"His course received the approbation of the whole posse"*: Ibid.

16 *Nash announced he would wait half an hour*: Ibid.; *New Orleans Republican*, March 3–10, 1874; McCain, "Looking Backward," 6; *Condition of the South*, 9.

16 *The Negroes had built two or three makeshift cannons*: Davis, "The Colfax Riot," 3.

16 *Nash split his force into three parts*: Watson, "An Incident," 4.

17 *"Old soldiers who were with Lee"*: "Important Testimony Concerning the Colfax Massacre," Louisiana *Democrat*, May 21, 1873.

17 *"pending a wholesale execution"*: Anonymous letter to Cammie G. Henry from Ferriday, Louisiana, September 4, 1934, Cammie G. Henry Research Center, Melrose Collection, Folder 100.

17 *"You all know you're going to be shot"*: Ibid.

17 *They soaked the rags in the oil*: Watson, "An Incident," 5.

18 *One man in the courthouse tore off his shirtsleeve*: Davis, "The Colfax Riot," 3; Watson, "An Incident," 6; *Condition of the South*, 9.

18 *In the white version, a few white men led by James Hadnot*: Davis, "The Colfax Riot," 3; McCain, "Looking Backward," 4.

18 *"exasperated beyond endurance"*: Committee of Seventy, "History of the Riot at Colfax," 11.

18 *"to believe this claim"*: *Condition of the South*, 9.

18 *even the white accounts of the event*: Davis, "The Colfax Riot," 3; McCain, "Looking Backward," 4.

18 *he expired some time after that*: McCain, "Looking Backward," 8.

18 *Hadnot was shot from behind*: *Condition of the South*, 9.

18 *"only to meet a savage and hellish butchery"*: "Horrible Massacre," 9.

18 *"pried up floorboards and tried, unsuccessfully, to hide"*: Judge Woods, quoted in Grant, "Message of the President," 3.

19 *White posses on horseback rode away*: Davis, "The Colfax Riot," 4; Watson, "An Incident," 4.

19 *some of the white men asked the crew*: "Horrible Massacre," 10.

19 *"dead beeves"*: "The Grant Parish Prisoners," *New Orleans Republican*, March 4, 1874.

19 *The whites gave them a tour:* "Horrible Massacre," 10.

19 *"It was a sorry blunder the negroes made":* Watson, "An Incident," 6.

19 *"That excesses were committed":* Committee of Seventy, "History of the Riot at Colfax," 12.

20 *When night fell: Condition of the South,* 9.

20 *"he did not come 400 miles":* Levi Nelson, trial transcript, *New Orleans Republican,* February 28, 1874.

20 *foiled escape attempt:* Davis, "The Colfax Riot," 4; Williams, "Judge Williams Writes," Vol.1, part 5; McCain, "An interesting review," 4.

20 *any Negro families who wanted to come to Colfax:* Woods, quoted in Grant, "Message of the President," 3.

20 *a boatload of "Metropolitan Police":* Davis, "The Colfax Riot," 4.

20 *the town was littered with unburied bodies:* Woods, quoted in "Message of the President," 3; *Condition of the South,* 9.

21 *"About one-third of a mile below the courthouse":* DeKlyne, "Report of T. W. DeKlyne," 23.

21 *"The corpses laid around indiscriminately":* William Wright, *New Orleans Republican,* April 18, 1873.

22 *"The place I found to be almost entirely deserted":* Captain J. H. Smith, letter to Captain W. S. Guidry, April 22, 1873, Record Group 393, Post of Colfax, Louisiana, National Archives.

22 *In his final report:* J. H. Smith, letter to A. A. General, Department of the Gulf, April 29, 1873, ibid.

22 *no white Republicans were harmed: Condition of the South,* 9; Woods, quoted in Grant, "Message of the President," 3.

22 *In June a federal grand jury in New Orleans:* McCain, "Looking Backward," 5.

23 *known colloquially as "Ku Klux laws":* John Hope Franklin, *Reconstruction After the Civil War* (Chicago: University of Chicago Press, 1994), 159–60.

23 *In July, a state Republican judge:* Sipress, "Triumph of Reaction," 110–11.

23 *In October, Louisiana's "state steamboat":* Ibid., 114.

23 *"Negroes knew long before we did":* "Rousterbouts," unsigned manuscript in the Cammie G. Henry Research Center, Melrose Collection.

23 *"Soon after the expedition":* Gust. Towle, letter to Apr. Adjutant General, Holly Springs, November 3, 1873, Record Group 393, Post of Alexandria, Camp Canby, National Archives.

24 *"he swam Red River on his horse":* Dunn, "Christopher Columbus Nash," 7.

24 *"This is the first time, and God grant it may be the last":* "The Grant Parish Prisoners," *New Orleans Republican,* March 13, 1874."

24 *three former Confederate soldiers:* Joe Gray Taylor, *Louisiana Reconstructed, 1863–1877* (Baton Rouge: Louisiana State University Press, 1974), 281.

24 *"[W]e, having grown weary":* H. Oscar Lestage Jr., "The White League in Louisiana and Its Participation in Reconstruction Riots," *Louisiana Historical Quarterly* 18, no. 3 (July 1935): 638.

25 *Nearly overnight the White League:* See Foner, *Reconstruction,* 550–58.

25 *"the military arm of the Democratic Party":* George C. Rable, *But There Was No Peace: The Role of Violence in the Politics of Reconstruction:* (Athens: University of Georgia Press, 1984), 132.

26 *"was regarded as establishing the principle":* Testimony of William Pitt Kellogg in "Condition of the South," House Report 261, part 3, 43rd Cong., 2nd Sess., 246.

26 *On the forty-eighth anniversary:* See "Program, Unveiling of Monument to Heroes of the Colfax Riot," Cammie G. Henry Research Center, Melrose Collection, Bound Volume 3, "Louisiana Miscellany." Also author's visits to Colfax.

27 *"A butchery of citizens was committed at Colfax":* Grant, "Message of the President," 3–4.

29 *"On Easter Sunday":* "Horrible Massacre," 4.

1. ADELBERT AND BLANCHE

31 Biographical details about Ames: Blanche Ames Ames, *Adelbert Ames: Broken Oaths and Reconstruction in Mississippi, 1835–1933* (New York: Argosy-Antiquarian, 1964). Also see Richard N. Current, *Three Carpetbag Governors* (Baton Rouge: Louisiana State University Press, 1967), chap. 3.

32 *"He was the beau-ideal":* Ames, *Adelbert Ames,* 188. The man quoted is Colonel Henry C. Lockwood.

32 *"consist of little more":* Ibid., 224.

33 *"In affairs of state":* Ibid., 235.

33 *"has not mounted so high":* Ibid., 235–36.

35 *"By the numerous reports":* Blanche Ames, ed., *Chronicles from the Nineteenth Century: Family Letters of Blanche Butler and Adelbert Ames,* 2 vols. (n.p., 1957), 1:37 (Adelbert Ames to James H. Fry, October 28, 1869).

39 *"The little children of New Orleans":* Grace King, *New Orleans; the Place and the People* (New York: Macmillan, 1925), 304.

40 *"His great genius":* Ames, *Chronicles,* 1:148 (Adelbert Ames to Blanche Butler, May 28, 1870).

41 *"a beauty that is the event":* Ibid., 127–28 (Adelbert Ames to Blanche Butler, May 18, 1870).

41 *"The papers say":* Ibid., 42 (Jesse Ames to Adelbert Ames, April 5, 1870).

42 *"Do you blacken":* Ibid., 145 (Blanche Butler to Adelbert Ames, May 27, 1870).

42 *"Old Jew":* Ibid., 131 (Adelbert Ames to Blanche Butler, May 19, 1870), 149 (Adelbert Ames to Blanche Butler, May 28, 1870).

42 *"I thought I had better write":* Ibid., 178 (Blanche Butler to Adelbert Ames, June 26, 1870).

43 *"Am I not getting":* Adelbert Ames to Blanche Butler, June 19, 1870, Ames Family Papers. This is one of the few letters not included in *Chronicles from the Nineteenth Century.*

44 *"The engines":* Ibid., 208–209 (Diary of Blanche Butler Ames, October 29, 1870).

44 *"Our lives have been marked":* Ibid., 173 (Adelbert Ames to Blanche Butler, June 22, 1870).

44 *"I should be a little careful":* Ibid., 195 (Sarah Butler to Blanche Butler Ames, September 7, 1870).

45 *"Are you glad":* Ibid., 160 (Adelbert Ames to Blanche Butler, June 10, 1870).

45 *"I don't know that I look forward"*: Ibid., 160 (Blanche Butler to Adelbert Ames, "Saturday morning").

45 *"the fleas"*: Ibid., 214 (Diary of Blanche Butler Ames, November 1870).

45 *"There are perhaps some twenty houses"*: Ibid., 215. (Diary of Blanche Butler Ames, "Saturday afternoon").

45 *"the baleful climate"*: Ibid., 217–18 (Diary of Blanche Butler Ames, November 20, 1870).

46 *"The malarious atmosphere"*: Ibid., 216 (Diary of Blanche Butler Ames, "Saturday afternoon").

46 *"This Mrs. Gill"*: Ibid., 214 (Diary of Blanche Butler Ames, November 1870).

47 *"buckle on his armor"*: Ibid., 165 (Adelbert Ames to Blanche Butler, June 17, 1870).

47 *"The colored girl"*: Adelbert Ames, letter to Blanche Butler Ames, May 16, 1871, Ames Family Papers, Sophia Smith Collection, Smith College Library, Northampton, Massachusetts.

48 *"Hatred to the Union"*: Ames, *Adelbert Ames*, 336.

49 *"Gen'l Ames will not"*: Ames, *Chronicles*, 1:237 (Blanche Butler Ames to Sarah Butler, March 31, 1871).

49 *"Alcorn is intensely disliked"*: Ibid., 315 (Adelbert Ames to Blanche Butler Ames, September 22, 1871).

49 *"I find the political situation"*: Ibid., 318 (Adelbert Ames to Blanche Butler Ames, September 26, 1871).

50 *"show that the power of the bayonet"*: Ibid., 334 (Blanche Butler Ames to Adelbert Ames, October 14, 1871).

51 *"Sometimes I feel like abandoning"*: Ibid., 337 (Adelbert Ames to Blanche Butler Ames, October 19, 1871).

52 *"My colleague is not connected"*: Ames, *Adelbert Ames*, 359.

54 *"As I look about"*: Ames, *Chronicles*, 1:393 (Adelbert Ames to Blanche Butler Ames, October 15, 1872).

54 *"You speak of running for Gov."*: Ibid., 399 (Blanche Butler Ames to Adelbert Ames, October 21, 1872).

54 *"It causes two different and conflicting emotions"*: Ibid., 410 (Adelbert Ames to Blanche Butler Ames, November 4, 1872).

55 *"When I took command"*: Adelbert Ames, Testimony of Adelbert Ames, in "Vicksburgh Troubles," House Report 265, 43rd Cong., 2nd Sess., 541.

56 *"Everyone on the street asks"*: Ames, *Chronicles*, 1:456 (Blanche Butler Ames to Sarah Butler, May 18, 1873).

56 *"Southrons"*: Adelbert Ames, letter to Blanche Butler Ames, April 19, 1870, Ames Family Papers.

57 *"I imagine early Christians"*: Ames, *Chronicles*, 1:585 (Adelbert Ames to Blanche Butler Ames, October 1, 1873).

57 *"I hope you have not felt obliged"*: Ibid., 491 (Blanche Butler Ames to Adelbert Ames, July 21 1873).

57 *"It is better to take care of the present"*: Ibid., 584 (Blanche Butler Ames to Adelbert Ames, October 1, 1873).

58 *"Could the victory be more decided?"*: Ibid., 540 (Adelbert Ames to Blanche Butler Ames, August 27, 1873).

59 *"About half past nine"*: Ibid., 499 (Blanche Butler Ames to Adelbert Ames, July 25, 1873).

59 *"After viewing the dancing":* Ibid., 527–28 (Adelbert Ames to Blanche Butler Ames, August 17, 1873).

60 *"I find I am producing":* Ibid., 590 (Adelbert Ames to Blanche Butler Ames, October 5, 1873).

60 *"it seemed as if every colored man":* Ibid. (Adelbert Ames to Blanche Butler Ames, October 5, 1873).

60 *"a sea of upturned faces":* Ibid., 600 (Adelebert Ames to Blanche Butler Ames, October 14, 1873).

60 *"My leadership of the party":* Ibid., 611 (Adelbert Ames to Blanche Butler Ames, October 22, 1873).

61 *"Money and whiskey":* Ibid., 617 (Adelbert Ames to Blanche Butler Ames, October 28, 1873).

61 *"Money, threats":* Ibid., 618 (Adelbert Ames to Blanche Butler Ames, October 28, 1873).

61 *"He had previously refused":* Ibid., 621 (Adelbert Ames to Blanche Butler Ames, October 30, 1873).

62 *"Never mind, my boy":* Ibid., 630 (Blanche Butler Ames to Adelbert Ames, November 7, 1863).

2. VICKSBURG TROUBLES

64 *She sent her mother little sketches:* Ames, *Chronicles,* 1:641–42 (Blanche Butler Ames to Sarah Butler, January 25, 1874), 651 (Blanche Butler Ames to Sarah Butler, February 13, 1874).

64 *Convicts under armed guard:* Ibid., 644 (Blanche Butler Ames to Sarah Butler, January 30, 1874).

64 *The cook was difficult to persuade:* Ibid., 643 (Blanche Butler Ames to Sarah Butler, January 30, 1874).

64 *"The colored people are not nearly as well trained":* Ibid.

64 *"All are lynx-eyed":* Ibid., 667 (Blanche Butler Ames to Sarah Butler, March 26, 1874).

64 *"A sallow, Southern woman":* Ibid., 646 (Sarah Butler to Blanche Butler Ames, February 6, 1874).

64 *Butler had undertaken to build:* Ibid., 674 (Sarah Butler to Blanche Butler Ames, April 20, 1874).

65 Ames's agenda as governor: Ibid., 635–40 ("Inaugural Address of Gov. Adelbert Ames to the Mississippi Legislature, Thursday, January 22, 1874").

68 *"[H]ere was a great heart":* Edward Mayes, *Lucius Q. C. Lamar: His Life, Times, and Speeches 1825–1893* (Nashville: Publishing House of the Methodist Episcopal Church, South, 1896), 166–67.

68 *"deliverance of the state from Military thralldom":* L.Q.C. Lamar, letter to Edward Clark, October 14, 1873; Clark Family Papers, Mississippi Department of Archives & History, Library Division, Special Collections Section, Jackson, Mississippi (hereafter cited as MDAH).

69 *"[Y]ou will find that his mission in Miss.":* L.Q.C. Lamar, letter to Edward Clark, October 16, 1873; ibid.

70 *"I think you act to do something":* "John," letter to Adelbert Ames, February 8, 1874, Ames Governor's Office Papers.

71 *"If we don't have better treatment":* L. D. Penn, letter to Adelbert Ames, January 30, 1874, Ames Governor's Office Papers.

72 *"Armed bodies of men are parading the streets"*: John Y. Simon, ed., *The Papers of Ulysses S. Grant*, 28 vols. (Carbondale: Southern Illinois University Press, 1967–2005), 25:157n.

72 *"Regret to inform you that I find"*: Ames telegram to Grant, July 29, 1874, ibid., 158n.

72 *his response came, tersely:* Ibid., 158–59.

73 *"Talk of bloodshed and slaughter of the whites"*: J. S. McNeily, "Climax and Collapse of Reconstruction in Mississippi, 1874–76," *Proceedings of the Mississippi Historical Society* 12 (1912): 297.

73 *"For four weeks or more"*: "Vicksburgh Troubles," House Report 265, 43rd Cong., 2nd Sess., iii.

74 *Secretary of War Belknap:* McNeily, "Climax and Collapse," 299.

74 *"I have tried to get troops"*: Ames, *Chronicles*, 1:693 (Adelbert Ames to Blanche Butler Ames, July 31, 1874).

74 *"This house . . . does not seem a natural place"*: Ibid., 695 (Adelbert Ames to Blanche Butler Ames, August 2, 1874).

74 *"The election at Vicksburg passed off quietly"*: Ibid., 698 (Adelbert Ames to Blanche Butler Ames, August 5, 1874).

75 *"The result, moral and political"*: McNeily, "Climax and Collapse," 299.

75 *Blanche shipped him a pistol in a box:* Ames, *Chronicles*, 1:691 (Blanche Butler Ames to Adelbert Ames, July 29, 1874).

75 *A Colfax-like incident occurred in Austin:* Ibid., 707 (Adelbert Ames to Blanche Butler Ames, August 12, 1874).

75 *"I suppose they will now hunt the Negroes"*: Ibid.

75 *"eight or ten" of the Negroes:* McNeily, "Climax and Collapse," 300.

76 *"Mississippi, which has commanded my thoughts"*: Ames, *Chronicles*, 1:707 (Adelbert Ames to Blanche Butler Ames, August 12, 1874).

76 *sent out a confidential feeler:* Adelbert Ames, letter to F. C. Harris, August 4, 1874, Ames Governor's Office Papers, MDAH.

76 *That summer President Grant was receiving reports:* Grant Papers, 25:144, 156–59.

77 *"Thae tak up the Corlded Peapel and Haung thim"*: Ibid., 188n.

77 *A letter from a "Committee of 1000 men"*: Ibid., 218–220n.

77 *he publicly instructed Secretary of War Belknap:* Ibid., 187–88.

77 *the White League had made its boldest move yet:* Ibid., 221–23n.

77 *"turbulent and disorderly persons to disperse"*: Ibid., 213–14.

78 *"The leaders here are some half-dozen"*: Major Lewis Merrill, October 25, 1874, "Letters Received by the Office of the Adjutant General," Senate, 43rd Cong., 2nd Sess., 5.

78 *"The condition of these poor people is pitiable"*: Ibid., 52.

79 *"there was abundant evidence"*: William Archibald Dunning, *Reconstruction, Political and Economic, 1865–1877* (Harper & Brothers, 1907), 254.

79 *"traitor," he wrote Blanche:* Ames, *Chronicles*, 2:48 (Adelbert Ames to Blanche Butler Ames, November 1, 1874).

79 *"They have beaten Ben Butler"*: Ibid., 52 (Adelbert Ames to Blanche Butler Ames, November 4, 1874).

80 *"What sorry times have befallen us!"*: Ibid.

80 *Adelbert's future political success:* Ibid., 69 (Sarah Butler to Blanche Butler Ames, December 11, 1874).

80 *"If Gen'l Ames can only be returned"*: Ibid., 58 (Blanche Butler Ames to Sarah Butler, November 11, 1874).
81 *A Negro farmer named Moses Kellaby*: Testimony of Moses Kellaby, *Vicksburgh Troubles*, House Report 265, 43rd Cong., 2nd Sess., 197–98.
82 *"taxpayers' leagues"*: Ibid., ii. For the Democratic view, see the minority report, xix–xxxvi.
83 *"a storm of cyclonic intensity"*: McNeily, "Climax and Collapse," 305.
83 *"The best known of those charged was Thomas W. Cardozo"*: *Vicksburgh Troubles*, xiii–xiv, xx. For more on Cardozo's background, see Euline W. Brock, "Thomas W. Cardozo: Fallible Black Reconstruction Leader," *Journal of Southern History* 47, no. 2, (May 1981): 183–206.
83 *"The grand jury report was the spark that fired the train"*: McNeily, "Climax and Collapse," 306.
84 *"I set to work"*: Testimony of Peter Crosby, *Vicksburgh Troubles*, 400.
84 *"general riot"*: George F. Brown, letter to Adelbert Ames, December 2, 1874. In Ames Governor's Office Papers.
84 *That night Ames convened a group of his advisers*: Testimony of Peter Crosby, *Vicksburgh Troubles*, 401–402; testimony of Adelbert Ames, *Mississippi in 1875: Report of the Select Committee to Inquire into the Mississippi Election of 1875*, Senate Report 527, 44th Cong., 1st Sess., 538–39. For a description of the meeting, those present, etc., see depositions of J. Tarbell, G. E. Harris, W. W. Dedrick, and W. W. Allyn, *The Testimony in the Impeachment of Adelbert Ames, as Governor of Mississippi* (Jackson: Power & Barksdale, 1877), 111–22.
85 *The reason for this special scrutiny*: *Vicksburgh Troubles*, xvi.
85 *"The blood of the martyrs is the seed of the church"*: Depositions of I. D. Shadd and W. M. Deason, *Testimony in the Impeachment of Adelbert Ames*, 209, 216; McNeily, "Climax and Collapse," 314.
85 *in an only slightly tamer version of the story*: W. W. Dedrick, *Testimony in the Impeachment of Adelbert Ames*, 114; W. W. Allyn, 124.
85 *Governor Ames of course hotly denied*: See Ames's testimony in *Mississippi in 1875*, 1:1–46.
86 *"Gen'l Ames is quite troubled"*: Ames, *Chronicles*, 2:68 (Blanche Butler Ames to Sarah Butler, December 5, 1874).
86 *In Jackson, Governor Ames issued a proclamation*: Adelbert Ames, "Proclamation," December 4, 1874, Ames Governor's Office Papers.
86 *"Citizens, shall we submit"*: *Vicksburgh Troubles*, xxiv.
86 *On Sunday, December 6*: Ibid.; see also testimony of Emily Boyd, 166; testimony of Moses Kellaby, 196; testimony of Peter Crosby, 402; testimony of Andrew Owen, 118.
87 *"The dread of Negro insurrection"*: "The Vicksburg Troubles," unsigned, undated manuscript, Vicksburg and Warren County Historical Society, Old Court House Museum, Vicksburg, Mississippi.
87 *December 7, a sentinel posted in the high cupola*: *Vicksburgh Troubles*, vii.
87 *In the white version of the story*: Ibid., xxvii.
88 *"With that curious inconsistency"*: Ibid., vii.
88 *Colonel Miller called out to Owen*: Testimony of Andrew Owen, ibid., 109.
88 *Crosby told him he had better disband his posse*: Testimony of Peter Crosby, ibid., 406.
88 *"Men, go right back home"*: Testimony of Andrew Owen, ibid., 109.

88 *"It was no battle; it was a simple massacre"*: Ibid., viii.
88 *"They were shot down like dogs"*: Ames, *Chronicles*, 2:69–70 (Blanche Butler Ames to Sarah Butler, December 14, 1874).
88 *"To lead eighty or one hundred men"*: *Vicksburgh Troubles*, vii.
89 *A Negro named William Wood:* Testimony of William Wood, ibid., 178.
90 *a Negro family named Banks:* Testimony of Louisa Banks, ibid.,169–71.
90 *"They have killed our husbands"*: Testimony of Louisa Banks, ibid., 171.
90 *Another Negro woman, Lucinda Mitchell, testified:* Testimony of Lucinda Mitchell, ibid., 317.
90 *A woman named Matilda Furman testified:* Testimony of Matilda Furman, ibid., 486.
91 *"Others were killed and eaten by buzzards"*: Testimony of William Wood, ibid., 176.
91 *Many Negro men left their families and hid:* Ibid., see also testimony of Emily Boyd, 163.
91 *The best estimate of the final death toll:* Ibid., xi.
91 *Ames greeted them:* Ames, *Chronicles*, 2:71–76 ("Message of Gov. Adelbert Ames to the Extraordinary Session of the Mississippi Legislature").
91 *Ames telegraphed to President Grant:* Grant Papers, 25:306–307.
92 *On December 24, Grant ordered Philip Sheridan:* Ibid., 26:16n.
92 *"The President says he believes in Gen'l Ames"*: Ames, *Chronicles*, 2:78–79 (Sarah Butler to Blanche Butler Ames, December 26, 1874).
92 *"I have to-night assumed control"*: Philip Sheridan to Grant, January 4, 1875, quoted in McNeily, "Climax and Collapse," 329.
92 *They removed A. J. Flanagan:* Testimony of A. J. Flanagan, *Vicksburgh Troubles*, 217–18.
93 *"The political condition of the State"*: Henry A. Morrow, "Letters Received," 73.
93 *"I think that the terrorism now existing"*: Philip Sheridan, letter to William Belknap, January 5, 1875, Grant Papers, 26:18–19n.
94 *"military interference in Louisiana"*: Carl Schurz, "Military Interference in Louisiana: Speech of Hon. Carl Schurz, of Missouri, in the Senate of the United States, January 11, 1875" (Washington, D.C.: GPO, 1875).
94 *In Boston, Charles Francis Adams"*: See William Gillette, *Retreat from Reconstruction, 1869–1879* (Baton Rouge: Louisiana State University Press, 1979), 236–58.
94 *"consign to the hands of their oppressors"*: Oscar Sherwin, *Prophet of Liberty: The Life and Times of Wendell Phillips* (New York: Bookman Associates, 1958), 625.
94 *"Sheridan was a little rash"*: Ames, *Chronicles*, 2:95 (Sarah Butler to Blanche Butler Ames, January 12, 1875).
95 *"Mother carries her endorsement almost to an absurdity"*: Frederick Grant, letter to Philip Sheridan, January 14, 1875, Grant Papers, 26:25n.
95 *"he would certainly not denounce it'"*: Hamilton Fish, diary entry of January 9, 1875, Grant Papers, 26:21n.
95 *"Military interfearence with a Legislative body"*: Ibid., 23n.
95 *"To say that the murder of a negro"*: Ibid., 8.
95 *"I have no desire to have United States troops interfere"*: Ibid., 13.
96 *"The President read his message"*: Ibid., 13n24.
96 *"It cannot be possible"*: Ames, *Chronicles*, 2:92 ("Message of Gov. Adelbert Ames to the Legislature of Mississippi, Session of 1875").

96 *"As if a community of murderers":* Ibid., 94–95 (Blanche Butler Ames to Sarah Butler, January 11, 1875).
97 *"will be an overwhelming vindication of your people":* L.Q.C. Lamar, letter to Edward Clark, February 1, 1875, Clark Family Papers.
98 *"A little learning is a dangerous thing in its application to them":* Vicksburgh Troubles, xxiv.
98 *"One of two things this nation must do":* Ibid., xvi.
99 *"I fear that Congress will not give the President power":* Jesse Ames, letter to Adelbert Ames, January 17, 1875, Ames Family Papers.
99 *"it was quite probable that you might have trouble":* Ames, *Chronicles,* 2:98 (Benjamin F. Butler to Adelbert Ames, March 3, 1875).

3. THE PEACE CONFERENCE

100 *Albert T. Morgan, sheriff of Yazoo County:* For details of Morgan's life, see his memoir *Yazoo; Or, On the Picket Line of Freedom in the South: A Personal Narrative.* (Columbia: University of South Carolina Press, 2000); for the whites' estimation of Morgan, see Robert Bowman, "Reconstruction in Yazoo County" (Jackson: Publications of the Mississippi Historical Society, 1903, 123–24.
101 *Whites nicknamed Morgan "Highgate Morgan":* McNeily, "Climax and Collapse," 383.
101 *When it came time for Morgan to take office:* For Morgan's perspective on the ensuing events, see Morgan, *Yazoo,* 382–91; for the white view, see the testimony of W. A. Drennan, J. C. Prewitt, and, especially, Walter Scott, *Testimony in the Impeachment of Adelbert Ames,* 99–101.
102 *From a "damp and cold" cell in the county jail:* Albert T. Morgan, letter to Adelbert Ames, January 11, 1874, Ames Governor's Office Papers.
102 *"Morgan was the idol of the Yazoo negroes":* Bowman, "Reconstruction in Yazoo County," 124.
102 *"Reason, facts, and figures":* Ibid., 127.
102 *secret white militia companies were forming:* Morgan, *Yazoo,* 436–40.
103 *In the summer of 1875, he went to Jackson:* Ibid., 456.
103 *had a private, friendly audience with President Grant:* Ames, *Chronicles,* 2:11 (Adelbert Ames to Blanche Butler Ames, July 24, 1875).
103 *In August a letter arrived from Vicksburg:* John Adams, letter to Adelbert Ames, August 10, 1875, Ames Governor's Office Papers.
103 *"The colored people are buyin ammonition":* Morgan, *Yazoo,* 452.
103 *"four-fifths of the colored population":* Ibid., 462.
104 *The killing of the Enforcement Act of 1875:* Wirt Armistead Cate, *Lucius Q.C. Lamar: Secession and Reunion* (Chapel Hill: University of North Carolina Press, 1935), 184–86.
104 *"Press where you see his white plume shine":* Mayes, *Lamar,* 248.
105 *On July 15, he went to a small railroad depot:* Ibid., 250.
105 *operated by Colonel William C. Falkner:* M. Thomas Inge, ed., *Conversations with William Faulkner* (Jackson: University Press of Mississippi, 1999), 10.
106 *"The true sentiment of the assembly was 'color line'":* Ames, *Chronicles,* 2:124 (Adelbert Ames to Blanche Butler Ames, August 4, 1875).
106 *He read Anthony Trollope's:* The Way We Live Now: Ibid., 139 (Adelbert Ames to Blanche Butler Ames, August 17, 1875).

106 *"I am fully determined not to accept the Senatorship"*: Ibid., 150 (Adelbert Ames to Blanche Butler Ames, August 29, 1875).

106 *A day later he reaffirmed this decision:* Ibid., 151–52 (Adelbert Ames to Blanche Butler Ames, August 30, 1875).

107 *Her practical-minded father:* Ibid., 151.

107 *Ames confided to a historian:* Adelbert Ames, letter to James W. Garner, January 17, 1900, James W. Garner Papers, MDAH.

107 *"Of course you hate it"*: Ames, *Chronicles*, 2:158 (Blanche Butler Ames to Adelbert Ames, September 3, 1875).

107 *"I have never seen such depravity"*: Ibid., 153 (Adelbert Ames to Blanche Butler Ames, August 31, 1875).

108 *On September 1, 1875, the Republicans of Yazoo City:* For an account of the meeting and ensuing events, see the testimony in *Mississippi in 1875*, 2:1662–1759; for the white perspective, see *The Testimony in the Impeachment of Adelbert Ames*, 78–152.

108 *"the human hornet"*: Morgan, *Yazoo*, 464.

108 *"a bitter denunciation of me"*: Ibid., 465.

108 *"As a careful surgeon"*: Ibid., 466.

109 *In Morgan's version of the story:* Ibid., 467.

109 *Adelbert Ames got a report of these events:* Ames, *Chronicles*, 2:155 (Adelbert Ames to Blanche Butler Ames, September 2, 1875).

109 *She gave Ames a fuller account:* Ibid., 2:159–60 (Adelbert Ames to Blanche Butler Ames, September 3, 1875).

110 *"We must have U.S. troops"*: Albert T. Morgan, letter to Adelbert Ames, September 4, 1875, *Mississippi in 1875*, 2:104.

110 *"Can nothing be done?"*: Albert T. Morgan, letter to Adelbert Ames, September 9, 1875, ibid., 97.

110 *One evening someone told Morgan:* Morgan, *Yazoo*, 476–77.

111 *On the following Saturday afternoon:* For a complete account of the events, see the testimony in *Mississippi in 1875*, 1:288–568.

111 *"I happily congratulate the speaker on his conservative tone"*: testimony of D. C. Crawford, *Mississippi in 1875*, 1:429. See Henry T. Fisher's own account of his speech in his testimony, 522.

112 *Most witnesses later testified:* Ibid., 430.

112 *"The thing opened just like lightning"*: Testimony of E. B. Welborne, ibid., 501.

112 *"I don't think I ever saw the same number of men"*: Testimony of John H. Estell, ibid., 319.

113 *One white person claimed to have seen eight hundred armed Negro men:* Testimony of W. A. Montgomery, ibid., 541, 543, 544.

113 *a column of seventy-five mounted Negroes:* Testimony of W. A. Montgomery, *Mississippi in 1875*, 1:557.

114 *"Seeing that there were so many men together"*: Testimony of W. A. Montgomery, ibid., 546.

114 *"For the next few days there was anarchy"*: W. Calvin Wells, "Reconstruction and Its Destruction in Hinds County," *Publications of the Mississippi Historical Society*, 9:100.

114 *"They moved around in the country"*: Testimony of Abel Alderson, *Mississippi in 1875*, 1:293.

114 *"They just hunted the whole country clean out"*: Testimony of E. B. Welborne, ibid., 494.

115 *"Then he said, 'If you don't tell'":* Testimony of Ann Hodge, ibid., 421.
115 *"Tell him when I saw him":* Testimony of Margaret Ann Caldwell, ibid., 439.
115 *"Before sunup, they went to a house":* Ibid.
116 *"What did it mean, their killing black people":* Ibid., 440.
116 *fifty or seventy-five men came to see William Haffa:* Testimony of Alzina F. Haffa, ibid., 483–89.
117 *Most estimates were that somewhere between thirty and fifty men had been killed:* Testimony of Abel Alderson, ibid., 300; testimony of Henry T. Fisher, 528.
117 *they made their way, usually by night:* Testimony of E. B. Welborne, ibid., 494; testimony of G. T. Swann, 310.
117 *The Republican justice of the peace:* His name was Peyton Robinson; the testimony he took is in the Ames Governor's Office Papers.
117 *"Captain William Montgomery fired on me":* Testimony of Alfred Moses, September 10, 1875, ibid.
117 *"On Sunday, September 5th, 1875,":* Testimony of George Holmes, September 10, 1875, ibid.
118 *"On Sunday morning about 10 or 11 o'clock":* Testimony of Eli Burnell, September 9, 1875, ibid.
118 *"When I got home Dave Henderson sent for me":* Testimony of Freeman Jones, September 10, 1875, ibid.
118 *"My mother in law . . . told me that Widow Currie":* Testimony of John Allison, September 10, 1875, ibid.
119 *"out of breath and out of heart":* Ames, *Chronicles,* 2:163 (Adelbert Ames to Blanche Butler Ames, September 5, 1875).
119 *"With the means now available":* William H. Harney, letter to Adelbert Ames, September 6, 1875, Grant Papers, 26:293.
120 *"You may read to your Father such portions of my letters":* Ames, *Chronicles,* 2:166–67 (Adelbert Ames to Blanche Butler Ames, September 7, 1875).
121 *"I cannot interfere with troops":* C. C. Augur, telegram to Adelbert Ames, September 5, 1875, Ames Governor's Office Papers.
121 *"Domestic violence, in its most aggravated form":* Adelbert Ames, telegram to Ulysses S. Grant, September 8, 1875, Grant Papers, 26:296.
121 *"the poor black people are lying now out in the woods":* E. C. Walker, undated letter to Adelbert Ames (September 1875), Ames Governor's Office Papers.
121 *"This county is now up in Raw":* E. C. Walker, letter to Ulysses S. Grant, September 7, 1875, Grant Papers, 26:294n.
121 *The then-brand-new attorney general:* See Gillette, *Retreat from Reconstruction,* 156.
122 *"I do not think that the Constitution & the laws":* Edwards Pierrepont, letter to Ulysses S. Grant, Grant Papers, 26:314n.
122 *"The necessity which called forth my dispatch of the 8th":* Adelbert Ames, telegram to Edwards Pierrepont, September 11, 1875, ibid., 297n.
122 *"I am somewhat perplexed":* Ulysses S. Grant, letter to Edwards Pierrepont, September 13, 1875, Edwards Pierrepont Papers, Manuscripts and Archives, Yale University Library; Grant Papers, 26:312–13.
122 *"I do not see how we are to evade the call":* Ibid.
122 *"I think on the whole a proclamation":* Ibid.
123 *"You see by this the mind of the President":* Edwards Pierrepont, letter to Adelbert Ames, September 14, 1875, Grant Papers, 26:314n; the original letter,

which is worth seeing because its elaborate Gothic calligraphy conveys so much, is in the Ames Governor's Office Papers.

124 *"I threw some kisses to the moon for my sweetheart"*: Ames, *Chronicles*, 2:170 (Blanche Butler Ames to Adelbert Ames, September 10, 1875).

124 *"I will look to the moon tonight"*: Ibid., 181 (Adelbert Ames to Blanche Butler Ames, September 16, 1875).

124 *She wrote to him that she was inclined to rush to Jackson:* Ibid. (Blanche Butler Ames to Adelbert Ames, September 17, 1875).

124 *Adelbert agreed:* Ibid., 191 (Adelbert Ames to Blanche Butler Ames, September 22, 1875).

124 *Ben Butler went to Washington:* Ibid., 190 (Blanche Butler Ames to Adelbert Ames, September 22, 1875).

124 *"quite exasperated me"*: Ibid., 183 (Adelbert Ames to Blanche Butler Ames, September 17, 1875).

124 *Ames had a cache of weapons:* Ibid., 200 (Adelbert Ames to Blanche Butler Ames, September 28, 1875).

125 *"The Democrats will gain the victory"*: "Three Hundred Voters," letter to Adelbert Ames, September 14, 1875, *Mississippi in 1875*, 2:87, "Documentary Evidence" section.

125 *"I have not been able to find even one man"*: Ames, *Chronicles*, 2:191 (Adelbert Ames to Blanche Butler Ames, September 22, 1875).

125 *The post's adjutant general:* Testimony of Frank Johnston, *Mississippi in 1875*, 1:334.

126 *On October 9, a militia company in Jackson:* Testimony of Frank Johnston, ibid.; Ames, *Chronicles*, 2:210–11 (Adelbert Ames to Blanche Butler Ames, October 8, 1875).

127 *Most Democrats believed that Governor Ames:* Testimony of Frank Johnston, *Mississippi in 1875*, 1:334–35.

127 *in September, just that had happened:* Testimony of George K. Chase, ibid., 2:1801.

127 *"to allow a squad of men to enter Jackson"*: W. Calvin Wells, "Reconstruction and Its Destruction in Hinds County" (Jackson: Publications of the Mississippi Historical Society, 1906), 105.

127 *"I had never seen Colonel Lamar so indignant"*: Ibid., 106.

127 *The chairman of the Mississippi Democratic Party was James Zachariah George:* See Gillette, *Retreat from Reconstruction*, 229.

128 *One member of George's telegraphic network:* See *Mississippi in 1875*, 1:381ff.

128 *"We learn here that Caldwell, with 100 armed men"*: William Montgomery, telegram to James Z. George, October 9, 1875, Ames Governor's Office Papers.

128 *"Caldwell's company left"*: U. M. Young, telegram to James Z. George, October 9, 1875, testimony of J. A. Galbreath, *Mississippi in 1875*, 1:387.

128 *"A difficulty should be avoided by all means"*: James Z. George, telegram to U. M. Young, October 9, 1875, ibid.

128 *"The wire was kept hot all day"*: McNeily, "Climax and Collapse," 404.

128 *A rumor quickly spread all through white Mississippi:* Frank Johnston, "The Conference of October 15th, 1875, Between General George and Governor Ames" (Jackson: Publications of the Mississippi Historical Society, 1902), 69.

129 *Chase was a friend of Pierrepont's:* See Grant Papers, 26:335n.

129 *"that I had some capacity for managing"*: Testimony of George K. Chase, *Mississippi in 1875*, 2:1810.

129 *Pierrepont had given him a modest budget:* Ibid., 1806.

129 *Chase adopted the role of neutral broker:* For Chase's impressions of the two sides, see ibid., 1801–1803, 1806, 1816.

129 *The reports about a coming confrontation:* Testimony of George K. Chase, ibid., 1803.

129 *Chase conceived of a plan:* Ibid., 1802.

130 *"It is possible that the purpose to send militia"*: A. J. McCormick, telegram to James Z. George, October 12, 1875, in testimony of J. A. Galbreath, ibid., 1:388.

130 *The peace conference took place on October 13, 1875:* For participants' accounts, see testimony of Frank Johnston, ibid., 333–36, and testimony of George K. Chase, 2:1803.

130 *One participant remembered that Chase said not a single word:* Johnston, "The Conference of October 15, 1871," 71.

131 *The only mild resistance he offered:* Ames, *Chronicles,* 2:217 (Adelbert Ames to Blanche Butler Ames, October 14, 1875).

131 *"The citizens expressed themselves well-satisfied"*: Testimony of George K. Chase, *Mississippi in 1875*, 1803.

131 *"The programme of the Democracy"*: Ames, *Chronicles,* 2:195 (Adelbert Ames to Blanche Butler Ames, September 24, 1875).

132 *"My demand must be made in writing"*: Ibid., 216 (Adelbert Ames to Blanche Butler Ames, October 12, 1875).

132 *"Yes, a revolution has taken place"*: Ibid.

132 *"My dread is that I fear somebody will think"*: Ibid., 220 (Adelbert Ames to Blanche Butler Ames, October 15, 1875).

132 *He told Blanche that the deal:* Ibid., 217 (Adelbert Ames to Blanche Butler Ames, October 14, 1875).

132 "No compromise": Albert Morgan, letter to Adelbert Ames, October 13, 1875, Ames Governor's Office Papers.

133 *Ames believed it possible:* Ames, *Chronicles,* 2:220 (Adelbert Ames to Blanche Butler Ames, October 15, 1875).

133 *One early hint had been about his knowledge:* Ibid., 215–16 (Adelbert Ames to Blanche Butler Ames, October 12, 1875).

133 *"Through the timely and skillful intervention"*: Adelbert Ames, letter to Edwards Pierrepont, October 16, 1875, Grant Papers, 26:335n.

133 *"The indications now are"*: Ames, *Chronicles,* 2:224 (Adelbert Ames to Blanche Butler Ames, October 18, 1875).

133 *"You can feel quite sure that this Department"*: Edwards Pierrepont, letter to Adelbert Ames, October 23, 1875, Grant Papers, 26:336n.

133 *moved into an unoccupied children's room:* Ames, *Chronicles,* 2:225 (Adelbert Ames to Blanche Butler Ames, October 18, 1875).

134 *Chase was a "talker"*: Ibid., 236 (Adelbert Ames to Blanche Butler Ames, October 24, 1875).

134 *"Do not get jealous"*: Ibid., 223 (Adelbert Ames to Blanche Butler Ames, October 17, 1875).

134 *"A more immoral picture thereof"*: Ibid., 236 (Adelbert Ames to Blanche Butler Ames, October 24, 1875).

134 *He managed to find a woman in Jackson:* Ibid., 239–40 (Adelbert Ames to Blanche Butler Ames, October 26, 1875).
134 *"On October 19, two weeks before Election Day":* Ibid., 220 (Adelbert Ames to Blanche Butler Ames, October 20, 1875).

4. REVOLUTION

135 *Mississippi in 1875 had two Negro members of Congress:* For more about the two men, see John R. Lynch, *Reminiscences of an Active Life: The Autobiography of John Roy Lynch,* ed. John Hope Franklin (Chicago: University of Chicago Press, 1970); John R. Lynch, *The Facts of Reconstruction* (New York: Neale Publishers, 1913); "Blanche K. Bruce of Mississippi: Conservative Assimilationist," *Southern Black Leaders of the Reconstruction Era,* ed. by Howard W. Rabinowitz (Urbana: University of Illinois Press, 1982); William B. Gatewood, *Aristocrats of Color: The Black Elite, 1880–1920* (Bloomington: Indiana University Press, 1990).
135 *Congressman Lynch went to the White House:* Lynch, *Facts of Reconstruction,* 147.
136 *"a good, capable, and efficient postmaster":* Ibid., 148.
136 *"According to Lynch, Grant told him":* Ibid., 150–51.
136 *"I should not have yielded":* Ibid., 152–53.
137 *"Whatever their motives may be":* Ibid., 155.
137 *Governor Ames had had a strong suspicion:* Ames, *Chronicles,* 2:215 (Adelbert Ames to Blanche Butler Ames, October 12, 1875).
137 *"I deem it my duty to give you facts":* George K. Chase, letter to Edwards Pierrepont, ca. October 27, 1875, Grant Papers, 26:336n.
138 *Now that he was living in the Governor's Mansion:* Testimony of George K. Chase, *Mississippi in 1875,* 2:1807.
138 *"I was met every time in that way":* Ibid., 1804.
138 *The worst of the incidents of early October 1875:* For an account of the incident, see the testimony of Adelbert Ames, ibid., 1:25–27, 42–44; for the white perspective, see the statement of Senator Alcorn, 67–71.
139 *also including Senator Alcorn's rebellious son:* Testimony of Adelbert Ames, ibid., 26.
139 *L.Q.C. Lamar was going to address the Democratic rally:* James B. Murphy, *L.Q.C. Lamar: Pragmatic Patriot* (Baton Rouge: Louisiana State University Press, 1973), 151–53; Cate, *Lucius Q.C. Lamar,* 217–20.
139 *"The colored people were to come in:* Testimony of John Brown, *Causes of the Removal of the Negroes,* 352.
139 *Senator Alcorn (who was armed):* Statement of Senator Alcorn, *Mississippi in 1875,* 70.
139 *"to sack and burn the town":* Ibid.
140 *"The colored men scattered all over the county":* Testimony of John Brown, *Causes of the Removal of the Negroes,* 354.
141 *"I have been driven from my county":* John Brown, telegram to Adelbert Ames, October 7, 1875, Ames Governor's Office Papers.
141 *"A perfect state of terror reigns supreme":* John Brown, letter to Adelbert Ames, October 8, 1875, ibid.
141 *Brown surreptitiously returned to Friars Point:* John Brown, October 24 and 26, 1875, documentary evidence in *Mississippi in 1875,* 2:20. John Brown,

letters to Adelbert Ames, October 24 and October 26, 1875. In *Mississippi in 1875*, Documentary Evidence, 2:20.

141 *General James Z. George was in telegraphic communication:* See telegram from H. P. Reid to James Z. George, October 5, 1875, in testimony of J. A. Galbreath, ibid., 1:386.

142 *"The sheriff of Coahoma County":* Ibid.

142 *"THE FRIARS POINT WAR":* See testimony of Adelbert Ames, ibid., 1:27.

143 *"Lawless bodies of armed men":* A. P. Merrill, letter to Adelbert Ames, October 9, 1875, *Mississippi in 1875*, 2:3, "Documentary Evidence" section.

143 *"we of the collorde voters of Amite":* William Deshields, letter to Adelbert Ames, October 23, 1875, ibid., 2:9.

143 *"Everything here is exceedingly warm":* A. Parker, Sheriff, letter to Adelbert Ames, October 24, 1875, ibid.

144 *"We, as Republicans of the State of Mississippi":* William Canly, letter to Adelbert Ames, October 9, 1875, ibid., 28–29.

144 *"It is utterly impossible":* W. F. Simonton, letter to Adelbert Ames, October 16, 1875, ibid., 46–47.

144 *"a rank old Demicrit":* N. R. Blackman, letter to Adelbert Ames, October 16, 1875, ibid., 44.

144 *"Ever since Saturday":* Anonymous letter from Vicksburg to Adelbert Ames, October 13, 1875, ibid., 85.

144 *"We are poor and cannot afford to buy guns":* Abraham Burriss, letter to Adelbert Ames, October 13, 1875, ibid., 86.

144 *Blanche Ames . . . was imploring her father:* Ames, *Chronicles*, 2:215 (Blanche Butler Ames to Adelbert Ames, October 12, 1875).

144 *"he saw Grant and he had half written the telegram":* Ibid., 228–29 (Blanche Butler Ames to Adelbert Ames, October 20, 1875).

145 *She urged him to resign the governorship immediately:* Ibid., 231–32 (Blanche Butler Ames to Adelbert Ames, October 22, 1875).

145 *Ames had sunk into a strange state:* See Adelbert Ames's letters to Blanche Butler Ames, October 22 and 23, 1875, ibid., 232–33.

145 *"Success is the only thing the world appreciates":* Ibid., 248 (Blanche Butler Ames to Adelbert Ames, October 26, 1875).

145 *wired Ames that the federal government:* Ibid., 244 (Adelbert Ames to Blanche Butler Ames, October 28, 1875).

146 *General Augur . . . saying he had ordered the troops in Mississippi:* C. C. Augur, telegram to Adelbert Ames, September 5, 1875, Ames Governor's Office Papers.

146 *Chase called upon the Democratic leaders:* Testimony of George K. Chase, *Mississippi in 1875*, 2:1809.

146 *Ben Butler reported to Blanche:* Ames, *Chronicles*, 2:237n (Benjamin Butler to Blanche Butler Ames, October 16, 1875).

146 *"The election ceases to have any interest":* Ibid., 245–46 (Adelbert Ames to Blanche Butler Ames, October 30, 1875).

146 *"This day has not been a happy one":* Ibid., 246 (Adelbert Ames to Blanche Butler Ames, October 31, 1875).

146 *One technique, the most benign:* Testimony of George K. Chase, *Mississippi in 1875*, 2:1808.

147 *"Their object was to destroy the leaders":* Ibid., 1806.

147 *"had a band of his own of about 100 armed men":* Ibid., 1805.
147 *"The intimidation and threatening of colored voters":* Charles Caldwell and
      N. D. Sneed, letter to Adelbert Ames, October 29, 1875, ibid., 2:32–33,
      "Documentary Evidence" section.
147 *lent the Democratic Party a cannon:* Testimony of George K. Chase, ibid.,
      2:1805, 1814.
148 *One of Ames's servants later testified:* Testimony of Polk Smith, ibid.,
      433–34.
148 *"The reports which come to me almost hourly":* Ames, *Chronicles,* 2:248 (Adel-
      bert Ames to Blanche Butler Ames, November 1, 1875).
148 *In Lowndes County:* Testimony of Joseph P. Billups, *Mississippi in 1875,* 1:817.
148 *In adjoining Colfax County:* Testimony of Lex Brame, ibid., 255.
148 *many of these young men had come across the border:* H. W. Lewis, Sheriff, let-
      ter to Adelbert Ames, October 22, 1875, ibid., 2:55–56, "Documentary Ev-
      idence" section; see also testimony of E. O. Sykes, 1103.
149 *in the Lowndes County seat:* See ibid., 1:790–831, for material on these events.
149 *"Town fired last night in fourteen places":* C. Gross, telegram to James Z.
      George, November 2, 1875. In testimony of J. A. Galbreath, *Mississippi in
      1875,* 1:400.
149 *"The voters did not get to vote":* Isaac Jones, letter to Adelbert Ames, Novem-
      ber 7, 1875, *Mississippi in 1875,* 2:57–58, "Documentary Evidence" section.
149 *ever since a Negro legislator:* Testimony of Edward H. Stiles, ibid., 1:159.
149 *On the Saturday before the election:* Ibid., 161–71. For the white perspective,
      see the testimony of J. D. Vertner, 191–220.
150 *who by some accounts had a cannon:* Ibid., 174, 188.
150 *"On the day of the election eighty men":* W. D. Sprott, letter to the Boutwell
      Committee staff (which produced *Mississippi in 1875*), July 19, 1876, Red-
      path Collection, Manuscripts and Archives Division, New York Public Li-
      brary.
150 *"the moment the first pistol was fired":* Testimony of Edward H. Stiles, *Missis-
      sippi in 1875,* 1:181.
150 *"Your dispatch satisfactory:"* James Z. George, telegram to J. D. Vertner, No-
      vember 2, 1875. In testimony of J. A. Galbreath, *Mississippi in 1875,* 1: 405.
150 *in Peytona, not a single Republican vote was cast:* Testimony of Edward H.
      Stiles, ibid., 1:178.
150 *"the democrats, just as they were commencing to count":* Ibid.
150 *The Republican vote total in the county as a whole* Election statistics, ibid.,
      2:144, "Documentary Evidence" section.
151 *"in manly and ringing tones he declared":* *Vicksburg Herald,* quoted in James
      M. Wells, *The Chisolm Massacre: A Picture of "Home Rule" in Mississippi*
      (Washington, D.C.: Chisolm Monument Association, 1878), 111–12.
151 *"The present contest is rather a revolution":* *Aberdeen Examiner,* October 7,
      1875, quoted in *Mississippi in 1875,* 2:1144.
151 *"Whoever eats the white man's meat":* *Aberdeen Examiner,* quoting R. O. Rey-
      nalds, ibid.
151 *"I won't give you meat and bread if you go against us":* Testimony of Miles
      Walker, *Mississippi in 1875,* 2:1132.
151 *"You are known to be a vile, corrupt, and thieving scoundrel":* Testimony of
      George T. Cook, ibid., 1047.
151 *rode up to the home of Howard Settle:* Testimony of James W. Lee, ibid., 1044.

151 *"Things are getting in an awful condition here"*: James W. Lee, letter to Adelbert Ames, October 23, 1875, ibid., 64–65, "Documentary Evidence" section.

152 *Sulphur Springs and Paine's Chapel:* See ibid., 1124, 1026, 1093.

152 *Black Republicans had a custom of bringing drums:* Testimony of James W. Lee, ibid., 1024–25; testimony of Washington Halliway, 1130.

152 *"Stop that; you cannot beat that drum"*: Testimony of James W. Lee, ibid., 1025.

152 *Democrats posted armed sentries at two fords:* Testimony of E. O. Sykes, ibid., 1107.

152 *the courthouse in Aberdeen:* Testimony of Reuben Davis, ibid., 1054, 1069; testimony of James W. Lee, 1027, 1030.

153 *the Negroes arrived at the courthouse early in the morning:* Ibid., 1056–57; see also the testimony of E. O. Sykes, 1098.

153 *"cover the yard with dead niggers"*: Testimony of Miles Walker, ibid., 1132; testimony of Scott Hughes, 1136.

153 *"Several hundred colored men were knocked down"*: Testimony of James W. Lee, ibid., 1030.

153 *Lee had been counting on fourteen hundred Republican votes:* Ibid.

153 *"I think the world is made up of various grades of life"*: Testimony of Reuben Davis, ibid., 1064.

154 *In Yazoo County, the most extreme case:* Election statistics, ibid., 145, "Documentary Evidence" section.

154 *"waited upon"*: Testimony of H. P. Scott, ibid., 1:589–90.

154 *"The Grave is not dug but can be easily done"*: "Committee of Thirteen," letter to Amos Sanders, October 28, 1875, Redpath Collection.

154 *In De Kalb, a Republican official wrote"*: W. W. Chisolm, letter to Adelbert Ames, November 3, 1875, *Mississippi in 1875*, 2:45, "Documentary Evidence" section.

155 *"Monroe County farmers' pledge of honor"*: The pledge was originally printed in the *Aberdeen Examiner*, November 4, 1875. Quoted in testimony of John E. Meek, *Mississippi in 1875*, 2:1141.

155 *At three in the morning on the Sunday after the election:* Ames, *Chronicles*, 2:252–53 (Adelbert Ames to Blanche Butler Ames, November 5, 1875).

155 *relatively little White Line activity:* Testimony of H. P. Scott, *Mississippi in 1875*, 1:589; testimony of W. D. Brown, 695.

155 *In mid-November, in a country store:* Testimony of Bowie Foreman, ibid., 600–601. For the white perspective, see testimony of William S. Farrish, 646–47, and W. W. Moore, 681.

155 *The Negroes were rumored to be in possession:* Testimony of William S. Farrish, ibid., 649.

155 *"We barricaded our doors"*: Testimony of D. B. Ball, ibid., 749.

156 *The cotton harvest was in by now:* Ibid., 753.

156 *"To arms, to arms!"*: Testimony of W. W. Moore, ibid., 684.

156 *"I heerd the white people say"*: Testimony of David M. Mickey, ibid., 732.

156 *"It was a fearful sight"*: Testimony of Bowie Foreman, ibid., 603.

156 *"do their utmost to arrest and deliver"*: Testimony of W. D. Brown, *Mississippi in 1875*, 1:699.

156 *one of them led by William S. Farrish:* Testimony of William S. Farrish, ibid., 650–51.

157 *Derry Brown was arrested and sent to Vicksburg:* Testimony of Derry Brown, ibid., 629.

157 *"If they did that, if it was not in a pitched fight":* Testimony of T. M. Miller, ibid., 667.

157 *a Negro teenager named David Washington:* Testimony of Margaret Ann Caldwell, ibid., 435. See also Blanche Ames's account in Ames, *Chronicles*, 2:257–59 (Blanche Butler Ames to Adelbert Ames, December 8, 1875).

158 *"Remember when you kill me":* Testimony of Margaret Ann Caldwell, *Mississippi in 1875*, 1:438.

158 *"We'll save him while we got him":* Ibid.

158 *"I was at my room until just nearly dark":* Ibid., 436–40.

159 *"Those who have seen Caldwell's corpse":* Ames, *Chronicles*, 2:258 (Blanche Butler Ames to Sarah Butler, December 8, 1875).

160 *"They all marched up to my house":* Testimony of Margaret Ann Caldwell, *Mississippi in 1875*, 1:438.

160 *"This is your time of political effort":* Ames, *Chronicles*, 2:260 (Sarah Butler to Blanche Butler Ames, December 15, 1875).

160 *Congressman Lucius Quintus Cincinnatus Lamar:* Murphy, *L.Q.C. Lamar*, 156–57.

161 *"Be not cast down or worried":* Ames, *Chronicles*, 2:263 (Benjamin Butler to Adelbert Ames, December 23, 1875).

161 *Senator Oliver P. Morton of Indiana:* Murphy, *L.Q.C. Lamar*, 159; McNeily, "Climax and Collapse," 433.

161 *"At night in the town here:* Ames, *Chronicles*, 2:259 (Blanche Butler Ames to Sarah Butler, December 8, 1875).

162 *A member of the white mob that had killed Charles Caldwell:* Ibid., 257–58.

162 *"His last idea is that they put a chain":* Ibid., 259.

162 *Ames gave a long, eloquent, carefully prepared address:* Ibid., 266–78 ("Annual Message of Gov. Adelbert Ames to the Legislature of Mississippi Session of 1876," January 4, 1876).

162 *In February, a legislative committee:* Ibid., 285–304 (majority and minority reports of the Mississippi House of Representatives).

162 *One article asserted that Ames's having put Charles Caldwell in charge:* Ibid., 287 (eleventh count in the bill of impeachment).

162 *another accused Ames of misconduct:* Ibid., 287, 288 (tenth count in the bill of impeachment).

162 *As soon as he got the news:* Ibid., 304–305 (Benjamin Butler to Adelbert Ames, February 25, 1876).

162 *Lamar wrote a friend in Mississippi:* L.Q.C. Lamar, letter to Edward C. Walthall, February 23, 1876, quoted in McNeily, "Climax and Collapse," 453–54.

163 *Lamar urged Butler to hire a lawyer friend of his:* Ames, *Chronicles*, 2:304–305 (Benjamin Butler to Adelbert Ames, February 25, 1876).

163 *"a double dealer upon whom no dependence can be placed":* Ibid., 344 (Blanche Butler Ames to Sarah Butler, March 14, 1876).

163 *Ben Butler engaged a different lawyer:* Ibid., 347–48 (Benjamin Butler to Adelbert Ames, March 25, 1876).

163 *"Of the principal men in Jackson":* Ibid., 310 (Blanche Butler Ames to Sarah Butler, March 1, 1876).

163 *his message in 1876 didn't mention the South:* McNeily, "Climax and Collapse," 429.

164 *"I will not conceal from you that the matter":* Ames, *Chronicles,* 2:353–54 (Benjamin Butler to Adelbert Ames, April 1, 1876).

164 *Ames's new lawyer, who dashed off a letter:* Thomas J. Durant, letter to Adelbert Ames, March 28, 1876, Ames Governor's Office Papers, MDAH.

164 *"Oh, if only I could see you":* William C. Pitt, letter to the Boutwell Committee staff, April 10, 1876, Redpath Collection.

165 *"These people expect to capture the Senatorial Committee":* J. Tarbell, letter to the Boutwell Committee staff, April 16, 1876, Redpath Collection.

165 *"A great many colored are intimidated":* Anonymous letter to the Boutwell Committee staff, June 18, 1876, Redpath Collection.

165 *one witness who did testify reported to the committee:* J. L. Edwards (West Point, Mississippi), letter to Senator George Boutwell, July 9, 1876, Redpath Collection.

165 *where Redpath interviewed Ames:* Ames, *Chronicles,* 2:364 (Adelbert Ames to Blanche Butler Ames, May 1, 1876).

165 *"due wholly to fraud, violence, and murder":* "Mississippi Democrats: Some Plain Words About Them," *New York Times,* May 2, 1876, in Ames Family Papers.

166 *"In one phrase—hostility to the negro":* Ibid.

166 *Just a few days later, bad trouble broke out:* Testimony of Hugh M. Foley, *Mississippi in 1875,* 2:1533–43; testimony of D. A. Weber, 1548–60.

166 *a region with unusually good Negro schools:* Testimony of D. A. Weber, ibid., 1552.

166 *"These Regulators in our section of the country":* Testimony of E. L. Weber, ibid., 1570.

166 *One evening in May two Negroes murdered a shopkeeper:* Testimony of D. A. Weber, ibid., 1549, 1558–59.

166 *Aaronson had actually been murdered by white men:* Ibid., 1552, 1562.

167 *"One was in bed and said he was sick":* Testimony of Kenner James, ibid., 1589.

167 *"These men told me that my republicanism":* Testimony of Alfred Black, *Mississippi in 1875,* 2:1584.

167 *A dispatch from E. L. Weber:* E. L. Weber, letter to the Boutwell Committee staff, May 18, 1876, Redpath Collection. In his testimony before the committee, Weber increased his estimate to fifty. See *Mississippi in 1875,* 2:1567.

167 *"For myself I had no doubt":* George S. Boutwell, *Reminiscences of Sixty Years in Public Affairs,* 2 vols. (New York: McClure, Phillips, 1902), 2:280.

168 *"While I was conducting the investigation at Jackson":* Ibid., 281.

168 *he was surprised to hear gunfire:* Adelbert Ames, September 8, 1876, *Chronicles,* 2:403–405.

169 *"Is it not strange that Mississippi":* Ibid., 405–406 (Adelbert Ames to Blanche Butler Ames, September 9, 1876).

169 *Cole Younger . . . said that the gang had come to Northfield:* Cole Younger, *The Story of Cole Younger by Himself* (St. Paul: Minnesota Historical Society Press, 2000), 74.

5. THE MISSISSIPPI PLAN

170 *Democrats had begun to talk about the possibility:* William Archibald Dunning, *Reconstruction, Political and Economic, 1865–1877* (New York: Harper, 1907), 305.

170 *James George and Ethelbert Barksdale:* James Ford Rhodes, *History of the United States from the Compromise of 1850,* 9 vols. (New York: Macmillan, 1900–28), 7:198.

171 *"The Negroes are now almost ready to take to the swamps":* T. J. Reed, letter to the Boutwell Committee staff, July 28, 1876, Redpath Collection.

172 *"I would not have believed that so many colored people":* Richard Zuczek, *States of Rebellion: Reconstruction in South Carolina* (Columbia: University of South Carolina Press, 1996), 150.

172 *the South Carolina state militia:* See the report of South Carolina Attorney General William Stone and D. H. Chamberlain's July 13 letter, both in *South Carolina in 1876,* Senate Miscellaneous Document 48, Vol. II, 44th Cong., 2nd Sess., 473–79; for a Dunning School historian's version of events, see John S. Reynolds, *Reconstruction in South Carolina, 1865–1877* (Columbia: State Company, 1905), 344–47.

173 *"regarded as ringleaders in bringing on the difficulty":* Reynolds, *Reconstruction in South Carolina,* 346.

173 *One had his tongue cut off:* R. B. Elliott et al., *Address of a Colored Convention on the Hamburgh Massacre,* Senate Miscellaneous Document 48, 494.

173 *"I cannot help waving the bloody shirt":* Quoted in William Gillette, *Retreat from Reconstruction, 1869–1879* (Louisiana State University Press, 1979), 307.

173 *"foreshadows a campaign of blood and violence":* D. H. Chamberlain, July 22, 1876, Senate Miscellaneous Document 48, 481.

173 *"The scene in Hamburgh":* U. S. Grant, July 26, 1876, Ibid., 483.

173 *a second, worse massacre occurred:* T. H. Blackwell and James Canten, *Depositions and Report Regarding the Ellenton Massacre,* ibid., 511–15.

174 *"rifle clubs":* Charles J. Babbitt, *List of Rifle-Clubs in South Carolina,* ibid., 499–509.

174 *A careful accounting by U.S. marshals:* Blackwell and Canten, *Report Regarding the Ellenton Massacre,* 513–14.

174 *One was a deaf and mute teenage boy:* Ibid., 513. The boy who had his ear cut off is a different person.

174 *A Negro state legislator named Simon Coker:* Ibid.

174 *the rifle club came upon a group of terrified and lightly armed Negroes:* Ibid., 512.

174 *President Grant issued a proclamation:* U. S. Grant, October 17, 1876, Senate Miscellaneous Document 48, 537.

174 *An anti-Reconstruction historian later estimated:* This is derived from John S. Reynolds, *Reconstruction in South Carolina, 1865–1877* (Negro Universities Press, 1969 [originally published 1905]).

174 *"the shot-gun policy":* *The Floridian,* August 31, 1876, quoted in William Watson Davis, *The Civil War and Reconstruction in Florida* (1913; repr., Gainsville, University of Florida Press, 1964), 694.

175 *Some Florida Negroes testified afterward:* Testimony of Stephen Thomas, 44th Cong., 2nd Sess., *Florida Election, 1876: Report of the Senate Committee on*

Privileges and Elections, with the Testimony and Documentary Evidence, on the Election in the State of Florida in 1876 (Washington, D.C.: GPO, 1877), 249.

175 *one local Democratic organization published a pledge:* Ibid., 24.

175 *"The substance of it was about like this":* Testimony of Benjamin Dilworth, ibid., 336.

175 *Jefferson County's Negro state senator:* Ibid., 24.

175 *In Levy County, shots were fired:* Ibid., 27.

175 *the Negro state senator, E. G. Johnson, had been assassinated:* Ibid., 25.

175 *Regulators murdered a black man named Moses Smith:* Ibid., 24.

175 *"The colored men had been marched from the road":* Ibid., 26.

175 *President Grant sent a small complement of troops to Florida:* Davis, *Civil War and Reconstruction in Florida,* 702.

176 *reinforced by allies from Georgia:* Ibid., 701.

176 *broke up Republican rallies:* Testimony of William Macnish, *Florida Election,* 243.

176 *a Democrat who worked for the railroad:* Davis, *Civil War and Reconstruction in Florida,* 708.

176 *Regulators on horseback stood out on the roads:* Testimony of Thomas Boyd, *Florida Election,* 247; testimony of George P. Fowler, 258.

176 *In the town of Monticello:* Davis, *Civil War and Reconstruction in Florida,* 706.

176 *Democrats printed "galvanized" sample ballots: Florida Election,* 19.

176 *"a boisterous and pressing crowd kept republicans":* Ibid., 22.

176 *"They were not over-scrupulous about means":* William Watson Davis, *The Civil War and Reconstruction in Florida* (Gainesville: University of Florida Press, 1964 [originally published 1913]), 703.

176 *"The atrocities of Saint Bartholomew": Louisiana in 1876. Report of the Sub-Committee of the Committee on Privileges and Elections of the United States Senate* (Washington, D.C.: GPO, 1877), 2.

177 *including one delivered in person in the White House:* Grant Papers, 27:239n (quoting the *New York Herald,* July 25, 1876).

177 *In Ouachita, a Republican named Dr. B. H. Dinkgrave: Vote for Electors in Louisiana,* Senate Executive Document 2, 44th Cong., 2nd Sess., 26.

177 *"Primus Johnson, a colored republican, was shot": Louisiana in 1876,* 17.

177 *"Upon arriving at Logwood's": Vote for Electors,* 26.

177 *"Another republican, by the name of Ferdinand Bynum": Louisiana in 1876,* 18.

177 *"the rifle-clubs took the field":* Ibid., 19.

178 *In West Feliciana Parish: Vote for Electors,* 11.

178 *In East Feliciana, the Bulldozers:* Ibid., 18.

178 *(Gair "was literally shot to pieces"):* Ibid.

178 *not a single Republican vote was cast:* Ibid., 8, 18.

178 *"April 13, 1876. Jerry Myers, hung": Vote for Electors,* 22.

178 *the parish coroner received a letter:* Ibid., 22–23.

179 *their chief weapon was control of the local "returning boards":* Lynch, *Facts of Reconstruction,* 160.

179 *Nationally, it was the closest presidential election:* Dunning, *Reconstruction,* 309–41; Lynch, *Reminiscences of an Active Life,* 193–98.

180 *But Blaine double-crossed his fellow Republicans:* Lynch, *Reminiscences of an Active Life,* 206–207.

180 *Blanche K. Bruce, paid a call on Lamar:* L.Q.C. Lamar, letter to Edward Clark, March 15, 1877, Clark Family Papers.

181 *voted for Lamar's admission:* Ibid.

181 *"I believe him to be a noble negro":* Ibid.

181 *Lamar and Bruce struck a deal:* Ibid.

181 *"You are right in your view that boldness":* L.Q.C. Lamar, letter to Edward Clark, March 30, 1877, Clark Family Papers.

182 *a former judge named W. W. Chisolm:* For the account of John W. Gully's murder and Chisolm's arrest, see Wells, *Chisolm Massacre,* 161–99.

183 *"a scene to have equaled in horror":* Ibid., 186.

183 *"Mrs. C.—'You know about my husband'":* Ames, *Chronicles,* 2:478–79 (Adelbert Ames to Blanche Butler Ames, March 20, 1878).

185 *Bruce named his son after a white politician:* Eric Foner, *Freedom's Lawmakers: A Directory of Black Officeholders During Reconstruction* (New York: Oxford University Press, 1993), 29–30.

185 *"Need I tell you I hold the state has gone":* Ames, *Chronicles,* 2:250 (Adelbert Ames to Blanche Butler Ames, November 4, 1875).

185 *"Redemption" was just the word:* See Rhodes, *History of the United States,* 7:177; John R. Lynch, "Some Historical Errors of James Ford Rhodes," *Journal of Negro History* 2, no. 4 (October 1917): 358; Dunning, *Reconstruction,* 303.

187 *Thomas Dixon, a Baptist minister, lawyer, politician:* For Dixon's background, see Sam G. Dickson's Introduction to Thomas Dixon Jr., *The Reconstruction Trilogy: The Leopard's Spots, The Clansman, The Traitor* (Newport Beach, CA: Noontide Press, 1994), ix–xx.

188 *"The Ethiopian can not change his skin":* Dixon, *The Leopard's Spots,* 237.

188 *one involving hanging, the other burning alive:* Ibid., 77, 196.

189 *"Henceforth there could be but one issue":* Ibid., 82.

189 *wrote a stage version of his second Reconstruction novel:* Dickson, Introduction, xv.

189 *"whose name was enough to start a riot:* Dixon, *The Clansman,* 321.

189 *President Grant dispatching troops to the South:* Ibid., 417.

189 *"Griffith made Dixon's play into* The Birth of a Nation": Dickson, Introduction, xvi.

190 *"It is like writing history with lightning":* Ibid., xvii.

190 *including the chief justice of the United States:* Ibid.

191 *although the South had been wrong to resist:* Burgess, *Reconstruction,* vii.

192 *"the North is learning every day by valuable experiences":* Ibid., viii–ix.

192 *"It was the most soul-sickening spectacle":* Ibid., 263.

192 *"it was now a choice between complete destruction":* Ibid., 275.

193 *"a credit to his race":* Rhodes, *History of the Unites States,* 7:156.

193 *He alluded only very lightly to the campaign:* Ibid., 157–58.

193 *"Like the men who had enacted Congressional reconstruction":* Ibid., 159.

194 *"The white men of the South were aroused":* Woodrow Wilson, *A History of the American People, Volume V: Reunion and Rationalization* (New York: Harper, 1908), 58.

194 *"the struggle through which the southern whites":* Dunning, *Reconstruction,* xv.

194 *"all the forces that made for civilization":* Ibid., 212.

195 *"The demoralization of the South was less political":* Ibid., 212–13.

195 *"A more intimate association with the other race":* Ibid., 213–14.

195 *"the hideous crimes against white womanhood"*: Ibid., 214.
195 *they were "extremists"*: Ibid., 86.
195 *"the picturesque details"*: Ibid., xvi.
195 *"The aggressive and violent element"*: Ibid., 278–79.
196 *Pinckney Benton Stewart Pinchback:* For more on Pinchback's life, see James Haskins, *Pinckney Benton Stewart Pinchback* (New York: Macmillan, 1973).
197 *"Here, under the protecting care"*: Pinckney Pinchback, undated speech (1876), Pinckney Benton Stewart Pinchback Papers, Manuscript Department, Moorland-Spingarn Research Center, Howard University, Washington, D.C., 3.
198 *"I fear that we will have to face the conclusion"*: Ibid., 1.
198 *"Of late it has become quite fashionable"*: Ibid., 15–16.
199 *"Now, sir, let me say that the South is proposed"*: John R. Lynch, "Southern Question: Reply to Mr. Lamar. Speech of John R. Lynch, of Mississippi, in the House of Representatives, August 12, 1876" (Washington, D.C., GPO, 1876), 11.
199 *Adelbert Ames ordered six copies:* John R. Lynch, letter to Adelbert Ames, May 14, 1914, Ames Family Papers.
199 *In 1917 Lynch contributed a long article:* Lynch, "Some Historical Errors of James Ford Rhodes," 345–68.
200 *in the exact amount of $315,612.19:* Ibid., 360.
200 *a Democrat named William L. Hemingway:* Ibid., 359–61.
200 *"The democrats, together with the radical element"*: Lynch, *Facts of Reconstruction*, 141.
200 The Atlantic Monthly *published an article of his:* "The Freedmen's Bureau," *Atlantic Monthly*, March 1901.
201 *"deadly dull"*: Claude G. Bowers, *The Tragic Era: The Revolution after Lincoln* (Boston: Houghton Mifflin, 1929).
201 *"Great masses moving from place to place"*: Ibid., 448.
202 *"There was no 'corruption' as the statistics prove"*: Adelbert Ames, letter to E. Benjamin Andrews, May, 24, 1895, Adelbert Ames Papers.
203 *Andrews did indeed correct his account:* See Elisha Benjamin Andrews, *The History of the Last Quarter-Century in the United States, 1870–1895* (New York: Scribner, 1896), 142–52. Andrews quotes extensively in the book from a letter Ames wrote him.
203 *The two men struck up the cordial but wary relationship:* The Ames-Garner correspondence can be found in the Ames Family Papers and in the James W. Garner Papers.
204 *"millstones about the neck"*: James W. Garner, letter to Adelbert Ames, December 4, 1899, James W. Garner Papers.
204 *"which trampled the State government"*: Adelbert Ames, letter to James W. Garner, December 21, 1899, ibid.
204 *"He who was a slave"*: Adelbert Ames, undated letter to John R. Lynch, Ames Family Papers.
204 *"The days are many before Christ's Sermon"*: Adelbert Ames, March 20, 1929; Adelbert Ames Papers.
206 *"a black nightmare the South could never forget"*: John F. Kennedy, *Profiles in Courage* (New York: Harper, 1956), 153.
206 *"a wave of popularity"*: Ibid., 163.
206 *"restitution of normal Federal-state relations"*: Ibid., 161.
206 *"No state suffered more from carpetbag rule"*: Ibid.

207 *"Imagine—if you were called upon to implement"*: Blanche Ames Ames, letter to John F. Kennedy, June 6, 1956, Ames Family Papers.

207 *"It is not anticipated that* Profiles in Courage": John F. Kennedy, letter to Blanche Ames Ames, July 13, 1956, ibid.

207 *overturning the Jim Crow laws:* It is worth saying a word here about C. Vann Woodward, the great historian of the South. Through a series of influential works about Reconstruction and the period that followed it—including *Tom Watson: Agrarian Rebel* (New York: Macmillan, 1938), *Reunion and Reaction* (Boston: Little, Brown, 1951), *Origins of the New South* (Baton Rouge: Louisiana State University Press, 1951), and *The Strange Career of Jim Crow* (New York: Oxford University Press, 1957)—Woodward argued that a biracial, economically populist political order had been a real possibility in the post–Civil War South but that business interests had played on racial prejudice to turn white voters against black enfranchisement in order to create a more conservative polity. In Woodward's version, the Jim Crow era was best understood as a tragic, but an eminently avoidable, turn of events.

Woodward's work became an important source of historical support for the civil rights movement. Martin Luther King, Jr., quoted Woodward copiously, for example, in his unforgettable speech on the steps of the Alabama state capitol in Montgomery in 1965 that ended the Selma-to-Montgomery march and preceded the reinstitution, through the passage of the Voting Rights Act, of federal enforcement of the Fifteenth Amendment's guarantee of voting rights for African Americans. The idea that Jim Crow had been a kind of unhappy accident helped to make its abolition seem possible. But Woodward's work tends to underemphasize significantly the extent to which the Southern Democratic Party had effectively nullified Negro rights in the 1870s, long before the Jim Crow laws, through the success of a conscious, coordinated program of political violence that the federal government declined to defeat.

208 *"Dear Grandma"*: George Ames Plimpton, undated letter to Blanche Ames Ames, Ames Family Papers.

208 *In August 1963 she received a polite off-putting letter:* Theodore Sorensen, letter to Blanche Ames Ames, August 5, 1963, ibid.

208 *a state dinner at the White House:* See George Plimpton, "A Clean, Well-Lighted Place," *New York Review of Books,* December 18, 1980.

A NOTE ON SOURCES

The literature on the post–Civil War Reconstruction period is vast, but this book focuses on a discrete set of events during Reconstruction about which there is a limited, though rich, supply of source material. I relied on one general history of Reconstruction constantly while working on this book: Eric Foner's *Reconstruction: America's Unfinished Revolution, 1863–1877* (Harper & Row, 1988). In the realm of primary sources, a similarly indispensable masterwork is the Southern Illinois University Press's complete edition of the papers of Ulysses S. Grant, edited by John Y. Simon. The Grant papers' long notes, which contain the texts of many letters written to him and other contemporary documents, are extraordinarily informative and helpful. Volumes 22 through 27 of the Grant papers were especially useful to me.

The Colfax massacre, in Louisiana, was a big story in its day, with extensive news coverage of it and subsequent events in the press. Where I have relied on the coverage (taking into account, of course, that most newspapers then functioned as political-party organs), I cite it in the following notes. *United States v. Cruikshank et al.* (1876), which ended in a Supreme Court decision overturning legislation that gave the federal government the authority to enforce Reconstruction in the states, arose from the Colfax massacre; there are hundreds of pages of material from and about the case. The original trial records, now at a National Archives and Records Administration facility in Fort Worth, Texas, were especially useful, though the trial transcript itself has apparently been lost. Contemporary reports on Colfax and other violence in the Red River valley of Louisiana from the Republican point of view can be found in "Affairs in Louisiana," Senate Executive Document 13, 43rd Congress, 2nd Session; "Condition of the South," House Report 101, 43rd Congress, 2nd Session; and "Horrible Massacre in Grant Parish, Louisiana," a collection of speeches published by the Louisiana Republican Party in 1873. Army records at the National Archives in Washington include some firsthand reports on Colfax and related matters, especially in Department of the Gulf, Record Group 393, post records for Colfax and for Camp Canby (Alexandria, Louisiana).

The papers of Pinckney Benton Stewart Pinchback, the Louisiana Republican who was America's first black governor (an office he held for six months), have a few references to Colfax and some interesting comments by Pinchback about the general situation in Louisiana at the time. They are at the Moorland-Spingarn Research Center at Howard University.

The Democratic point of view about Colfax can be found in "Condition of the South," House Report 261, 43rd Congress, 2nd Session (a dissent from the report of the same name mentioned above), and also in the Melrose Collection, a large, eccentric body of material assembled by a Louisiana doctor named Milton Dunn, whose father had been a member of the white militia that fought at Colfax. It is housed at the Cammie G. Henry Research Center, Northwestern State University, Natchitoches, Louisiana. The reminiscences of E. E. Davis, Jr., John I. McCain, O. W. Watson, and J. A. Williams—all white—are particularly interesting. The manuscript of the unpublished novel "From Blue to Gray," by Kate K. Grant, who lived on a plantation near Colfax, is in the Layssard Family Papers at the Louisiana State University archives in Baton Rouge. Though certainly not a conventional history, it does fairly represent the white participants' mythologized version of events; at the end of it is an affidavit signed by Christopher Columbus Nash and the other leaders of the white forces vouching for its accuracy. Another Democratic source is "History of the Riot at Colfax," by the Committee of Seventy, a New Orleans group (Clark & Hofeline, 1874).

For many years the only work of scholarship devoted to the Colfax massacre was a predictably anti-Reconstruction 1929 Southern Methodist University master's thesis by Manie White Johnson, "The Colfax Riot of April, 1873." In 1993, fortunately, a serious contemporary scholar, Joel M. Sipress, completed a Ph.D. dissertation at the University of North Carolina titled "The Triumph of Reaction: Political Struggle in a New South Community, 1865–1898," which, because the community Sipress studied is Grant Parish, Louisiana, contains by far the best and most reliable account of the Colfax massacre.

On the events in Mississippi in 1874–75, three primary sources stand out. The nearly daily correspondence between Adelbert and Blanche Ames, an extraordinary gift to historians, is in the Ames Family Papers at the Sophia Smith Collection, Smith College. In 1957 the Ames family privately published a two-volume edition of these letters, edited (and very slightly sanitized) under the title *Chronicles from the Nineteenth Century: Family Letters of Blanche Butler and Adelbert Ames*, copies of which can be found in research libraries. Ames's governor's office papers, at the Mississippi Department of Archives and History in Jackson, make up another first-rate set of documents. The Boutwell Report—"Mississippi in 1875: Report of the Select Committee to Inquire into the Mississippi Election of 1875," Senate Report 527, 44th Congress, 1st Session—comprises more than two thousand pages of contemporary evidence on the 1875 election, mostly testimony from eyewitnesses, compiled by a committee friendly to Ames but with a combative minority always attending to the point of view of the Mississippi redeemers.

Other manuscript collections containing useful material on the end of Reconstruction in Mississippi and related matters include the papers of Edwards Pierrepont, at Yale University; the Adelbert Ames Papers, a small post-gubernatorial collection at the Mississippi Department of Archives and History; the papers of Blanche Ames Ames, daughter of Adelbert and Blanche, in the Ames Family Papers (especially the material pertaining to her unsuccessful attempts to get John F. Kennedy to revise his chapter on the Mississippi Redeemer L.Q.C. Lamar in *Profiles in Courage*); the Redpath Collection, a box of letters received by the veteran abolitionist editor James Redpath in connection with the investigation that produced the Boutwell Report, at the New York Public Library; and a small collection of letters from L.Q.C. Lamar to Edward D. Clark, at the University of Mississippi in Oxford, with a set of copies at the Mississippi Department of Archives and History. Blanche Ames Ames wrote a biography of her father, *Adelbert Ames: Broken Oaths and Reconstruction in Mississippi, 1835–1933* (Argosy-Antiquarian Press, 1964), which is useful, though hardly dispassionate.

In December 1874 the U.S. House of Representatives produced a quick report, with eyewitness testimony, called "Vicksburgh Troubles," House Report 265, 43rd Congress, 2nd Session. A complete record of the testimony in Ames's impeachment trial in 1876, in manuscript form, is at the Mississippi Department of Archives and History and, in printed form, in *The Testimony in the Impeachment of Adelbert Ames, as Governor of Mississippi* (Power & Barksdale, 1877). The Mississippi records of the Army's Department of the Gulf, especially in "Letters Received by the Adjutant General," are also useful. The U.S. Senate's "Exoduster Hearings" of 1880 (Senate Report 693, 46th Congress, 2nd Session), on the migration of Negroes from the Deep South to Kansas, contains testimony by blacks on conditions during late Reconstruction; especially useful are the long interviews with the leading Exoduster, Henry Adams, who lived in the Red River valley of Louisiana during Reconstruction, and John M. Brown, who was, until he was run out of the state in 1875, the Republican sheriff of Coahoma County, Mississippi.

Eyewitness testimony on the implementation of the Mississippi plan in other Southern states in 1876 can be found in "Florida Election, 1876," Senate Report 611, 44th Congress, 2nd Session; "Louisiana in 1876," Senate Report 701, 44th Congress, 2nd Session; "Vote for Electors in Louisiana," Senate Executive Document 2, 44th Congress, 2nd Session; and "South Carolina in 1876," Senate Miscellaneous Document 48, 44th Congress, 2nd Session.

Three Mississippi Republicans wrote valuable memoirs of the Reconstruction period. Albert T. Morgan, the carpetbagger sheriff of Yazoo County (whose copious letters to Governor Ames are in the governor's office papers), self-published a memoir in 1884 called *Yazoo; or, On the Picket Line of Freedom in the South, a Personal Narrative*, which the University of South Carolina Press republished in 2000. James M. Wells, a federal tax collector, wrote *The Chisolm Massacre: A Picture of Home Rule in Mississippi* (Haskell House Publishers, 1877), an account of the murder of a Republican county sheriff by White Liners. John R. Lynch, Mississippi's first black congressman, wrote *The Facts of Reconstruction* (Neale Publishing, 1913), as well as, a few years later, a useful article titled "Some Historical Errors of James Ford Rhodes" (*Journal of Negro History* 2, no. 4, Oct. 1917). During the early years of the twentieth century, the Mississippi Historical Society published a thirteen-volume set of *Proceedings*, in which Reconstruction is a major theme. Most of its articles are not really histories but memoirs by Redeemers about events in which they participated, which are useful as pure representations of the Redeemer point of view. The most ambitious of these is the book-length "Climax and Collapse of Reconstruction in Mississippi, 1874–76," by J. S. McNeily, in volume 12 of the *Proceedings* (1912). Also useful for my purposes were "The Clinton Riot," by Charles Hillman Brough (volume VI, 1902); "The Conference of October 15, 1875, Between General George and Governor Ames," by Frank Johnston (volume VI, 1902); and "Reconstruction in Yazoo County," by Robert Bowman (volume VII, 1903). One step away from a memoir, and quite valuable as a passionate expression of Redeemer sentiment, is *Lucius Q.C. Lamar: His Life, Times, and Speeches, 1825–1893*, by Edward Mayes, who was Lamar's son-in-law and a former chancellor of the University of Mississippi (Publishing House of the Methodist Episcopal Church, South, Barbee & Smith, Agents, 1896).

Works of scholarship that discuss late-Reconstruction events in Louisiana and Mississippi in some detail begin with two books from the pro-Redeemer Dunning school of Reconstruction history, named after Professor William Archibald Dunning of Columbia University: *Reconstruction in Louisiana After 1868* by Ella Lonn (G. P. Putnam's Sons, 1918) and *Reconstruction in Mississippi* by James Wilford Garner (Macmillan, 1901). The latter is one of the fairer and more careful of the state histories by Dunning's protégés. The big, synthetic histories of Reconstruction by Dunning himself and other anti-Reconstruction historians of the early twentieth century are useful for the picture they give of mainstream academic opinion on the subject. These include John W. Burgess's *Reconstruction and the Constitution, 1866–1876* (Charles Scribner's Sons, 1902), Dunning's *Reconstruction, Political and Economic, 1865–1877* (Harper & Brothers, 1907), and the portions devoted to Reconstruction in two multivolume American histories, Woodrow Wilson's *A History of the American People*, volume V (Harper & Brothers, 1902), and James Ford Rhodes's *History of the United States*, volume VII: *1872–1877* (Macmillan, 1906).

Popular, rather than scholarly, anti-Reconstruction works include Thomas Dixon's novels *The Leopard's Spots* (Doubleday, Page & Company, 1902), *The Clansman* (Grosset & Dunlap, 1905), and *The Traitor* (Doubleday, Page & Company, 1907); D. W. Griffith's film version of Dixon's books, *The Birth of a Nation*, and Claude Bowers's *The Tragic Era: The Revolution After Lincoln* (Houghton Mifflin, 1929).

The first significant revisionist history of the period, W.E.B. Du Bois's *Black Reconstruction in America, 1860–1880* (Harcourt, Brace, 1935), has a chapter on Mississippi and Louisiana. Vernon Lane Wharton's *The Negro in Mississippi, 1865–1890* (University of North Carolina Press, 1947) contains a detailed, anti-Redeemer account of the events of 1874–75. *Retreat from Reconstruction, 1869–1879* by William Gillette (Louisiana State University Press, 1979) is still the most complete account in book form of Redemption in Louisiana and Mississippi. George C. Rable's *But There Was No Peace: The Role of Violence in the Politics of Reconstruction* (University of Georgia Press, 1984) has a chapter on each state. *The Road to Redemption: Southern Politics, 1869–1879* by Michael Perman (University of North Carolina Press, 1984) also discusses Reconstruction politics in Louisiana and Mississippi. Christopher Waldrep's *Roots of Disorder: Race and Criminal Justice in the American South, 1817–80* (University of Illinois Press, 1998), a study set in Vicksburg, Mississippi, has a section on the "Vicksburg troubles" of 1874. *A Nation Under Our Feet: Black Political Struggles in the Rural South, from Slavery to the Great Migration*, by Steven Hahn (Harvard University Press, 2003), has one chapter on the "Negro uprisings" of the late Reconstruction period and another on Henry Adams and the Exoduster movement. Recent social histories I found useful include *Freedom's Women: Black Women and Families in Civil War Era Mississippi*, by Noralee Frankel (Indiana University Press, 1999) and *Degrees of Freedom: Louisiana and Cuba After Slavery*, by Rebecca J. Scott (Harvard University Press, 2005).

Other modern histories of Reconstruction in Louisiana and Mississippi are *Louisiana Reconstructed, 1863–1877*, by Joe Gray Taylor (Louisiana State University Press, 1974); *The Day of the Carpetbagger: Republican Reconstruction in Mississippi*, by William C. Harris (Louisiana State University Press, 1979); and Richard

Nelson Current's *Three Carpetbag Governors* (Louisiana State University Press, 1967), one of whose chapters is about Adelbert Ames. There is no one book entirely devoted to the material I have covered in this one, but the books listed here, all of which cover it in the course of attending mainly to other business, represent the most substantial treatment between hard covers of the Mississippi plan.

Historical events as important as those of the Reconstruction period constantly change in valence retrospectively depending on what is going on in the present. The civil rights movement, which represented as direct and literal a revisiting of the main themes of Reconstruction as it is possible to imagine, led to a great scholarly reworking of the subject, which extended roughly from the publication of John Hope Franklin's *Reconstruction: After the Civil War* (University of Chicago Press) in 1961 to that of Foner's *Reconstruction* in 1988 and includes many other books and articles. This body of work treats the goals of Reconstruction, especially Radical Reconstruction, much more sympathetically than the writing of previous historians had. Since the publication of Foner's book, Reconstruction itself has not undergone a major historical reexamination, but the fall of the Soviet Union and the subsequent unrest in many parts of the world have produced much interesting scholarship, mostly by political scientists rather than historians, on subjects like ethnic conflict, terrorism, asymmetric warfare, weak states, democracy creation, and strategies for concluding civil wars, and these themes seem to me to bear on the events in this book. One book I found especially useful was *The Deadly Ethnic Riot* by Donald L. Horowitz (University of California Press, 2001). A rare and interesting example of a political scientist from this school discussing the American Civil War and Reconstruction directly is "The End of the American Civil War," by Stephen John Stedman, in *Stopping the Killing: How Civil Wars End*, edited by Roy Licklider (New York University Press, 1993). Stedman treats Reconstruction as a continuation of the Civil War rather than as a postscript to it, which is a way of looking at the subject that seems appropriate to the story I have told here.

ACKNOWLEDGMENTS

Twenty years ago, when I was researching my book *The Promised Land*, I spent a lot of time driving through rural Mississippi. When I would arrive in a town, I would go to the public library and see if there was a local-history room. Often there was, and often it would have material, gathered from white townspeople years later, about the "redemption" of Mississippi in 1875. The stories lodged themselves in my mind, because their plot line was so consistent, and so implausible, from town to town—the fearsome "Negro uprising," always coincident with that year's political campaign, and always successfully repulsed with little or no white bloodshed.

I might have just put the subject away except that my wife, Judith Shulevitz, when I told her about it, insisted that I return to it and find out more about the events of 1875 in Mississippi. I owe this book to her unerring editor's instinct, and more broadly I am grateful to her for pushing me, on this and all other subjects, to think about things in fresher and deeper ways than I would have on my own.

Three people helped me with the research for this book: in the earliest stages, Kim Phillips-Fein, at the time a graduate student in American history, served as a guide to the literature and the archives. My oldest son, Alex, spent the summer of 2002, when he was between high school and college, chasing down archival material for me, mainly in the Army records housed in the National

Archives in Washington. At the very end of the process, Julia Ioffe, a fact-checker at *The New Yorker*, helped me put together the endnotes. My assistant at Columbia Journalism School, Susan Radmer, has been enormously helpful in all sorts of ways, including handling a high volume of requests from me for materials from Columbia's library system.

I'd like to thank especially three of the research librarians I met while working on this book: Ida E. Jones at the Moorland-Spingarn Research Center at Howard University in Washington, D.C.; Anne Lipscomb Webster at the Mississippi Department of Archives and History in Jackson; and Mary Linn Wernet at the Cammie G. Henry Research Center, Northwestern State University, Natchitoches, Louisiana. I am also grateful to the New York Public Library for permitting me to work in its Frederick Lewis Allen Room, birthing room to many books, during the spring and summer of 2003.

Lee Bollinger and Alan Brinkley, for whom I work at Columbia University, have been extraordinarily generous in giving me enough time away from an administrator's job to finish this book. Lawrence Powell, of Tulane University, gave me invaluable advice throughout my research. Eric Foner, of Columbia's history department, read the book in manuscript and suggested many ways of improving it. Jeffrey Frank, my editor at *The New Yorker*, also read portions of the book in manuscript and made suggestions that have improved it greatly. Stephen John Stedman, a political scientist at Stanford, was helpful in acquainting me with the recent academic literature on the aftermaths of civil wars and suggesting that it would be useful to think about the Reconstruction period in that light. My agent, Amanda Urban, did her usual superbly professional job in guiding the book through the publishing process.

I have dedicated this book to Elisabeth Sifton, who edited *The Promised Land*; then my next book, *The Big Test*; and now *Redemption*. I owe my life as an author to Elisabeth, who brings to her work an unusual combination of literary discernment, intellectual rigor, and moral passion. For me, writing books is never a solo activity, because of Elisabeth's unfailingly loyal and supportive, but never easygoing, ever-presence at the other end of the transaction.

INDEX